HITS and MISSES

OF THE

TRAPSHOOTING and SKEET WORLD

•

HUNTING TIPS

By

JIMMY ROBINSON

TRAPSHOOTING AND SKEET EDITOR
SPORTS AFIELD MAGAZINE

•

MINNEAPOLIS
JIMMY ROBINSON, PUBLISHER

Printed in the United States of America by the Bureau of Engraving. Inc.
Minneapolis. Minnesota.

Dedicated to
My Loving Mother

PAST AND PRESENT PRESIDENTS OF THE

Ned Lutz

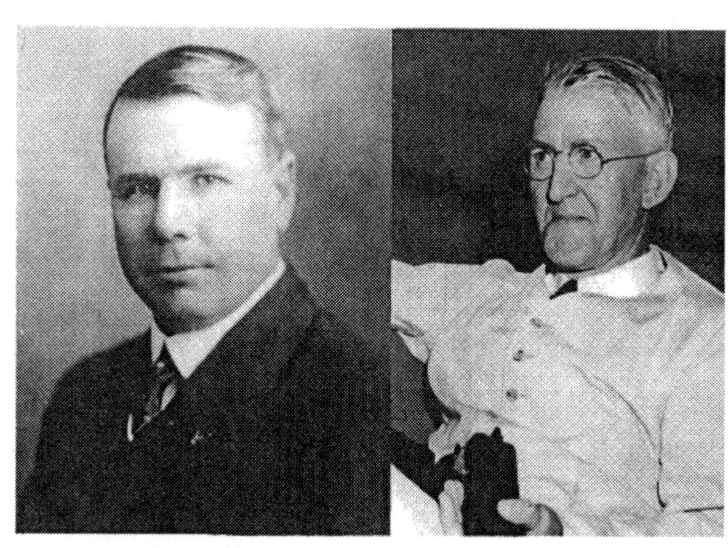

F. D. Stoop

T. C. Marshall

Ernie Maetzold

Uley Brooks

Sam Sharman

ɔck Jenkins—Ike Andrews

AMATEUR TRAPSHOOTING ASSOCIATION

Bob Coffey Fred King

Guy Dering George S. McCarty John Eshelman

CONTENTS

FOREWORD

In this book, we have tried to gather as many records on the clay target sport as possible. We have contacted shooters in all parts of the country for our information.

We have made every effort to be accurate; however, here and there we may have slipped. We will appreciate it if we may be advised of any inaccuracies so that corrections may be made in a supplement which we propose to publish in the future.

We have used a great many photographs in this book and have tried not to duplicate the winners, but in some cases this was impossible. It has been difficult to print all the pictures that we wanted to; these may come in the proposed supplement.

The writer acknowledges, with thanks, the aid extended him by Ray Loring, Henry Ahlin, Dick Hecker, Clyde Mitchell, Guy Nichols, Harold Russell, the officers of the Amateur Trapshooting Association, Ben J. Field, Henry Brown, Bill Mayfield, Fred Nordin, J. M. Hawkins, Fred Etchen, Charlie Dockendorf, Hunter Dempsey, J. A. Johnson, Dave Flannigan, Vic Bracher, Charlie Hopkins, Gus Peret, Mac Allen, Harry Maginnis, R. H. Coleman, Lou Smith, Gail Evans, Clarence Hutt, Stewart Comeaux, and many more who helped with this book.

If you like it, tell your friends. If you wish to order more books, write me personally, at 710 Phoenix Building, Minneapolis, Minnesota. Price is $3.00.

Thank you!

Jimmy Robinson.

PART I

THE HISTORY OF TRAPSHOOTING

No naturalist discovered the clay "bird." Like many other good things it was discovered in America. For more than sixty years this inanimate, mechanically propelled, swift and fragile little flying target has afforded keen sport for thousands of virile men and women the length and breadth of the land. Every day in the year trapshooters with leveled guns are calling for its catapult flight from its roosting place in the gun club "traphouses."

The first mention of trapshooting as a sport is found in an old English publication called the Sporting Magazine issued in 1793. Popinjay had been indulged in by bow and arrow marksmen for practice upon flying or moving game, but it is hard to imagine where any shotgun shooting could have been indulged in up to about 1619 when the first gun stock was made. It is true the match lock gun, arquebuses, harquebuses and muskets had been used before this, but none of them were shotguns.

The flint lock muzzle loader was no doubt the first gun used in trapshooting and likely was used in the gatherings mentioned in 1793. However, it certainly could not have gotten very far because it took at least an hour to load the gun in order to fire 10 shots.

The first trapshooting club was formed in 1810 at the Hornsey Wood House Pigeon Club in England. The earliest record of trapshooting in the U. S. was at the Sportsmen's Club in Cincinnati in 1831 and live pigeons were used. In those days there was an abundance of game, and no doubt trapshooting and releasing game from traps gave the hunters practice. Domestic pigeons gradually replaced wild birds and wooden blocks; tin cans and bottles were used, being thrown in the air from behind a barricade and practically straight up.

Charlie Portlock of Boston introduced the first glass ball competition mentioned as trapshooting in 1866. There were lots of matches shot in those days at glass balls. The first glass ball champion was Captain A. H. Bogardus. These balls were the first inanimate substitutes for pigeons, and they attained wide popularity in the 70's.

However, none of the glass balls satisfactorily simulated the flight of the bird, and the first really successful substitute was not found until George Ligowsky of Cincinnati invented the original clay target, which the targets of present-day trapshooting closely resemble. Along with the target, Mr. Ligowsky produced a practical ground trap for throwing it. The Ligowsky target and trap, first perfected in the early 80's, gave trapshooting, as we know it today, its real start. Substitutes and improvements soon came, but the "clay" target in present use, even though no longer made entirely of clay, and the trap that throws it, have not been altered in principle.

The First National Championship took place at New Orleans, February 11th - 16th, 1885. Captain Bogardus was a good trapshoot, but Dr. Carver took the championship from him. Then followed in order, J. A. R. Elliott, Rollo Heikes, Harvey McMurchey, Bill Crosby, and they held the sway until Fred Gilbert from Iowa entered the game.

The Interstate Trapshooting Association was organized in 1890. This gradually developed into the present Amateur Trapshooting Association that built a permanent home for the sport at Vandalia, Ohio, in 1924, where the Grand American Trapshooting tourney is held each year.

Trapshooting is one of the most popular of American outdoor competitive sports today. To the hunter it calls forth happy days he has spent afield and puts him in practice for days that will come afield.

GRAND AMERICAN HANDICAP KINGS

1900—R. O. HEIKES

Rollo O. "Pop" Heikes of Dayton, Ohio, won the first Grand American at clay targets back in the year 1900. The world's series of trapshooting was held that year at the Interstate Park, Queens, Long Island, New York, June 12 to 15. "Pop" went through all the stages of trapshooting from the glass balls to the clay targets of the present time; from the old black powder days to the present smokeless powder.

Heikes was born on Christmas day, 1856, on a farm near Dayton. As a boy, his spectacular triumphs with a gun were the envy of many an American youth. On account of his skill with both shotgun and rifle in the grim, early days of the West, the Ute Indians christened him "White Chief."

When Rollo was 21 years old, the Heikes family moved to Nebraska because "Rolly" had weak lungs, thinking the change might benefit him. He already had defeated many of the country's greatest live bird shots. On July 1, 1880, he broke his first 100 straight at clay targets.

From Nebraska he migrated to Utah, where he purchased a cattle ranch. There he did a great deal of game hunting, both big and small game. But the following year Heikes moved back to Dayton, and he was married a few months later. In 1886 he became a professional and shot as one for many years.

Heikes' winning of the first Grand American at clay targets came as no surprise to the target world, as he was generally recognized as one of the greatest all-around shots in the country at that time. In winning the 1900 Blue Ribbon race, Heikes broke 91 out of 100, shooting from the 22-yard line. A shooter by the name of Hood Waters took second honors, with 89. He lived in Baltimore, Maryland.

Trapshooters named Heikes "The Daddy of 'em all," and

At the 1900 Grand American: *(Left to right)* Charlie Young, Pop Heikes (the winner), Woolfolk Henderson, Les German and Tom Marshall

Pictured with this group taken at the Grand American, are Marie Kautzky Grant, Alice Crothers, Mrs. J. Murphy, Mrs. J. C. Wright and Georgianna Hobson, all former National Women's champions

NATIONAL WOMEN'S CHAMPIONS

Mrs. H. E. Grigsby, Oklahoma City, 1932 Women's champion, took part in the 1940 Texas state shoot. Here we snapped her with *(top row, left to right)* Mrs. W. C. Morris, Mrs. Watty Watkins, Mrs. W. B. Barnhill, Mrs. H. E. Grigsby, Mrs. W. F. Stanton, Mrs. N. V. Pillot; *(Sitting)* La Del Murphree, Frances Gardner, Mrs. George Cameron and Mrs. John Loffland

what a fitting name it was. Not only was he one of the greatest shots that the world has ever known, but a more honest and fair shooter never finger-itched the trigger.

It might be well to mention those who worked on the first handicap committee. Elmer Shaner, then manager of the Interstate Trapshooting Association, controlling body of both trapshooting and live bird shooting, was assisted by Jacob Pentz of Shooting and Fishing; Bernard Waters of Forest and Stream; W. R. Hobart of American Field, and Will Park of Sporting Life.

The 1900 Grand American marked the first time in the history of trapshooting that handicapping by distance was applied at any clay target tourney on a large scale. Amateurs and professionals, side by side, fought it out for the supreme honors of the target world. The 1900 Grand American attracted 74 of the best shots of that era in the country.

Heikes won many honors, both at live birds and at clay targets. He once told me he received his greatest thrill when he won the world's professional championship at Grant Park, Chicago, in 1915. Years before, he broke the world's record at live birds when he killed 99 out of 100. He attended 25 Grand Americans and shot for 55 years. It was W. T. Den of Brownsville, Nebraska, who started him in the shooting game. Mr. Heikes died several years ago.

Grand notes . . . Jack Fanning and J. A. R. Elliott were given the supreme handicap penalty at this shoot, 23 yards, so you can see how they were regarded in those days. . . . Charlie Young (then shooting as Robin Hood) along with C. Landis, J. H. Willey of Laconia, New York, and G. O. Henderson of Hingham, Massachusetts, broke 88's to tie for third place that year. . . . Rollo Heikes received 16 per cent of the purse for his victory, which was $130.25. . . . H. C. Bridges, known as "Tarheel," won the Preliminary Handicap with 89 out of 100 from the 19-yard stripe.

1901—E. C. GRIFFITH

E. C. Griffith of Pascoag, Rhode Island, won the second Grand American, the big shoot again being staged at the Interstate Park, New York. Several months before the Grand American "Griff" had carried away high honors at the Live Bird Grand American, marking the first and only gunner who

NATIONAL WOMEN'S CHAMPIONS

Bunny Sanders

Jeanette Jay

Lela Hall

Mrs. Wm. Gilbert

Kitty Boyer

Toots Randall

Mrs. E. L. King

Mrs. Harry Harrison

Gladys Reid

ever stalked away with these two major wins. It is a record that will no doubt stand forever, as live bird Grand Americans have been discontinued.

Griffith's live bird win was nothing short of spectacular. When the smoke had cleared away in this race, it was found that the eastern star was locked in a tie with 22 other "world knowns" of that time. This big event called for 25 handicap birds. Twenty-three had killed them all. "Griff," shooting from the 28-yard line, won first place by snuffing 18 more.

J. L. D. "Don" Morrison, then of Minnesota and in later years a resident of Los Angeles, won second place, at 29 yards, dropping his 18th bird. R. R. Bennett, at 27 yards, took third place, missing his 15th pigeon. There were 200 actual shooters who took part in the big race that year. This Blue Ribbon event was known as the Ninth Grand American at Live Pigeons.

Griffith won the clay target Grand American with 95 breaks from the 19-yard line. Let it be said that scores were much lower in those days, and his high score easily outdistanced the field. Targets were much tougher at that time and the ammunition was not up to the present day standard.

A shooter by the name of Keystone came in for second honors when he eliminated 93 of his 100. Seventy-five shooters, the best in the country at that time, took part in the meet. Rollo Heikes, the previous year's winner, turned in 84 from 22 yards. Fifty-six thousand seven hundred fifty clay birds were dished up to the gunners at the 1901 competition. A stiff breeze blew from the south during the shoot and the day was hot and sultry.

Mr. Griffith stated in a recent letter that he still shoots the odd clay target. He runs the Star theater in Pascoag, and was 80 years of age on November 22. He is in the best of health.

Grand notes . . . Paul North, prominent sportsman of those days, helped with the shoot . . . Charlie Phellis (still shooting) and Luther Squier shot the program . . . Charlie Young again shot well, breaking 91 out of 100 to tie Ed Banks, the trapshooting scribe of the time, for fourth place . . . Griffith received $128.96 for his Grand American win . . . Ed Fulford, Utica, New York, copped the Preliminary Handicap with ease, breaking 95 out of 100 from the 18-yard line.

Mr. and Mrs. Ad Topperwein

1902—C. W. FLOYD

The late C. W. Floyd captured the third Grand American at clay targets with a score of 94 out of 100, shooting from the 18-yard line. Floyd at that time was connected with the Seventh Regiment Armory of New York City. The Blue Ribbon event was staged for the third consecutive time at the Interstate Park, New York, May 6 to 9.

Ninety-one gunners took part in the 1902 Grand. Ideal weather prevailed. It marked the first time that a Grand American winner had crashed straight in his first event. By events, Floyd turned in 25, 22, 23 and 24. Approximately 66,430 targets were trapped at this competition.

The late Elmer Shaner, then secretary-manager of the Interstate Association, conducted the tourney in his usual capable manner just as he had the other Grand Americans at live birds and clay targets.

There was another Grand American held that year, and it marked the finish of Grand Americans at live pigeons. The big shoot that year, which attracted 456 actual shooters, was held at the Blue River Shooting Park, Kansas City, Missouri, on March 31 to April 5. Herman C. Hirschy of Minnesota was the winner, with 25 straight and 53 straight in the shoot-off. Thirty-three gunners broke 25 straights to tie for the championship.

Grand notes . . . Rollo Guy and C. Bissett broke 92's to follow Floyd in the Grand American . . . Despite the fact that A. W. Kirby of Greenville, Ohio, broke his gun, he broke high scores in every event . . . Dr. O. F. Britton, known as "Partington," won the Preliminary Handicap, but only after winning a shoot-off from big Ed Rike of Dayton, Ohio. They broke 92's in the main event . . . It was H. G. Wheeler, Marlborough, Massachusetts, in the Consolation Handicap, with 92

These are the shooters who killed 25 straight pigeons to tie for the 1902 Grand American Live Bird race: Herman Hirschy (the winner of the shoot-off), Charlie Spencer, Pop Heikes, J. D. Pollard, L. Owen, George Roll, Guy Dering, S. Snyder, Don Morrison, G. W. Clay, Luther Squier, Fred Gilbert, Russell Cool, G. V. D. Darby, Tom Nichols, H. E. Boltenstern, Ed Bingham, T. Dockson, Ed Troeh, J. H. Boisseau, B No. 27, Hood Waters, J. H. Holmes, H. B. Hill, Bill Crosby, Pat Adams, J. E. Avery, Slim Glover, W. H. Herman, Ed Banks, W. W. Turner, S. Eugenia and J. Kaintuck

out of 100, but it took a shoot-off with Rollo Heikes to turn the trick . . . Bill Crosby won the All-around championship with 402 out of 430, followed by Herbert, Heikes and Mink.

1903—MARTIN DIEFENDERFER

The 1903 Grand American moved to the west for the first time. It was staged at Elliott's Blue River Shooting Park, Kansas City, Missouri, April 14 to 17.

The Grand American Handicap race was shot on April 16. Like the year before, ideal weather conditions prevailed.

Martin Diefenderfer of Wood River, Nebraska, won fame that year by breaking 94 from 16 yards to lead the increased field of 192 of the world's greatest shots. Diefenderfer was born in Mercer County, Pennsylvania, and at an early age moved to Nebraska, where he entered the hardware business. He is now living in South Pasadena, California, and from the latest reports is enjoying the best of health.

M. E. "Max" Hensler, the "boy wonder" from Beaver Dam, Wisconsin, broke 93 to cinch second place. Hensler shot like a house on fire at this shoot. On the previous day he had won the Preliminary Handicap title with 91. Max died years ago in Colorado Springs, Colorado.

Grand notes . . . Dr. D. A. Quick, Eldorado Springs, Colorado, copped the Consolation Handicap with 95 out of 100 from 16 yards, with A. C. Connor, Pekin, Illinois, and H. Pearse, Chicopee, Kansas, next with 93's . . . A prominent squad was made up of A. Gambell, Charlie Phellis and Luther Squier from Ohio, J. T. Atkinson, New Castle, Pennsylvania, and D. S. Daudt from South Bethlehem, Pennsylvania . . . The Humane Society wired in "You are kindly requested on behalf of the Humane Society to have all crippled birds immediately destroyed." So the shooters did their level best to destroy every clay bird . . . Fred Whitney, of Des Moines, was the cashier . . . Lakefield, Minnesota, sent a squad headed by young Frank Kalash. Frank was hailed as a comer by the scribes. Others in squad were Harry Morrison, Clifford Darr, Henry Winter and Lenny Rue . . . Fred Gilbert won the All-around, followed by Crosby, Powers, Elliott and Russ Klein.

1904—R. D. GUPTILL

Had it not been for the late Tom Marshall, R. D. Guptill, a Minnesota shooter, might not have won the 1904 Grand American Handicap race at Indianapolis. Guptill was persuaded by Marshall to attend the Grand American that year. Marshall thought he had a chance. The rest is history.

In the feature race, the Gopher trigger-puller tied up with W. W. Randall of Colorado. Each had finished their century with 96 hits. The shoot-off for world honors in the shotgun field was as bitter as it was worth watching. Twenty target events were shot in those days and the two crack shots tied up in their first two frames with 17 each. The third frame was a different story, with Guptill losing but one clay, while the Colorado gunner let five go by. Guptill stood on 19 yards, while Randall shot from 17.

Ben J. Field, author "Random Shots," and his pal, Tom Davis *(right)*, who has run bulletin boards at shoots for 40 years, both live in New York City.

Moderate weather conditions prevailed at the 1904 Grand American. The attendance, 336 entries, was nearly twice as great as at any previous meets, with 150,000 targets trapped in all events.

GRAND AMERICAN WINNERS

E. C. Griffith (1901)

C. W. Floyd (1902)

M. Diefenderfer (1903)

Dick Guptill (1904)

Russell Barber (1905)

F. E. Rogers (1906)

J. J. Blanks (1907)

Fred Harlow (1908)

Fred Shattuck (1909)

Riley Thompson (1910)

Father of Pacific Coast Trapshooting—
Hy Everding

Mr. Guptill still shoots occasionally. He attended the 1941 Grand American and broke 95 out of 100 in the Veterans' race. He is a fishing guide at Paynesville, Minnesota, and is enjoying the best of health.

Grand notes . . . Alex Mermod was drumming up business for his big live bird shoot at DuPont Park in St. Louis . . . L. A. Cummings, Bunker Hill, Illinois, and W. H. Clay, St. Louis, Missouri, tied for the Preliminary Handicap with 98 out of 100, the former winning the shoot-off and title . . . Don Morrison of St. Paul, Minnesota, won the high average for the tourney . . . Bill Heer, Guthrie, Oklahoma, copped the Consolation Handicap from 20 yards with 98 out of 100. Harvey McMurchie of Fulton, New York, was next, with 97.

1905—RUSSELL BARBER

When it comes to outstanding Grand American achievements, Russell Barber of Long Beach, California, takes a back seat to none of them. At the time of the 1905 Grand classic of scattergun champs and near champs, at Indianapolis, Russ Barber was living in the little town of Paulina, Iowa.

Just before Russ boarded the train for the Grand American, which was held at Indianapolis, his wife pinned a fourleaf clover on his gun stock.

Bill Heer

Now a four-leaf clover is said to mean luck, but it is not claimed that Barber was in any way lucky at the 1905 Grand. However, it is certain that the Iowa boy had his shooting togs on and what he did to those targets was a-plenty.

What did he do? He hung up a record that has stood since Grand Americans began in 1900, by winning both the Grand American Handicap race with 99 hits from the 16-yard line and the Preliminary Handicap on the previous day. Then, to top off a week of success, he took second honors in the Consolation race.

In winning the Grand American Handicap proper, Barber crashed 20 in his first event, dropped one in his second frame and ran the rest without a skip. His 99 score, by the way, was by far the highest yet scored. A 98 was scored to take second place alone. Ohio won the State Team race with 474 out of 500. This was a new feature. The following gunners represented the Buckeye state that year: J. Orr, Stanley Rhodes, D. A. Upson, F. H. Snow and F. D. Alkire.

Colonel O. N. Ford, Del Monte, California *(right)*, explains the famous Ford purse system to *(left)* Albert Elasho, Dr. J. H. Bradfield, Addison Stillwell and A. H. Remington

Fred Stone, one of America's leading comedians, shot through the entire program. Fred was playing in "The Wizard of Oz" at that time.

Another attraction at the 1905 Grand American was the squad made up of the five DuPont boys.

Three hundred and fifty-two shooters took part in the 1905 Blue Ribbon event. Barber, who was the big winner, was connected with powder and ammunition companies for 20 years. He has won many honors and trophies on the firing line. Twice he tied for the World's Professional championship; once with the late Fred Gilbert at the Columbus, Ohio, Grand American, and the other time with the great Homer Clark at Chicago. In 1932 at the Minnesota state shoot we watched him break 48 out of 50 mixed targets to tie up for the Minnesota Diamond Badge championship. Barber makes his home in Long Beach, California.

1906—FRED ROGERS

Fred Rogers, a St. Louis shooter, won the 1906 Grand American Handicap race with 94 breaks from 17 yards. The Grand American Handicap attracted 290 gunners that year and was held for the third consecutive time at Indianapolis.

In winning the big race, Rogers broke a 19, 20, 18, 19 and 18. The well known George Lyon, then of Durham, North Carolina, and George Roll of Blue Island, Illinois, shared runner-up honors at the 1906 classic with 93 each. Both shot from 19 yards. The scores were exceptionally good, considering the weather. A regular hurricane swept over the traps. Chan Powers, Decatur, Illinois, one of the greatest amateur shots in the country at that time, carried off the Preliminary Handicap at this shoot. We might add that we watched Chan tie for the Preliminary title at Dayton, Ohio, in 1926. At the 1906 Grand, Chan tied up in this race with two other crack shots of that time and defeated them in the shoot-off. They scored 93 out of 100. Powers shot from 20 yards.

Illinois won the Team race that was represented by Jay Graham, still as tough as leather; B. Dunnill, Chan Powers, H. Dunnill and B. T. Cole. They were all crack shots in those days. They broke 470 out of 500.

Guy Ward, who is still shooting, broke 144 out of 150 to win the Amateur Clay Target championship. He stood on 18

Guy Ward—National trapshooting champion, 1906

yards. At that time he made his home at Walnut Log, Tennessee. It is said that Guy used his old duck gun. He was considered then, and still is, one of the greatest duck hunters in the country. He was brought up on the shores of the famous Reelfoot Lake, Tennessee, and was practically unknown as a shooter up to this Grand American Handicap.

This marked the beginning of the Amateur Clay Target championship race. That year it was decided on 150 clays at 18 yards rise; the following seven years on 200 targets; five years on 100 clays, and from then on it has been decided on 200 targets at 16 yards rise.

Fred Rogers became a pro after the 1906 Grand American and was widely known in Missouri and Kansas, where he traveled. He died a good many years ago.

Grand notes . . . Walter Huff, Macon, Georgia, won the Professional championship with 145 out of 150 . . . C. O. LeCompte added more friends to his already long list . . . Les German captured the All-around but was closely pressed by Delaware's Wm. Foord . . . It was Ed Voris and Dr. F. M. Edwards who tied Chan Powers for the Preliminary Handicap title . . . Two best scores turned in by back yardage men were made by the famous Ed O'Brien of Kansas and John Taylor of Ohio . . . Three gunners, J. A. R. Elliott, Don Morrison and Walter Huff busted 193's in the Open 200 . . . And, Fred Rogers bet on himself in the Grand American pool, a 100 to one shot, which wasn't bad side pickings.

1907—JEFF BLANKS

The 1907 Grand American Handicap was staged on the old Chicago Gun Club grounds, Chicago, and it furnished the first example of the fact that the handicap is any man's race, because in that year it was won for the first time by an 80 per cent shooter—something, however, that has happened several times since then.

The little town of Trezevant in western Tennessee, near Memphis, was put on the trapshooting map in that good year of our Lord by Jeff Blanks, one of her substantial citizens, well known locally as a business man. He was the owner of a large department store but little known as a trapshooter, especially outside the state. He was a brother of H. B. Blanks of Vicksburg, Mississippi, better known at the southern shoots than Jeff.

When the Grand American Handicap proper had been shot, little Jeff Blanks, the unknown, had become famous, for he was one of the tie men in the big race. And it was on a good score, 96 out of 100.

In some way Jeff had gone down the line with a loss of only four targets. He broke a 20 straight the first time up, then a 19, 18 and 19, and a 20. In those days the Grand American Handicap was shot in 20-bird events. Tied up with Blanks were two of the country's best shots, Chan Powers of Decatur, Illinois, a veteran of many tournaments, one of the noted shooters; and Miles Maryott, Fort Collins, Colorado, widely known as one of the best in the west. No one had considered Blanks seriously in the main event, and it was only after the tie was announced that he was given a thought, and then the consensus of opinion was that he had about as much chance as the proverbial snowflake in that warm region.

But "Old Tennessee" was game and the fact that he was pitted against two of the greatest shooters in the land held no terrors for Jeff. Of course, he was at 17 yards, while Powers and Maryott were back almost as far as they put 'em at the time.

The crowd gathered around and breathlessly watched Blanks calmly break 18 out of 20 to win, while the crackerjacks, Powers and Maryott, lost four and three respectively.

O. H. Nutt *(left)* and Chan Powers *(right)*, Preliminary Handicap winners in 1926 and 1906

The crowd cheered, and Blanks took his place as one of the immortals of the shooting world whose name has been broadcast over the country as a Grand American winner. He lives yet at his Tennessee home.

Illinois again won the State Team race—Jay Graham, Jesse Young, B. Dunnill, Hugh Clark and H. Dunnill making up the team. Their score was 458 out of a possible 500. Hugh Clark of Urbana, Illinois, won the Amateur Clay Target championship with 188 out of 200 from 18 yards. John R. Taylor, Newark, Ohio, still going strong, was high on the week's program. George Lyon of Durham, North Carolina, won the Preliminary Handicap with the same score, 96.

Four hundred and ninety-five shooters, the greatest number of entries a Grand American had brought out up to then, shot in the main race. This was the first time that the big city on the lake had staged the Grand American Handicap, but it was the scene of many subsequent Grands. Ideal weather conditions prevailed at this Grand American.

1908—FRED HARLOW

Fred Harlow, of Newark, Ohio, recognized as one of the leading trapshots of his day, crashed 92 out of 100 from a 16-yard line to capture the 1908 Grand American, staged that year at Columbus, Ohio. Harlow, a dark horse, did not have a walk-away. When the 100 targets were finished, he was found tied up with the peerless Woolfolk Henderson, the Lexington, Kentucky, gunner.

Fred, a distinctive new shooter, was hardly given a look-in by the gallery of shoot fans who assembled to see a new king of trapdom crowned. But the Newark trigger-puller stood the strain in the shoot-off like a veteran and defeated the Blue Grass star by one target.

During the Handicap race a strong wind swept over the traps in such a way that the targets at times were very erratic in their flight, causing many to soar away untouched.

"Duck Call" C. H. Ditto of Keithsburg, Illinois, won the Preliminary Handicap event at the 1908 Grand American with 95 breaks from 18 yards, after shooting out the well known Charlie "Sparrow" Young, who finished with the same score from 20 yards. Henderson and Harlow were next with 94.

The Illinois team again came through with flying colors in the state team race. The quintette scored 470 out of 500 to win. This marked the third straight victory for the Illinois squad. The 1908 team was composed of Jay Graham, who broke 94; George Roll, 97; Lem Willard, 90; Jesse Young, 94, and Chan Powers, 95. George Roll, who shot well all week, captured the amateur clay target championship with 183 breaks out of 200, shooting from 18 yards. George Maxwell, Hastings, Nebraska, the one-armed pro, won high average for the entire tournament with 485 out of 520.

Harlow, winner of the Grand American Handicap event, has been a target shooting star since the day he won the Grand American. Although Fred shoots but little, he turns in a good average of victories. When he is on the shooting grounds you know there will be fireworks. He won the Ohio state championship three times. Fred's occupation is that of district supervisor for the state fish and game department. In 1931 he averaged .9916 on 600 clays to top all gunners of North America in the 500 to 1,000 class.

Grand notes . . . Captain A. H. Hardy of Colorado gave an exhibition of fancy shooting . . . Ray Loring never missed a Grand in those days, this being his fourth . . . Denny Upson, C. H. Ditto and H. E. Buckwalter tied George Roll for the National championship. Buckwalter, who lived in Royersford, Pennsylvania, took second place after the shoot-off . . . L. I. Wade, Dallas, Texas, was one of the most popular shooters of this era and one of the best.

World's record squad at Yorklyn, Delaware—499 x 500: *(Left to right)* Bill Eldred, Joe Hiestand, Hale Jones, Ned Lilly and Art Cuscaden

1909—FRED SHATTUCK

Fred Shattuck of Columbus, Ohio, chalked up the third Buckeye Grand American Handicap win in 1909 at Chicago when he crashed 96 out of 100 from the 18-yard line in the regular program and 20 straight in the shoot-off. Three well-known gunners, John R. Livingston, Springville, Alabama, one of the state's greatest shots, 19 yards; George E. Burns, Cleveland, Ohio, 16 yards; and Billy Wettleaf, Nichols, Iowa, at 19 yards, had all tied with Shattuck in the regular race.

The shoot-off, which was short and sweet, showed the Columbus trigger-puller with 20 straight. Livingston dropped one and Burns two, while Wettleaf finished with 17 out of 20.

Four High Average kings: *(Left to right)* T. K. Lee, Alabama; Joe Cotant, Idaho; Art Risser, Illinois, and Boyd Duncan, Tennessee

Frank Fisher, Eagle Grove, Iowa, won the Preliminary Handicap race with 94 breaks from 18 yards. Mrs. Ad Topperwein shot like a house on fire all week. She was a member of the squad which broke 100 straight on the first day. The other four well knowns who shot in this squad were Harve Dixon, Missouri; Woolfolk Henderson, Kentucky; George Mackie, Kansas, and Homer Freeman, Atlanta, Georgia.

In the Amateur Clay Target championship race the well-known amateur expert, D. A. Upson of Cleveland, Ohio, won with a score of 188. F. E. Foltz of McClure, Ohio, took second place with 187, and the dangerous Woolfolk Henderson broke 185 to place third.

The late Fred Gilbert, then of Spirit Lake, Iowa, copped the Professional championship, scoring 193 out of 200, while Bill Heer of Oklahoma, a terror in those days, crashed 191 to take runner-up honors. Of the 457 gunners who attended the Grand American Handicap at Chicago that year, 142 were Illinois shooters. There was no team race in 1909.

The powerful "Southern Gin Squad" was on hand, composed of Nash Buckingham, J. B. Snowden, Jeff Blanks, J. B. Goodbar and B. H. Finley.

Although Shattuck, winner of the big event in 1909, shot much after this, he gradually dropped out of the shooting game. At the 1926 Grand American at Vandalia, Ohio, he shot in the Grand American Handicap race and crashed 72 out of his first 75.

Grand notes . . . Dr. C. E. Cook, now a prominent Chicago physician and noted fisherman as well, proved to the shooters that his shooting glasses were the best . . . H. E. "Ed" Winans,

J. A. R. "Jim" Elliott started the Kansas City Gun Club in 1888. R. S. "Uncle Bob" Elliott took it over in 1894 and operated it until his death in 1932. Russ Elliott now runs the club. Here we have pictured the Kansas City Gun Club members at the Grand American. *(Top row)* Carrick Mustion, Geo. Nicolai, Guy Nichols, Rudy Etchen, Russ Elliott, Joe Davison, Dick Williams, Ernest Jelly, Dave Henry, Lela Hall, T. S. Poquette, Chrissy Elliott, Paul Heitman, Mike Beard, J. J. Bunch, Harry Davis, Bert Metzger; *(Seated)* O. E. Grecian, Paul Trower, Skip Williams, Odd Williams, Dud Dickinson, R. E. Michaels, Guy Harryman, Hugh Golden

of Illinois, was one of the best men in the shooting game at that time.

1910—RILEY THOMPSON

The first hundred straight in Grand American history was turned in at the 1910 Grand American tussel, which was staged at the Chicago Gun Club, Chicago, Illinois. Riley "Farmer" Thompson, then known as one of the best amateur shots in the country, especially in the west, made the little town of Cainsville in northwestern Missouri famous by winning that year. He stood on the 19-yard mark.

This was a record for this event, and a record that stood up for 15 years, or until 1926, when Charlie "Sparrow" Young, the Springfield, Ohio, veteran, broke 100 straight from 23 yards. The score sheet at the 1910 tourney shows Charlie Young in action on the 19-yard line and he crashed 91 out of 100.

The day was perfect for high scores at the 1910 Grand. Not a breath of wind prevailed, and the slight haze that hung over the traps did not prevent high scores from being rolled up. I might add that Harvey McMurchy, a professional shot of that era, broke his first 80 straight, but dropped one in his last 20. Professionals were allowed to shoot for the money at that period.

For several months prior to the Grand American, Thompson had been in a slump, due to a bad case of "fudging," and he came to the shoot undecided as to whether he would enter the Grand American Handicap race. But he was finally persuaded to enter. Everybody knew that when Riley was right, no one had anything on him. He shot in the last squad on No. 5 peg.

Riley got off to a flying start. His "fudges" were not in evidence, and be broke his first 80 straight. Before he came up for his last 20 targets, Harvey McMurchy's 99 had been posted on the bulletin board, and Riley knew that to win he must break his last 20 straight.

It was almost dark when his squad came up for this last round and a great crowd gathered around to see the finish. The excitement was intense. The spectators watched breathlessly. It was said that you could have heard a pin drop. Hundreds of dollars and the winning of the Grand American Handicap, world's greatest shooting event, was at stake. Few could have stood the strain, but "Farmer" Riley had no more nerves than a fish. He went through that last string of 20 targets, powdering every one of them without even a close call. He shot them just like he had been shooting them out back of the barn at Cainsville. Shooters who knew Riley knew that if he missed a target it would not be due to stage fright but to a "fudge"—and the "fudge" didn't come. And so Riley made history that day, breaking the first 100 straight ever made at a Grand American.

The great gathering of shooters surged around Thompson with congratulations on one of the greatest exhibitions of stamina the sport of trapshooting has known. McMurchy's 99 took second place. He shot from 18 yards. McMurchy died in Florida years ago. Jay Graham, standing at 20 yards, and George Volk at 18, shared third place, with 98's.

W. J. Raup, Portage, Wisconsin, and C. E. Shaw, Chicago, tied for high honors in the Preliminary handicap race with 99 out of 100, both standing on 16 yards. Raup won the shoot-off with 20 straight. The late Guy Dering of Columbus, Wisconsin, carried off the National Clay Bird title with 187 out of 200 at 18 yards. Jay Graham, still going strong both at target shooting and fishing at Ingleside, Illinois, who had shot like a house on fire all week, broke 188. So did the late Jim Day, then of Texas. A squad composed of Jay Graham, John W. Garrett, Homer Freeman, Harve Dixon and Fred Ellett broke 100 straight from the 20-yard mark in one of the races. This was a world's record.

On the first day of the tournament John Garrett, Colorado Springs, Colorado, broke 80 straight singles and 10 pairs of doubles, which was another world's record at this record-smashing Grand American. The professional race was hotly contested. Charlie Spencer, St. Louis, Missouri, J. W. Garrett and H. E. Clark tied on 190. Two shoot-offs were needed to decide the winner. In the first frame all broke 20 straight and in the second Spencer broke 'em all while Clark and Garrett finished with 19.

Spencer died years ago. Riley Thompson still lives at Cainsville. To the best of my knowledge, I think Riley visited his last Grand American in 1926 and watched Charlie Young break his 100 straight.

1911—HARVE DIXON

Judge Harve Dixon, known for many years as the hard-shooting Oronogo wonder, carried off the twelfth Grand Amer-

A PERFECT SCORE—These Indiana gunners: *(Left to right)* Ferd Kahler, Ren Heaton, Ralph Jenkins, H. L. Cheek and Rock Jenkins, broke 125 straight

ican at clay targets held at Columbus, Ohio, June 22. The old reliable Harve broke 99 from the 20-yard mark. It was the greatest score made up to that time at this yardage.

The weather during the Columbus Grand was ideal for target shooting. Dixon dropped one clay in his first event, then finished without a loss. Close on the heels of the Missouri veteran came four other well-known shooters. They were T. E. Graham, brother of Jay; A. J. Hill, Dawson, Georgia; O. H. Nutt, Ohio, who won the Preliminary Handicap at Dayton, Ohio, some 15 years later, and E. C. Irwin. They broke 98's.

One of the outstanding shooters of the meet was the great ball player and professional trapshooter of those days, the late Lester German, then of Aberdeen, Maryland. Les won the Professional championship with 198 out of 200, running his first 192 straight. He also won the Doubles championship with 89 out of 100. C. C. Collins, Aldine, Indiana, shooting from 18 yards, won the Amateur championship with 196. C. B. Eaton, Fayette, Missouri, one of the state's best at that time, and H. F. Buckwalter, of Royersford, Pennsylvania, tied for high gun in the Preliminary race, with 98 each. Eaton at 18 yards won the shoot-off, scoring 20 to Buck's 18. The Keystone shooter shot from 19 yards. George Maxwell, Hastings, Nebraska, the one-armed pro, was High-over-all professional at this meet. He shot well in every event.

Harve Dixon, the winner, was a great shooter from boy-

Harve Dixon, Oronogo, Missouri, 1911 Grand American victor *(middle)*, pictured with a "Show Me" squad at the Grand American. The others are *(left to right)* C. Ziller, Count Smythe, A. M. McRae and Frank Folmer

hood days. The official record book shows Harve shooting his last registered clays in 1930, when he shot at 100 for an average of 96 per cent.

He won his state championship at singles and doubles on several occasions. Before his retirement he turned in creditable averages each year. In 1927 he finished the season with a mark of 96 per cent flat on 1,100 targets. Like most trapshooters, he is an excellent field shot. He is said to be one of the best bass fishermen in his part of the country. He fishes for them in the many streams of the Ozarks.

Famous Western squad at the Grand American: *(Left to right)* John Taylor, Frank Huseman, Spencer Olin, Homer Clark, and J. M. Hawkins. Hawkins, Taylor and Clark were stars at the 1911 Grand American. These five shooters are still going strong

Like Riley Thompson, he carries the name of "Farmer." Harve comes from a shooting family. His father, the late Judge Dixon, of Joplin, Missouri, was a trapshooter for 50 years, and his brother, Chester, was well known at the traps. Harve succeeded his father as County Judge. He now lives at Webb City, Missouri.

Three shooters who attended the 1911 Grand American are still going strong. We refer to J. M. Hawkins, Homer Clark and John Taylor. Hawkins won the Introductory race at the 1911 Grand with 100 straight, and incidentally, Homer Clark and John Taylor were next with 99's, topping such great shooting stars as Bill Heer, Jay Graham, Charlie Spencer, Les German, Dick Clancy and Fred Gilbert.

1912—W. E. PHILLIPS

All roads led to Springfield, the capital of Illinois, the third week in June, when the old Interstate Association's thirteenth Grand American Handicap Tournament was held on the grounds of the Illinois Gun Club.

It was the late W. E. Phillips, then a Chicago building contractor, who furnished the thrills that year when he busted 96 out of 100 from the 19-yard line and 17 out of 20 in the shoot-off.

Phillips did not have a walk-away in winning the feature race, which was shot in a rain and wind storm. At the conclusion of the 100 targets in the handicap he was found locked in a tie with an Ohio shooter, H. D. Duckham of Kenton. Phillips, however, stood the ordeal of the shoot-off better and won over the Buckeye shooter by two targets. He broke 17 out of 20, while the Kenton star turned in 15.

Three hundred and seventy-seven different shooters took part in the Grand American Handicap that year. By events Phillips broke a 20, 19, 17, 20, and 20. Duckham slipped one in his first frame, three in the second and he went out with 60 straight.

Max Kneussl, Ottawa, Illinois; J. A. Campbell, Tulsa, Oklahoma, and the famous Charlie Young of Springfield, Ohio, each broke 95. It might be noted that Charlie Young was close to the top at several of the earlier Grand Americans. His turn came to win later, in 1926.

Billy Hoon of Iowa, who tied for the National Clay Bird

title with 200 out of 200 at the Grand American at Dayton in 1932, broke high scores in all races at the 1912 Grand American Handicap classic. He won the Preliminary Handicap with 94 out of 100 from the 19-yard line, and was high amateur for the meet with 348 out of 400. Hoon had to step on the gas to win the preliminary, as he was tied up at the conclusion of this race with three other good amateur shots, all of whom lived in Illinois. They are, L. R. Stockley, Chicago, 19 yards; Jim Gray, Bloomington, 18 yards, and C. E. Orr of East Alton, who stood on 16. In the shoot-off the scores on 20 targets read something like this: Hoon, 18; Stockley, 17; Gray, 17, and Orr, 16.

Mark Arie won the Doubles championship with 89 out of 100, while the late Fred Gilbert took the pro honors with 84 after tying and shooting out J. S. Day, Texas; Walter Huff, Macon, Georgia, and the late Ed O'Brien, then of Florence, Kansas. H. G. Taylor, Meckling, South Dakota, won the high average for professional gunners with 742 out of 800.

There was a close and interesting race for the Amateur championship, which resulted in a tie for first place between E. W. Varner of Adams, Nebraska, and Billy Hoon, each of whom scored 192. Varner won the shoot-off by the narrow margin of one target.

Bill Crosby, one of the great professionals of that time, won the pro title with the fine score of 198 out of 200. Fred Gilbert and Rollo Heikes tied for second, with 195.

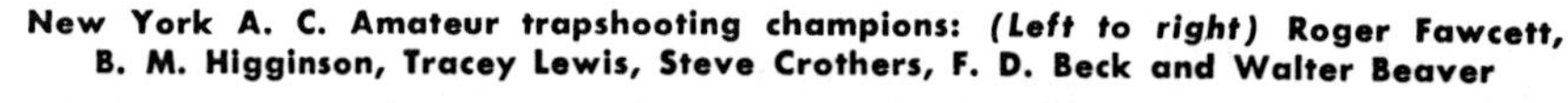
New York A. C. Amateur trapshooting champions: *(Left to right)* Roger Fawcett, B. M. Higginson, Tracey Lewis, Steve Crothers, F. D. Beck and Walter Beaver

Badger gunners at the Grand American: *(Front row, left to right)* Vic Reinders, George Gillette, John Kurth, A. F. Brighton, Bob Whepley, Art Roth, John A. Peterson, H. P. Nicklas; *(Second row)* Frank Mazanet, Ed Hanson, Frank Vyvyan, J. B. Schuyler, Ray Spink, Bobbie Vyvyan, Frank Bossman, Harry Billett, A. H. Fuller, Harley Waterman, Eddie Newburg, J. G. Brunkhorst, George Bluell, Mrs. Wm. Gilbert, Wm. Gilbert

Phillips, victor in the big race, was born in Wheeling, West Virginia. He moved to Naperville, Illinois, at the age of 10. His family owned a large farm about a mile from Naperville and it was there that Phillips first learned to use a shotgun. At that time game was very plentiful in that locality. During the early nineties, he attended many of the live bird shoots held at Grand Crossing Park, near Chicago. Later, when clay targets became popular, he took up the sport. He, along with John Egermann and Phil Hammersmith, were the prime boosters of the old Naperville Gun Club.

Along about the year 1907, trapshooting was started at the South Shore Country Club, Chicago, and Mr. Phillips was one of the organizers. When the Grand American Handicap was held at Grant Park in 1915, he was one of the men who took an active part in bringing the shoot to Chicago and staging the tournament. On April 28, 1921, he passed on to the Great Beyond.

1913—MARK HOOTMAN

A dark horse, Mark Hootman, an Ohio entry, stunned gunners and spectators by winning the 1913 Grand American

GRAND AMERICAN WINNERS

W. E. Phillips (1912)

L. B. Clarke (1915)

J. F. Wulf (1916)

C. H. Larson (1917)

J. D. Henry (1918)

G. W. Lorimer (1919)

A. L. Ivins (192

E. F. Haak (1921)

Jack Frink (1922)

Mark Arie (1923)

Mark Hootman, the 1913 Grand American winner, is shown with four other nationally known shooters: *(Left to right)* Charlie Young, George Peter, Sam Sharman, Mark Hootman and Charlie Bogert

Handicap race. The tourney that year was staged at the N. C. R. Gun Club, Dayton, Ohio.

It was Mark's first year at clay target shooting. In the spring of 1913 Mark thought that he would try a few of those clay targets. He was already, at that time, a handy man in the field with both shotgun and rifle, and he figured his chances were as good as the next fellow's at the traps. He attended a small shoot and made a fair score. His next attempt was at the Ohio state shoot. His gun pounded his face so hard that he quit the program after he had fired a few shots.

That year the Grand American was held in June. Mark thought that he would take it in and see what real competition

***(Left to right)* Sam Jenny, Harry Schomerus, T. Vail, Bart Lewis and Bob Prather. Jenny and Lewis were former National Doubles champions—Schomerus won the Preliminary Grand American Handicap in 1931**

was like, and enter a few of the races if his face did not bother him. Before long the bug seized him, and he took his place in the Grand American Handicap race along with 501 of the leading shotgun exponents of the world.

The rest is history. Hootman broke 97 out of 100, which placed him in a tie for high honors with F. A. Graper, Custer Park, Illinois, and J. A. Blunt, Greensboro, Alabama. In the shoot-off at 20 targets, Mark broke them all, while Blunt and Graper dropped one each. Hootman stood on 17 yards and Graper and Blunt on 20 yards.

At this shoot the late George L. Lyon of Durham, North Carolina, broke 94 out of 100 to win the Amateur Doubles title. Charlie Young, Springfield, Ohio, crashed 197 out of 200 to top the professionals while Bart Lewis, Auburn, Illinois, won the amateur clay bird crown with 195 out of 200.

The Preliminary Handicap race was a thriller. A. B. Richardson of Dover, Delaware, copped this title only after a heated shoot-off with the late Andy Meaders of Nashville, Tennessee, then 73 years old. In the regular race, with Richardson at 20 yards and Meaders at 18, they scored 96's. In the shoot-off, the Delaware gunner broke them all, while "Old Tennessee" let five go by unharmed. That year Jay Graham won the pro doubles championship with 88 out of 100.

Hootman has been a shooting star since the day he won the Grand American. The versatile Ohio target expert has won the Buckeye state high-average several times, has copped the state championship and has been high-over all at several state shoots. His average last year was .9642 on 1,400 clays.

1914—WOOLFOLK HENDERSON

The 1914 Grand American, staged at the N. C. R. grounds at Dayton, Ohio, brought to the front Woolfolk Henderson, the Lexington, Kentucky, gunner, who had been knocking at the championship door for several years.

Henderson's achievements at the 1914 classic had never been experienced before. He gave the greatest all around exhibition of target shooting the world had ever seen.

What did he do that caused a furore? First, he captured the Grand American Handicap race with the remarkable score of 98 out of 100 from 22 yards, unheard of in those days; second, he won the amateur clay bird championship with 99 out of 100; and third, he copped the Doubles title of the world with 90 out of 100. Henderson's three major wins still stand alone. But, at that, they came as no surprise to the shotgun world, for Woolfolk Henderson was a mighty shooter in those days.

Before we go any farther with our story, we might review how Woolfolk Henderson carried off the Amateur high-average title of North America that year with a mark of .9663 on 2,050 registered targets. His sensational Grand American triumphs, followed by his winning of the National high-average, stamped him clearly as the greatest shot of the 1914 trapshooting season. The Kentucky marksman had demonstrated it beyond a doubt.

The 1914 Grand American was the greatest held up to that time, with 186,000 targets being trapped. The tourney, which was staged September 8 to 11, was the second to be held at Dayton and the late John R. Patterson, president of the National Cash Register Company, left nothing undone to please the shooters. Elmer Shaner, manager of the shoot, often told me that the 1914 Grand was the best equipped gun meet up to that time.

Dark horses and mediocre gunners had been carrying off the Grand American Handicap races. The 1914 Blue Ribbon event clearly demonstrated that the crack shot had a chance. This marked the second time that a 22-yard man had won the big money. It will be remembered that "Pop" Heikes had won in the year 1900 at Madison Square Garden, New York, from 22 yards.

In the Handicap race, which Henderson won with 98, two shooters, A. C. Blair and O. P. Goode, tied for second place with 97's. The Lexington "tornado" had rather easy sailing in the National Amateur championship race. He broke the first frame of 25 targets straight, dropped one in his second string and ran out without a slip. In the second place, with 97's, came J. M. Barrett of Augusta, Georgia, and W. S. Behm of Pittsburgh.

The "fair haired boy" from the south side of the river had no walk-away in the Doubles race, however. As stated before, Woolfolk won with 90, but close up was the dangerous Sam Huntly with 89. The latter had one bad event, his third, when he dropped four targets.

Famous Southern professionals at the 1940 Texas State Shoot: *(Back row)* Herman Ehler, John McCullough, Frank Ponce, Walter Scott, and J. R. Hinkle; *(Bottom)* Dewey Godfrey, R. D. Fouse and W. C. Morris *(right)*

C. F. Riffe, Kenova, West Virginia, and hard-shooting Tony Chezik of Portal, North Dakota, broke 96 each to tie for the preliminary crown. Riffe, who stood on 17 yards, won the shoot-off by the narrow margin of one clay. Chezik, at 19 yards, broke 17 out of 20. Close on the heels of the 96's were C. E. Demitt, Morrow, Ohio; H. E. Wiedenbusch, Fairmont, West Virginia, and H. F. Whilon, each of whom broke 95. Wiedenbusch won the shoot with 19 out of 20.

They still talk about Henderson's wins at the 1914 Grand American. They will long be remembered in trapshooting history. In a recent letter Mr. Henderson stated that his health is fine. He's shooting groundhogs with his .22 for pastime.

New Jersey at the Grand: *(Back row)* E. Mount, A. E. Cooper, Johnny Flagg, A. F. Streelman, W. Fields, Paul Holloway, D. W. Thomas, M. H. Apgar, Mrs. H. J. Miller, H. J. Miller, W. B. Stillwagon; *(Bottom)* J. H. Lore, Walter F. Johnson, Fred Glaser, E. J. Lisk, W. W. Gearhart, Lewis Slocum

1915—L. B. CLARKE

E. Field White of Poly Choke fame and Charlie Newcomb, the 1915 National Trapshooting Champion

A wealthy Chicago banker, L. B. "Lou" Clarke, won the 1915 Grand American, which was held at Grant Park, right off of Michigan Boulevard, Chicago. This shoot had an unprecedented entry record of 884 shooters in the big event, which was not only a record up to this time, but a record that stood for many years. In fact, it stood until 1926, when 932 gunners lined up in the feature race at Vandalia, Ohio.

Clarke had been shooting clay targets but two years. He won the 1915 honors only after a heated shoot-off with three other shooters. They are: Dr. C. C. Hickham, Yeoman, Indi-

20 degrees below zero didn't bother the boys at the Milwaukee Gun Club: *(Front row, left to right)* A. J. Baum, Herman Zillgett, H. A. Dunham, Dr. H. Pannetti, Carl Koeffler, Dr. C. M. Vandenbergh; *(Back row)* John Fraser, Sr., Dr. L. C. Scharnhorst, Kurt Gustafson, C. McConnell, C. Huebschen, Dr. M. J. Bach, George Gillett, William E. Quinn, J. E. Johnson, Charles Hayden

ana, who, by the way, had tied for the Grand American Handicap twice in his trapshooting career; Jess Randall, then of Greensburg, Kansas, and Monte Dewire of Hamilton, Indiana. Randall is now a pro in Nebraska and is still shooting at a fast clip. Dewire carried off the amateur title at the 1932 Grand American.

In the shoot-off, Clarke won with 20 straight from 18 yards, Dewire broke 19 at 18 yards, Randall broke 18 at 19 yards and Hickman broke 17 at 19 yards.

R. H. Morse, another Chicago shooter, won the preliminary handicap with 95 breaks from the 18-yard line. Three gunners tied for second place: C. A. Gunning, Longmont, Colorado; George K. Mackie, Scannon, Kansas, and Ed Schendel of Milwaukee. The late Guy Dering of Columbus, Wisconsin, carried off the Doubles championship with 91 out of 100.

Charlie Newcomb, Philadelphia, then one of the greatest amateur shots in the country, captured the Amateur championship title with 99 out of 100. R. A. Fred King, Delta, Colorado, and A. B. Richardson, Dover, Delaware, broke 98 to divide second place. Billy Hoon of Iowa broke 196 out of 200 to win the Grand Park Introductory race. Bart Lewis was high-average pro of the tourney with 485 out of 500.

The last time I saw Mr. Clarke was at Pasadena Gun Club shooting skeet with Mel Morgan, Bob Wilfong and George Hamilton. He was still shooting "Mary Lou" that won the Grand for him. Mr. Clarke died a few years ago.

Grand notes . . . Henry B. Rebhausen, North Platte, Nebraska, won the Chicago overture with 98 out of 100. . . . Carl Hammersmith of Milwaukee won the Consolation Handicap with 91 out of 100, but only after shooting out Sam Leever, the former Pittsburgh baseball star from Goshen, Ohio. Fred Koch, Brookville, Ohio, a well known shot in those days, was third with 90 out of 100. . . . Tom Hale, young Tennessee star, shot well in the Champ of Champs race. . . . Dell Gross and Guy Dering staged a special race on 100 pairs of doubles, with Guy Dering winning by one target. . . . Denny Holland, who busted 100 straight to win the Missouri state championship, shot below his usual great form in the Champ of Champs competition. . . . The Kansas boys, George Mackie, Pete Hood, Jack Wray, George Grubb and Walter

Frank Troeh, Portland, Oregon, at the extreme right, has won more National championships than any other trapshooter. Here he is pictured with five other western stars: *(Left to right)* C. W. Wood, Cal Ray, T. H. Carpenter, C. G. Hiltibrand and J. H. Martin

Huscher, took back $1,700 in cash. . . . The perfect squad of 100 straight had J. R. Hinkle, F. G. Bills, E. W. Daniels, Bart Lewis and Charlie Young in their lineup.

1916—JACK WULF

The 1916 Grand American Handicap tournament, held under the auspices of the St. Louis Trapshooters Association, on August 21 to 26, was the next largest in the history of the world's great annual target classics up to this time. There were 683 actual starters. This was not a dark horse year. A veteran of the traps, widely known in the middle West, attired in a Palm Beach suit and wearing a Mexican sombrero, went down the line to become the winner of the big event of the meet.

He was Captain Jack Wulf of Milwaukee, known through the sportsmen's papers as "Captain Jack," and he landed the prize on a score of 99, from the 19-yard mark. Only once before had this score been beaten. Two shooters had equalled it in previous years.

Captain Jack was so confident that he was going to win the premier event that year that he had announced he was going to win and had even brought along his picture.

Eli Maland, an Iowa shooter, standing on 16 yards, broke a 98 to take second honors. Eli, John and Henry Maland, brothers, were well known in the Corn State. Three men turned in scores of 97 to tie for third place: H. C. Daley, Carlinville, Illinois, 16 yards; Charlie Atkinson, Creighton, Nebraska, 17 yards, and D. C. Rogers, an Indiana shooter, 19 yards. Ten gunners broke 96.

Al Koyen put the little town of Fremont, Nebraska, on the map at this shoot by winning the Preliminary Handicap title with 97 breaks from the 19-yard mark. L. S. Rambo, Delong, Illinois, came next, with 96. He stood on the same mark as Koyen.

Harve Dixon, the Oronogo, Missouri, veteran, again proved that he had few superiors with a shotgun. Harve broke some fine scores that week, his best being 197 out of 200 in the Introductory race, which was good enough to cop the bacon. The great Frank Troeh, then of the state of Washington, carried away the National Amateur championship. This was a 100-target affair in those days, and Frank broke 99. C. B. Eaton, Fayette, Missouri, then a cracking good shot, took second honors with 98 out of 100.

Allen Heil, Allentown, Pennsylvania, won the Doubles championship with 89 out of 50 pairs. Frank Troeh took runner-up honors to Heil by breaking 88 out of 100. The Consolation race was one of the hottest of the week. At the finish of the 100 targets two shooters had tied for high honors with 96: H. E. Furnas, then of Pittsburgh, Pennsylvania, and a 16-year old boy, W. E. Phillips, Jr., Chicago, son of the 1912 Grand American Handicap winner. Furnas, who stood on 16 yards, defeated the Chicago boy, shooting from 18 yards, by the narrow margin of one target.

The well known Mrs. L. G. Vogel, Detroit, Michigan, shooting from 18 yards, broke 95, to take third place. There will probably never be a more spectacular Consolation race than this, featuring as it did a 16-year old boy who had tied for high score and a woman shooter taking third position.

As for Jack Wulf, big winner of the week, he started shooting targets in 1895. Although never ranked as a great shot, he has always proven tough in shooting competition. He lives now in Milwaukee.

Grand notes . . . H. W. Cadwallader from Decatur, Illinois, could shoot as good with one eye as most shooters can with two. . . . Sam S. Foster, Mason City, Iowa, was master of ceremonies. . . . Pete Carney of Philadelphia was the trapshooting scribe at that time, and a good one, too. . . . Mrs. L. G. Vogel, Detroit, a great woman shooter in those days, won the Women's High Average. . . . Mrs. Jesse Dalton, Warsaw, Indiana, won the Women's championship. . . .

These gunners, all members of the Izaak Walton gun club at Casper, Wyoming, O. E. Spangler, J. T. Irick and H. E. Nickum, flew to the 1940 Grand American

Harvey Carlisle, Salt Lake City *(left)*, Tommy Lovett, Houston *(center)*, the 1939 National High Average leader, and J. O. Bates of Fort Worth. Gene Robertson *(extreme right)*, Los Angeles. Carlisle and Robertson, both Junior shooters, won their state championships

Clarence Parker, the well known Minot, North Dakota, hotel man, broke 192 out of 200 in the Preliminary race.

1917—CHARLIE LARSON

Two state champions, Charlie Larson of Wisconsin and the renowned Mark Arie of Illinois, tied for the big Handicap at the 1917 Grand American, which was staged at the South Shore Country Club, Chicago. Each broke 98 out of 100, Arie standing on 22 yards, Larson on 20.

NEBRASKA GUNNERS AT THE GRAND: ***(Top row)*** **Wayne Bailey, Glenn Bailey, John Davidson, Bailey girls, Mrs. Bailey, Mrs. Davidson, J. A. Walden, M. A. Burtan, J. A. Sabata, L. E. Berck, Mrs. Berck;** ***(Bottom)*** **M. S. Gray, Buford Bailey, Ernie Bihler, Eilene Davidson, Lester Stecker, Eddie Dygert, Dayton Dorn, Art Carmody, J. H. Bolin, Charlie Keller**

Eight hundred eight different shooters, most of them well known to the shotgun world, shot the feature race, the Grand American proper. In spite of a cold rain which at times swept over the traps, the scores were good. It took two days to shoot the big race that year. In the shoot-off Elmer Shaner, the veteran shoot manager, refereed. The two men, with much at stake, took their places. The outcome, with yardages considered, was an even bet. Larson, a state champion and splendid shot, with an advantage of two yards, was sure to make it interesting for the great Arie.

Walter Peterson ***(extreme right)*** **won the Champion of Champions race at the Grand in 1939. Here Bill Mayfield snaps him with** ***(left to right)*** **A. Peterson, Illinois; H. Peterson, Vermont; John Peterson, Iowa, the 1917 Preliminary Champion; and Archie Peterson of Minnesota**

Larson appeared a trifle nervous at first and dropped the first target that popped out of the traphouse. Not so with the pudgy boy from Illinois. He was as cool as usual, shooting quick, and broke his targets up in fine, snappy style. Larson let them go farther away, riding them out, but broke them remarkably well. At the end of the eighth round, Arie was one to the good. It looked like it was all his race and that he wouldn't miss one, but he did, his ninth, and at the end of 20 they found themselves just where they started. The Wisconsin boy apparently had regained his composure, if he ever had been nervous, for he lost no more; neither did Mark, and they were out with 19 each.

In the second 20 of the shoot-off, Arie quickly sprung into the lead when Larson missed his second clay. Again the odds were shifted. It was a two to one bet on the famous Arie. Everything went well until Mark's 13th bird, which he let go by. Then he missed two more, his 15th and 16th. Larson muffed his 14th, Arie his 18th, then they went out straight. The score at the end of the frame read: Larson, 18; Arie, 16.

Two 97 scores followed Arie and Larson. They were made by R. S. Smith of Mounds, Illinois, from the 19-yard line, and I. C. Norwood, Davenport, Iowa, who shot from 17 yards.

The Grand American tournament was held the last week in August and all the races were featured by big scores and surprises. Mark Arie was the most outstanding gunner of the week. The "Flying Dutchman" won the National Amateur championship with 99 out of 100 in the regular race and 75 straight in the shoot-off. Jay Clarke, Jr., state champion of Massachusetts, and Roy McIntyre, champion of Pennsylvania, tied Arie in this race. Clarke was eliminated in the second frame, while Arie and McIntyre went through a third string before Arie won. C. B. Platt, Bridgeton, New Jersey, a well known expert and later member of the 1924 American Olympic trapshooting team, carried away the Doubles title that year. Platt turned in the good score of 96. Arie came second with 95.

John Peterson, Randall, Iowa, shooting at 18 yards, won the Preliminary Handicap with 99 breaks. Roy Nutt of Chicago, standing on 19 yards, won the Consolation handicap with a score of 96.

In the Grand American proper, Max Emery of Chicago, 14 years of age, broke 83, while Andy Meaders of Nashville, Tennessee, then 76, turned in an 88.

Charlie Larson, winner of the Grand American Handicap race, started shooting clay targets in 1914. He won the first shoot he attended, which was held at Fond du Lac, Wisconsin. To win this event he broke 138 out of 150, and his score included a long run of 70. In 1917, the year he won the Grand, he captured the Wisconsin state championship with 99 out of 100, and was high-over-all on 16-yard targets, with 391 out of 400. He repeated his state championship the following year by breaking 97 out of a possible 100.

In 1922 Oscar Larson, Charlie's brother, won the Badger state crown with 198. Charlie was runner-up, with 197. In all of his trap experiences up to the time I last checked in 1933, he never lost a shoot-off. In 1921 Charlie averaged .9766, which I think was the greatest average he ever compiled for a season. He attended six or seven Grand Americans. The last time we saw Charlie was at the Wisconsin state shoot several years ago. He is a butcher in Waupaca.

O. N. Ford, then of Iowa, a great shot in those days, traveled 12,000 miles to shoots, shot at 6,025 targets for an average of .9546, breaking three 200 straights, unusual in those days of hard targets. Ford now runs the Del Monte Gun Club.

1918—J. D. HENRY

It does not matter whether you are the butcher, the baker or the candlestick maker in trapshooting—everybody has a chance. The Grand was won in 1918 by a barber, J. D. Henry by name, and he made his home at Elkhart, Indiana.

Henry was very much the dark horse. He came to the Grand, staged at the South Shore Country Club, Chicago, that year, unnoticed and unheralded. But we'll bet his many friends in Elkhart were at the train to welcome him home.

For Henry crashed from the 16-yard mark 97 targets in the regular race to tie up the famous Hank Pendergast of Phoenix, New York, a money shooter, if there ever was one. Hank stood on 22 yards, as he was one of the greatest shooters in the country. In the shoot-off, Pendergast, quick and confident, snuffing out his targets, looked like a sure winner. Henry, letting them get away, was chipping them. A moving picture machine was touched off right at Hank's ear and he lost two targets. He was too good a sport to claim a balk or make an alibi, but to close observers this seemed to have caused him to lose the race. The final check-up on the shoot-off revealed

Western Professionals at the Grand American: *(Back)* J. B. Grier, Paul Lewis, Mac Allen, Emmett Hines, Joe Davison, Don Flewelling, G. H. Oswald, Cap. Hopkins, Al Ormsbee, Guy Nichols, Homer Clark and Fred Bills

Henry with 18 and Pendergast with 17. However, Pendergast had been a big winner all week and Henry's victory was a great thing for the sport.

Six hundred twenty shooters took part in the Grand American Handicap proper, which was the fourth largest up to this time. It was the sixth time that the Grand was staged at Chicago.

Henry's average read 80 per cent on his registered targets in 1917 and 1918.

Four shooters broke 96 to tie for third place: Mark Arie; the late Johnny Black then of Winnipeg, Manitoba; R. C. Rains of West Frankfort, Illinois, and Billy Wettleaf of Nichols, Iowa.

E. J. Buck, Davenport, Iowa, carried away the Preliminary Handicap crown at this shoot with a score of 96 after a hot shoot-off with the world renowned E. F. Woodward of Houston, Texas. Buck stood on 18 yards and broke 19 in the shoot-off, while "Woody," on 21, broke 17.

Hank Pendergast won the South Shore Introductory race with 198 out of 200. This event was shot from 18 yards in those days. Pendergast's shooting was not a flash in the pan. He had won the New York state championship a few weeks before, making the fifth time that he had won that honor.

The well known Jean Pope from East Moline, Illinois, finished with 197 to take second honors in the Introductory race. Years ago—if my memory serves me correctly, it was

1926—Pope and Pendergast hooked up in the trap dual at the Grand American at Vandalia. Each had broken 199 to tie for the A class championship. It was one of the funniest shoot-offs this writer has ever seen.

I just can't recall the scores of the shoot-off, but I know that the tie was to be decided the next day on the regular 200 program. Pope was up in an early squad and broke his first two frames straight. So did Pendergast. I think it was the third event in the first 100 that caused the trouble. Pope dropped two targets in one event. Coming into the club house, the smiling Jean said he had blown up and lost the race. Thinking this was funny, I asked him, "Has Hank shot yet?" "No," said Jean, "but you can bet your last dollar that he will not drop two targets." Well, to shorten a long story, Hank missed three targets in his next event, which gave Pope the title. After dropping but one target in 250, it seems strange that they should both have blown up in the same event. But that is trapshooting.

Thirty-six states were represented in the National championship that year. Billy Heer, Oklahoma, and Fred Tomlin, New Jersey, tied for high gun with 98 out of 100. Heer copped the shoot-off. The Consolation Handicap was won by the well known R. R. Rosensteil of Freeport, Illinois, with 96 from 17 yards. A. R. Chezik, North Dakota, "Kip" Elbert of Iowa, and Dave Fauskee of Minnesota tied with 99 out of 100 each for the Chicago Overture. Chezik won the shoot-off with 19 out of 20.

Frank Troeh, Portland, Oregon, ace, broke 90 to win the Amateur Doubles title. The late J. S. Day took second place with 88. E. J. Buck, the Preliminary winner, came close to duplicating Russ Barber's feat of several years ago when Barber ran away with both the Preliminary and Grand American races. Buck broke 95 in the Grand American Handicap race.

Grand notes . . . Eugene DuPont of Wilmington was an entry. Several weeks before the Grand, Mr. DuPont used a 20 gauge gun to win the weekly shoot at the DuPont Trapshooting School, Atlantic City, with 97 and a 99 out of 200, running over 100 straight.

Iowa was represented by Bill Hoon, Bill Ridley, Bill Wettleaf, Sam S. Foster, later Vice President of the A.T.A.,

W. F. Harder, 1940 National High Average king, lines up with four other famous Nebraska gunners, J. Sanmann, W. L. Yeaman, F. D. Daily and Eddie Dygert

and Kip Elbert who had won the Team Wing Championship at the International Live Bird shoot at Kansas City a few months before. The Winklers of Chicago were prominent in those days. Mrs. Winkler won many championships and Mr. Winkler won the Hercules All-Around Championship Cup in 1918.

1919—G. W. "BILL" LORIMER

The late G. W. "Bill" Lorimer, then of Troy, Ohio, an old time shooter, but who had been out of the sport for the preceding 10 years until only two months before the 1919 event, captured the Grand American that year.

Bill's health was none too good in 1919. In fact, all hope for him had been given up only a few months before. It was after his physician had urged him to take up some form of recreation that he went back to his old love—target shooting.

But Bill had no idea of attending the big shoot, which was to be staged at Chicago that year. He thought he was too weak to stand the strain. In the month of July Lorimer went to a few small shoots around home, and this lay-off seemed to do him a lot of good. He turned in some fine scores. He was shooting so good in fact that little H. B. Greenmayer of Piqua tried to induce him to go to the Grand American. Lorimer contended it was out of the question, but the lure of the big event as it approached proved too much for him and he boarded the train for Chicago. The rest is history.

That year the Grand American proper attracted 848 shooters. Lorimer finished his 100 in the Grand American

Handicap race with 98 breaks, which placed him in a tie with two other good shots and champions of their states that year, Ed Hellyer, Pennsylvania, and W. E. Gordon, Alabama. Lorimer's many friends who were pulling for him thought it nearly impossible for him to win the shoot-off. But Lorimer's Scotch—it must have been good stuff—pulled him through. He won by the narrow margin of one target. Lorimer, who shot from 18 yards, broke 18 out of 20. Gordon, at 19 yards, broke 17. Hellyer, at 21, finished four down.

Mark Arie, always dangerous, broke 97 in the same event from 22 yards. Anyone who cares to review the Grand Americans will find Mark Arie the most consistent handicap shot of all time. The great Frank Troeh won the Amateur 18-yard championship with a perfect score of 200 straight. The Troeh-Arie combine is without peer when it comes to all around target shooting. Their records over a period of the preceding 20 years speak for themselves.

Joe Jennings of Todmorden, Ontario, a Canadian ace in the old days, broke 198 out of 200 in the 18-yard race to take second place to Troeh. The National Amateur championship race was hotly contested that year. Three state champs went out with 199 out of 200. They were: "Klondike" R. D. Morgan, representing Maryland-D.C.; the great Frank Wright of New York and Bill Akard of Missouri, all finished but one down. Wright, in good form as usual, broke 50 straight in the shoot-off to win.

A new race, which is so popular now, the Classification, was started at this Grand American. Chan Powers, Decatur, Illinois, a powerful amateur in those days, broke 100 to win A class. Paymaster F. P. Williams of Washington, D. C., came through with 99 to win B honors. The late Indian shooter, E. C. "Chief" Wheeler of Oklahoma, won C class with 98 and the well known D. C. Hayward of Wisconsin broke 95 to win in D. Each of these wins came only after spirited shoot-offs.

The late Nic Arie of Menard, Texas, brother of the famous Mark, won the world's Doubles champion with 91 out of 100.

Seventeen boys, ranging in age from 10 to 17, took part in the Junior championship at 50 targets. The honors were won by little George Miller, aged 10, of Brewton, Alabama, youngest shooter at the meet. He stood up like a veteran and dropped but one target in his 50.

The Women's championship race attracted a lot of attention. Mrs. A. H. Winkler, a well known Chicago shooter, won the title with 90. Mrs. C. E. Groat, who broke good scores in California for many years to come, took second, with 87. Mrs. "Toots" Randall of Lima, Ohio, who was starring on the stage at that time, took time off to visit the Grand that year. She broke 87 out of 100 to win the Ladies Grand American Handicap race. Mrs. Winkler was second in this race, with 85.

Bill Lorimer, hero of the week, passed on to the Happy Hunting Grounds at his Troy, Ohio, home in 1932. Lorimer had shot at traps for many years. An inventor by profession, he had something like 52 inventions to his credit. He was mayor of Piqua at one time.

1920—AL IVINS

The 1920 Grand American, staged at Cleveland, Ohio, the last week in August, attracted 715 different gunners in the feature Grand American Handicap race, which was won

Indiana won the Grand American State Team championship in 1940. Here they are: *(Left to right)* L. C. Wise, Ralph Jenkins, Phil Miller, Junior Johnston, Herschel Cheek

At the North Dakota State: Guy Nichols, L. L. Mikkelson, Johnny Jahn, C. B. McDowell, C. Lukkason, Forest Saunders, Bob Dickey, Gene Secord, Otto Gullingsrud

by a veteran of the traps and at live bird shooting, Al Ivins of Red Bank, New Jersey. Ivins was the first easterner to win the Grand American Handicap since C. W. Floyd of New York won it in 1902. In winning the 1920 Grand, Ivins broke 99 from the 19-yard line, and 25 of them, which he broke without a skip, were carried over from Friday to Saturday morning because of the terrific rain storm that broke over the grounds late in the afternoon on Grand American Handicap day. For the first time in many years, the race was shot in 25-bird events. The Red Bank veteran broke his first 52 straight on Friday, dropped his 53rd, and then ran out without a miss. By a coincidence, Friday was his 52nd birthday.

A Canadian shooter, Ed Stuart of Hamilton, Ontario, stood on the same yardage as Ivins and turned in a 98 for second place. Mark Arie and Woolfolk Henderson broke 97's to tie up with other gunners for third position. Nic Arie of Texas at 21 yards broke 74 of his first 75 and was the only possible tie for Ivins, but lost two in his last 25.

The Preliminary Handicap was won on the same score as the Grand. Three shooters ended their 100 with 99's. They were H. K. Mitton, Fort Collins, Colorado, who shot from 19 yards; Dr. J. R. Pence, Minot, North Dakota, who stood on the 18-yard line, and C. A. Rice of Erie, Pennsylvania, who shot from 16 yards. Mitton, the crack Colorado shot, carried away the title and honors with 25 straight in the shoot-off. Rice dropped one, while Pence let a couple slide by.

History repeated itself when Frank Wright, the Buffalo veteran and 1919 National champion, again came through a winner with a score of 197—two less than the year before—shooting out Oscar Hanson of Nebraska. Wright died many years ago, while Hanson passed away in 1931.

Mrs. Judd H. Bruff, Pittsburgh, Pennsylvania, broke 85 out of 100 to win the Women's championship, while Teddy Beem, Jr., West Frankfort, Illinois, broke 48 out of 50 in the regular program and won the shoot-off to capture the Junior championship. Mark Arie, as usual, scored a win at this tournament. He won the 18-yard championship with 198 breaks out of 200. Johnny Noel, Nashville, Hank Pendergast, Phoenix, New York, and Sam Vance, Tilsonburg, Ontario, broke 197. They were well known and popular shooters. Four gunners broke 92 out of 100 in the Doubles race to tie for first place. Pete O'Brien won in the shoot-off and took the championship back to Butte, Montana.

Al Ivins, Grand American Handicap winner, started shooting in 1890. He won many live bird and target honors in his day. In 1895 he topped a large field in the Hollywood, New Jersey, Futurity event at live birds with 24 out of 25 in the main program and 10 straight in the shoot-off, shooting from 28 yards. One year later he won the Phil Daly, Jr., live bird cup at Hollywood, New Jersey, with 25 straight from 30 yards. In 1897 he killed 49 out of 50 to carry away the Grand National

Remington Professionals at the Grand American: *(Top row, left to right)* Dunny Reynolds, Al Riehl, Frank LeFever, Carl Stevens, Earl Feitz, Arnold Katenhuesen, Ed McCormick and Carl Mos; *(Bottom row)* George Gray, E. C. Palmer, Dewey Godfrey, Clyde Wells, Clyde Mitchell, "Hap" Holoday and Fred Tomlin

Handicap at Elkwood Park, New Jersey. Ivins has many other live bird honors to his credit. His most important clay target win was, of course, the Grand American. In 1925 he averaged .9608 to win the high average title of New Jersey.

Twelve traps, fronting on Lake Erie, were used at the 1920 Grand American. The thunder and rain storm that came up on Friday evening was one of the worst any Grand American Handicap event has had. The rain flooded the tents and soaked those unfortunate enough to be caught on the firing line, and the squads that finished their 25 in it nearly all missed so many targets that they didn't show up for the finish Saturday morning. At this Grand American Handicap the late Charlie Spencer won the Professional championship on 195 out of 200 after a heated shoot-off with the "vet" Pop Heikes.

1921—E. F. HAAK

E. F. Haak, a Canton, Ohio, automobile dealer, won the 1921 Grand American Handicap race with 97 out of 100 from the 21-yard mark. This marked the eighth time that a Grand American had been held in Chicago. The shoot was staged at the South Shore Country Club. Haak was the sixth Buckeye shooter to win the Grand American.

In winning the big race of the program, Haak, from 21 yards, broke his first two events without a bobble, dropped

Dave Fauskee, Worthington, Minnesota, won the National Clay Target championship in 1922

Monte De Wire, Hamilton, Indiana, won the National Clay Target championship in 1932 with 200 straight

two in the third string and went out with 24 out of 25. There were 637 entries in the Grand American proper.

When E. F. Haak, the winner, had finished his 100, in mid afternoon, only one man had a chance to beat him. Three could tie him. They were: Frank Stanton, Ingleside, Illinois, with two down in 75; Jack Frink, Worthington, Minnesota; J. O. Goodwin, Baxter Springs, Kansas, and Ed Dubrava, Monroe, Nebraska, with 72 out of 75. All lost out in their last 25 birds.

Ed Dubrava had the toughest luck of the quartet. He had shot the first three strings in a two-man squad, and then, with a chance to tie if he could break the last 25 straight, his squad mate quit and Dubrava had to shoot his fourth string alone, with a great crowd of spectators looking on. At that, he broke 23 and was among the 95's.

Those who finished with 96's were: Big Frank Etchen of the shooting family of Etchens from Kansas; G. H. Griffith, Helena, Arkansas, who had shot well in the Preliminary Handicap race; Jake Fries, Buffalo, New York, and O. E. Faxon, Plano, Illinois.

On Monday, the first day of the Grand American Handicap tournament, Haak broke a 98. Tuesday he came through with another 98. Wednesday he crashed 192 out of 200 from the 18-yard line. Thursday it was 95 out of 100 from 21 yards in the Preliminary Handicap race. Friday he shot 97 to win the Grand.

Wisconsin copped the 1937 State Team championship at the Grand American: *(Left to right)* Rolly Schroeder, Dr. O. B. Hinz, Vic Reinders, Claude Olney and Harry Billett. Olney won the National Doubles championship in 1925—Vic Reinders won this same title in 1941

D. C. Hayward, Weyauwega, Wisconsin, won the Grand American Preliminary Handicap in 1923. Hayward is pictured here with *(left to right)* Ed Chase and Don Mihills of Wisconsin and A. F. Jones and H. R. Patterson of Minnesota at the Wisconsin State shoot at Madison

After 1921, Haak devoted very little time to trapshooting. However, until recently, at least, he made up for it in the field. He is an expert wing shot and made annual jaunts to Canada for duck shooting. He did a great deal of fishing, especially bass, using a fly-rod almost entirely. He has said that the most pleasant days of his life were spent at the traps and he always enjoyed the association of the high class shooting men that are in the game.

The 1921 Grand American was a thriller. In the Preliminary Handicap, shot on Thursday, 485 shooters lined up in quest of gold and more trap honors. M. L. Fox of Emery, South Dakota, was the winner on 99 breaks from the 19-yard mark. This was his first Grand American tournament, but, like other hard-shooting South Dakotans of that time, such as Jerry Wilson, Frank Hughes, George Kreger, Harry Thoman, Archie French and Harry Taylor, he was there with the goods. Two shooters, G. H. Griffith, Helena, Arkansas, a fairly new man at the traps, on the 19-yard mark and Ed McCormick of Libertyville, Illinois, on the 20-yard mark, came through with scores of 98 to tie for second place. McCormick won the shoot-off.

Fred Tomlin, the crack New Jersey professional, won the Professional 18-yard championship with 199 out of 200. He outshot Fred Gilbert in the shoot-off, 25 straight to Gilbert's 24.

Nic Arie was in great form. He won the National Amateur championship with 198 out of 200 and the 18-yard championship with the same score. Mrs. "Toots" Randall broke 98 out of 100 to win the Ladies' championship. Elmer Herrold of Ashkum, Illinois, crashed 48 out of 50 to tie the 12-year old Jimmy Bonner of New York in the Junior contest. Herrold won the shoot-off.

Fred King of Colorado and Sam Sharman of Salt Lake City, Utah, broke 94 each to tie for the Doubles championship. King won the shoot-off and honors that went with it.

The Professional championship was won by Art Killam, Missouri, but only after three shoot-offs with Mark Arie, a pro that year. In the regular race they broke 198 out of 200, while in the shoot-off Killam crashed 75 out of 75 and Arie broke 74.

E. F. Woodward, Texas; Fred Harlow, Ohio; Harry Thoman, South Dakota; G. D. Williams, Florida; C. E. Bonner, New York; Frank Hughes, South Dakota, and G. H. Ford, Indiana, all broke 100 straight in the South Shore Introductory the first day. Sam Sharman, Utah; the late Fred Plum of New Jersey; John Underwood, Missouri, and C. D. Coburn of Ohio crashed 100 straight in the Lake Michigan Special the following day.

Perfect weather conditions prevailed at this shoot, with 355,000 targets trapped.

1922—JACK FRINK

Minnesota trapshooters were firmly chiseled on the all-time records of trapshooting at the 1922 Grand American, held at Atlantic City, New Jersey. The little town of Worthington sent two men who were to become winners, Jack Frink, who captured the Grand American Handicap race with 96 out of 100 from 22 yards and the famed Dave Fauskee, who won the National Clay Bird title with 197 out of 200 in the main event and 25 straight against Frank Troeh in the shoot-off.

Mrs. E. L. King, Winona, Minnesota, big game hunter, expert field shot and trapshooter of ability, took the Women's race with 187 out of 200.

In the main race at the 1922 Grand, Frink was tied up in the regular race with three other gunners, E. T. Hall of Philadelphia (who died in 1928); H. B. Simpkins, Camden, New Jersey, and L. G. Sefing, Allentown, Pennsylvania. Frink,

The late Earl Donahue *(second from left)* of Minneapolis won the Grand American Professional championship in 1928, 1929 and 1931. *(Left to right)* Bob Coffey, former president of the A.T.A., who now lives in Orlando, Florida; Donahue; C. E. Bonner, New York; Elliott Pugh, Cincinnati, and Jimmy Bonner, New York. Jimmy won the Junior championship in 1923, 1925 and 1926

the only western man in the tie, won the shoot-off with 25 straight to win the premier honors of trapdom.

After the first 50 had been shot in the Grand American Handicap race, not even Frink himself believed that he had a chance to win. He had dropped four in his first 50. However, the fat man from Worthington pulled himself together and staged a great finale by crashing 50 straight. His 25 straight in the shoot-off gave him a straight run of 75 out of 75 from the 22-yard mark. And they were tough targets, too, because it was rainy and windy that day.

In this same race, Jimmy Bonner, then 13 years old, broke 49 out of his first 50 from 18 yards. In his third event the strain began to tell and he muffed four and ended the 100 with a 22 in the last 25, which was remarkable shooting for a youngster.

Phil Miller, Dallas, Texas, was one of the big guns at this shoot. He was high on all targets for the week, with 939 out of 1,000. He won the Amateur 18-yard championship with 194 out of 200, after shooting out Mark Arie, who had tied him. In the class A championship he broke 195 out of 200 to tie Frank Hughes for high gun. Miller won the shoot-off.

Jay Graham, Ingleside, Illinois, carried away the Professional 18-yard title with 194. For the second straight year,

R. A. King, Colorado, won the Amateur Doubles championship. With the rain, some wind and poor light, "nobody could hit 'em." King won on a score of 170 out of 200.

Dudley Shallcross, Massachusetts, then 15 years of age, won the Junior championship with 96 out of 100. This boy Shallcross was a classy little gunner. He was an exceptionally fine doubles shooter and tough on 16-yard clays. "Dud" quit trapshooting some years ago. He is now an expert skeet shot.

Art Killam of St. Louis, breaking 197 out of 200, won the Professional championship. Art has won this title three times. As usual, Mark Arie stood up well in all races. He tied for both the Preliminary Handicap and 18-yard championships, losing the latter after four shoot-offs with Phil Miller, and the former to H. C. Taylor of Tybee, Georgia.

The score in the Preliminary race read 97 out of 100. Taylor stood on 16 yards while Arie, the world renowned Illinois Dutchman, toed the 23-yard line. Taylor was a new shooter.

Jack Frink, the big noise of the week, was one of the most popular gunners in the game. He served 28 years as a trapshooter and won many important races. He was a retired plumber. He died several years ago.

The 1922 Grand American marked the first and only time since its earlier years that the Grand American Handicap was held on the eastern coast. Sixteen traps, fronting a marshy stretch of country, were used at the Atlantic City classic.

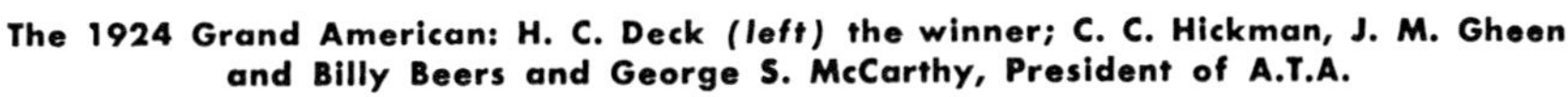

The 1924 Grand American: H. C. Deck *(left)* the winner; C. C. Hickman, J. M. Gheen and Billy Beers and George S. McCarthy, President of A.T.A.

WORLD'S RECORD WESTERN SQUAD, 993 x 1000: Joe Davison, Homer Clark, Cap. J. B. Grier, F. H. Woodcock, Karl Maust

1923—MARK ARIE

Mark Arie's turn finally came. This gunner, conceded by everybody to be the greatest handicap shot of all time, who had tied for both the Preliminary title and Grand American Handicap crown in former years, came through at the 1923 Grand American in the big race with a score of 96 breaks from the 23 yard line to win top place. This was the first time that a Grand American had been won from the 23-yard mark.

The 1923 Grand American was again staged at the South Shore Country Club, Chicago, in the last week in August. It was the first Grand American Handicap under amateur control and the officers of the Amateur Trapshooting Association outlined the attractive program and demonstrated that they were equally as efficient as the manufacturers.

Five hundred and thirteen gunners participated in the big race, which was shot on Thursday. At first there was little or no wind and the sky was clear. Later the wind came up rather strong from off the lake and the air was hazy, but most of the day it was bright and just cool enough for comfort.

Shooting in squad No. 1 and on peg No. 1, Arie started with a 23. He next broke a 24, then a 25, and a 24 in his final frame—49 out of his last 50 at a time in the day when the wind was bearing the targets down and hundreds of them were drowned in the lake along the line of the 12 traps.

The big event was over by three in the afternoon. Long before the last squads had shot their closing strings, it was known that the Illinois wizard had it sewed up. Frank Hughes, another of the country's best shots at that time, also on the 23-yard mark, which was the penalty at that time, broke 73 out of his first 75. On his last trap he missed two and went out with 95, which clinched second place.

Mrs. A. H. Winkler, the crack Chicago woman shooter, broke 90 in the Handicap race to win the Women's trophy. The scores, on the average, were among the lowest of any Grand American. The wind, which grew stronger from early afternoon to mid afternoon, was mainly responsible. Arie's victory was a popular one. He had been shooting at Grand Americans for 10 years. He tied for the prize in 1917, but lost in the shoot-off to Charlie Larson of Wisconsin.

Arie, year after year, has turned in high scores in the Grand American Handicap race. He has always taken the handicaps and hard conditions without kicking and is universally admired by shooters who want the best man to win. Arie has not done much shooting the past two years.

Walter Warren won the Lake Michigan Special at this meet. He broke 198 out of 200 to tie Bill Lambert of Oklahoma City for the honors, and defeated him 24 to 23 in the shoot-off.

Again Phil Miller shot well. This Texas star won the Doubles championship with 181 out of 200. Miller broke 199 the following day to win the Amateur Clay Target championship. Mrs. E. L. King of Winona, Minnesota, who had won the Women's Championship in 1922, again came through with flying colors, scoring 186 out of 200 to lead the field. Jimmy Bonner of New York, 14 years old, broke 88 out of 100 under the most adverse weather conditions to cop the Junior title.

Mark Arie made a conspicuous start on Wednesday when he broke 196 out of 200 to tie E. W. Ted Renfro, Montana, in the State Champions race. Arie won the shoot-off with a 24 out of 25 score to the Montana state champ's score of 23.

George McCarty, New Jersey, then vice-president of the Amateur Trapshooting Association, and Jay Clarke of Massachusetts, broke 195 out of 200 each to pave the way for an Eastern Zone team race win. The quintet broke 956 out of their 1,000 targets. The Pacific Zone team took second place with 954.

D. C. Hayward of Weyauwega, Wisconsin, had a walkaway in the Preliminary Handicap event. He broke 99 from

Chas. L. Horn

the 20-yard line to top the field by the narrow margin of a couple of city blocks.

Frank D. Stoop, Spokane, Washingington, was president of the A.T.A. Boyd Duncan, Lucy, Tennessee, an entry in the Professional race, broke 621 straight targets a few weeks before the 1923 Grand. The former record was 591 straight, turned in by Fred Gilbert in 1919.

This was the first time that I met up with Charles L. Horn, who at that time was getting a good start with the Federal Cartridge Company at Minneapolis. At this writing Mr. Horn is handling the big job of production at the New Brighton Defense Plant at Minneapolis. He is President of the Federal Cartridge Corporation.

1924—H. C. DECK

The 1924 Grand American marked the dedication of the new permanent home of trapshooting at Vandalia, Ohio.

A little, 63-year old carpenter with a $16 rabbit gun won the feature race that year. His name—H. C. Deck. His home—Plymouth, Ohio.

These five gunners, *(left to right)* George Slaughter, Michigan; Walter Beaver, Pennsylvania; Ralph Smoots, Ohio; Steve Crothers, Pennsylvania, and Ken Leech, Alberta, broke 200 straight at the Grand American

GRAND AMERICAN WINNERS

E. C. Starner (1925)

Otto Newlin (1927)

A. E. Sheffield (1932)

.. G. Dana (1934)

J. B. Royall (1935)

F. G. Carroll (1937)

O. B. West (1938)

B. L. Ritchie (1939)

Ernie Wolfe (1940)

Walter Tulbert (1941)

At the conclusion of the 100-target race it was found that four shooters—Deck, Billy Beers of Hartford, Connecticut, Dr. C. C. Hickman of Logansport, Indiana, and J. M. Gheen of Jersey Shore, Pennsylvania, had tied. In the shoot-off at 25 targets, Deck smothered all but one. Hickman finished second with a 23 score. Beers broke 22 and Gheen dropped four clays.

Deck's average at this time was not more than 80 per cent and he stood on the 16-yard line. The Plymouth veteran had been active at the traps for 30 years. He usually averaged about 80 per cent and sometimes recorded an average around 90. He shot targets merely for the love of the sport. Only once before in more than a quarter of a century of target shooting did he step into the limelight and that was at the Okoboji shoot years before. He broke 99 to tie Fred Harlow in the main race and defeated him in the shoot-off. This was his highest score at the traps.

Deck's Grand American Handicap win was a popular one. He was as cool as the proverbial cucumber in the shoot-off. He was the seventh Ohio shooter to win the Blue Ribbon classic. Deck still lives at Plymouth, Ohio.

Perfect weather conditions prevailed at the 1924 meet. Remarkable scores were turned in in all races. Frank Hughes, Chicago shotgun sensation, who had just returned from France with the American Olympic team, won the Amateur Clay Target championship with 199 out of 200, missing his first bird. The noted Texan, Phil Miller of Dallas, won the Doubles championship of North America with 191 out of 200, the highest score recorded in this event up to this time.

H. L. "Mike" Weisman, another popular Ohio shooter, came through in great style to steal the show in the Preliminary race with 99 out of 100. "Dud" Dickenson of Kansas and E. K. Kiefhaber of Buffalo broke 97's to tie up for second place. T. K. "Tachole" Lee, famous Alabama all around shot, and Tony Chezik of Portal, North Dakota, broke 198 to tie for the Dayton Introductory. Lee won in a long drawn out shoot-off. Art Killam of St. Louis and J. M. "Mal" Hawkins of Pittsburgh tied for the Professional championship with 197 each. Killam broke 25 straight to win the shoot-off.

One record was broken at this Grand American, and that was the number of targets trapped. More than 400,000 targets were thrown in the various events throughout the week. The gunners were pleased with the new shooting plant and it was the general opinion that the Grand American tournaments would grow larger from year to year, and this opinion has since been verified. George S. McCarty, Newfield, New Jersey, was the president of the trapshooters that year, with Ray Loring their secretary.

1925—E. C. STARNER

E. C. Starner of Ithaca, New York, a hotel man, won the 1925 Grand American, which was staged for the second time at the Vandalia permanent grounds. Starner broke 98 from 17 yards to capture this great event.

Eight hundred and thirty-seven different gunners participated in the various events during the week and shot at 550,000 targets, which was a record. Perfect weather conditions again prevailed. Seven hundred and ten shot the Grand American race.

S. A. Green, an old veteran of Waterville, Maine, carried off the high honors in the Preliminary Handicap race with 99 breaks from 18 yards. Green died several years ago. The Junior championship was won by that shooting sensation, young Jimmy Bonner of New York City, with a score of 197 out of 200, the highest score recorded in this race up to this time. Steve Crothers, Philadelphia, hit up a great gait at this shoot. He broke 200 straight the first day to win the Introductory and 200 without a skip the following day to win the Champion of Champions race.

Gladys Reid, widely known Portland, Oregon, shooter, shot her usual pace and topped the woman gunners in the championship race with 185 out of 200. Claude Olney, West Allis, Wisconsin, live bird and target star, won the Doubles championship with 191 out of 200. He had a long run of 116 straight.

Homer Clark, East Alton, Illinois, led the pros and captured the Professional championship with 199 out of 200. This win gave Homer his third Professional championship. It is interesting to note that up to this time Homer Clark and Art Killam led professionals with three Grand American wins each. Clark won in 1917, 1918 and 1925. Killam scored victories in 1921, 1922 and 1924.

Starner, the Grand American Handicap victor, could be classed as a dark horse. He came to the big shoot unknown, except in a local way in his home state. His average on registered targets was around the 86 per cent mark. But he had a winning streak that day and placed the town of Ithaca more clearly on the trapshooting map. Starner had been a shooter for eight years and his 98 score at the Grand American was his highest at the traps. He received $1,000 in cash for his Grand American win; a cash prize in the Ford purse race; a fine silver trophy and much national publicity. At that time Uley Brooks was president of the Amateur Trapshooting Association.

Starner is still a busy man with his hotel. He does some trout fishing in the streams near Ithaca and shoots a few game birds in his locality each hunting season.

1926—CHARLES A. YOUNG

The 1926 Grand American Handicap race was won with 100 straight from the 23-yard line by the famous veteran, Charles A. Young of Springfield, Ohio.

Charlie Young has attended every Grand American. At this writing, Charlie, nearing the 80 mark, is just as great as ever. In the opinion of this writer, Young is the greatest example of trapshooting and outdoor living that has ever lived. No other gunner, living or dead, has stood the strain like Charles A. Young.

The 1926 winner, Charles "Sparrow" Young, is known in every state in the Union and the provinces of Canada. He has averaged between 95 and 97 per cent for many years.

Dave Smyers, the L. C. Smith "gent," Oxford, Ohio, has visited 21 consecutive Grand Americans

Charlie Goodrich has charge of the Ithaca tent at the Grand American

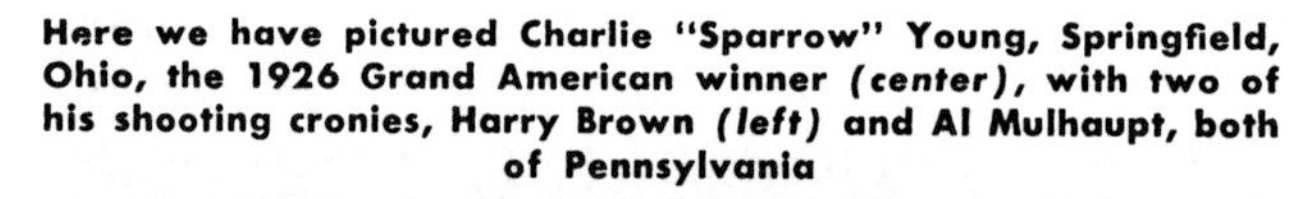

Here we have pictured Charlie "Sparrow" Young, Springfield, Ohio, the 1926 Grand American winner *(center)*, with two of his shooting cronies, Harry Brown *(left)* and Al Mulhaupt, both of Pennsylvania

This marked the second time that a Grand American was won with 100 straight. In 1910 Riley Thompson of Cainsville, Missouri, turned in a perfect score from the 19-yard mark, four yards closer up than Young.

Nine hundred and thirty-two of America's best shots lined up on the firing line the day that Young won the Grand. I watched him break his last 25 straight and it gave me one of the greatest thrills of my life. The weather was ideal for target shooting. This was the third straight year that perfect weather conditions prevailed, and the unprecedented entry and the fine equipment, indispensable in a shoot of this type, was a most emphatic answer to the question of whether a permanent home was needed, if any doubt remained in anyone's mind. The wisdom of building the home at Vandalia, in the center of the trapshooting population, was definitely proven.

Other outstanding scores were made at the 1926 Grand American. Bart Lewis, the sensational Illinois gunner, broke 192 out of 200 to win the Doubles championship. This was the highest score ever recorded by an amateur in this event.

Fred Tomlin, Glassboro, New Jersey, broke 200 straight to win the Professional championship.

Sam Jenny, Highlands, Illinois, had one of his good days and won the North American Clay Bird title with 199 out of 200, but only after a heated shoot-off with four other crack shots—E. F. Woodward of Texas, D. M. Hudson of Indiana, Ed Smith of South Dakota and Walter Warren, Chicago.

Jimmy Bonner of New York City again came through and won the Junior award. Adolph Werre of Wood River, Illinois, and Bonner broke 97's in the main race. Bonner crashed 25 straight in the shoot-off, while Werre let one soar away untouched.

The Preliminary Handicap race was a thriller. O. H. Nutt, a veteran Ohio shooter, and the late Chan Powers. out of Decatur, Illinois, tied up with 99 each. Nutt, who stood on the 19-yard mark, won the shoot-off with 24 out of 25, while Powers at 21 yards let three get away from him.

Illinois won the Team race, in which nearly every state in the Union and some Canadian provinces were represented. Mark Arie, with 199 out of 200; Frank Hughes, 197; Dr. A. Aszmann, 194; Jean Pope, 193, and Roy Nutt, 193, comprised this famous Illinois quintet.

More than 1,000 gunners shot during the week and 692,000 targets were trapped, another record up to this time.

We saw Charlie Young at the 1941 Grand American. He was still shooting good and enjoying fine health. He won the Veterans' race, with 99 out of 100.

Guy Dering, Columbus, Ohio, was named president of the Amateur Trapshooting Association and served in this position until his death in 1932.

Ray Middaugh, famous Nebraska shooter, was Manager of the A.T.A. in 1926. Ray broke 198 out of 200 to take high gun honors in the Ohio State Championship race staged at the Vandalia grounds, but did a real sportsmanlike deed by refusing to accept the title, inasmuch as he was employed by the Amateur Trapshooting Association.

1927—OTTO NEWLIN

A former big league baseball pitcher, Otto Newlin of Georgetown, Illinois, broke 98 out of 100 from the 20-yard mark to win the 28th Grand American Handicap race. It was held again at Vandalia. Eight hundred seventy-three shooters competed in the big race that year.

It was the opinion of many that the 1927 winner would have to break 100, as in the year before, but when the smoke had cleared away, two dark horses were tied on the winning score, 98. They were Otto Newlin and C. H. Reynolds, also a new shooter, from Royal Oak, Michigan.

In the shoot-off, Newlin broke 22 out of 25 to win, while Reynolds finished with 21, dropping four targets. Their true averages were revealed in the shoot-off, proving that the handicap committee had placed them correctly.

Bill Harris of East Alton, Illinois, handles the traps at the Grand American

Newlin started shooting in 1924. His Grand American score of 98 was the greatest of his career as a trapshooter. Like Starner's score in 1925, it was a great day to turn it in. In the shoot-off he was as cool under

(Left to right) **Bill Fienup, Missouri; Chet Schneider, Texas; Ray Fienup, Missouri; Billy Jenkins, Indiana; J. L. Kleeschulte, Missouri. Billy Jenkins won the National Junior championship in 1927—Ray Fienup won it in 1941**

fire as he used to be when he pitched professional baseball in the old days. He was a pitcher for 11 years, 1902 to 1912. He played with the Chicago White Sox, with Tacoma in the Coast league, with Indianapolis in the American Association and with Albany in the Eastern league. He once pitched a game for Albany against Troy in 78 minutes; he shut them out, 2 to 0—a world's time record up to that time. That same year the Utica team felt the sting of this great pitcher's arm in a 17-inning duel, which Newlin won 3 to 0. When on the slab for Indianapolis, he once shut out Ithaca 1 to 0 and allowed but one scratch hit.

Newlin visited his first Grand American in 1925. He shot poorly, but had a good time, so he came back in 1927, not expecting to win anything, but to enjoy a little vacation.

Guy Dering of Columbus, Wisconsin, shared the limelight with Newlin at this tournament. He duplicated all of Steve Crothers' 1925 feats. On the first day of the tourney Dering came through with 200 straight to win the B class title. He scored 200 without a miss on the following day to capture the North American Clay Bird crown, and on the third day he broke 36 straight, which gave him a straight run of 436. This tied Crothers' Grand American performance of two years before.

The strange part of it all was that Dering missed the same target and on the same trap that ended Crothers' long run.

Ten hundred and seventy different shooters took part in this meet, which broke all previous Grand American records, and the number of targets trapped was 743,000. Twenty-six traps were used and ideal weather conditions prevailed.

Fred Tomlin again won the Professional championship with 198 out of 200; C. E. Leek of Port Republic, New Jersey, copped the Preliminary Handicap with 98 out of 100 from 19 yards; Frank Troeh won the Doubles with 188 out of 200; Frank McGanney of Salt Lake City captured the Pro Doubles with 187 out of 200; the late Oscar Hanson of Nebraska won the Champ of Champs race with 197 out of 200; Mrs. Harry Harrison of New York won the Women's race with 192 out of 200; Billy Jenkins of Orleans, Indiana, took the Junior award with 98 out of 100; Howard Keifer of Ohio won the Sub-junior with 95, and Illinois took the Team race with Bart Lewis, Harry Schomerus, the late Charlie Armes, "Doc" H. E. Timm and Sam Herzog in the lineup. Their score was 960 out of 1,000.

1928—IKE ANDREWS

Isaac Andrews, Spartanburg, South Carolina, a veteran of 30 years of trapshooting, who had visited more than a dozen Grand Americans, won the 1928 Grand American with plenty to spare. Andrews' score of 95 out of 100 stood out like a lighthouse, for the day was windy, rainy and most disagreeable. He led the entire field by two targets.

The second place score was turned in by one Herman Schnell, the Wapakeneta, Ohio, rabbit hunter, who broke 93 from 18 yards.

Here is the picture of the race. Andrews, always an early riser, started out in squad No.1 in the morning when most of the lads were either sleeping in their tents or at the hotel. His start was anything but sensational. In fact he broke only 23's in his first two frames and Colonel Earl Feitz racked up a 46 out of 50 on his huge bulletin board. Several topped this mark. There were George Alling of Connecticut with a 48, Les Troeh of Minnesota, Ross Miller of Michigan and Herman Schnell of Ohio. All but Alling had 47's.

To make a long story short, Andrews crashed 49 out of the last 50 to score his 95, while the other leaders fell one by one along the wayside.

Paul Earle, of Starr, South Carolina, one of the greatest shots the South has ever produced

A word about this southern gunner, who, by the way, shot thousands of targets this year, and is still going strong. Ike was born in 1876. He started shooting in 1902 and had visited 18 Grand Americans up to this time. His count now reads 31 Grand Americans. He has won many sectional honors at the traps, including the Pinehurst Midwinter Preliminary Handicap, the Pinehurst North and South Handicap, the Pinehurst Doubles and many more.

"Ike," as we have many times told, was in on the ground floor of basketball. This was in the early 90's when Dr. Neismith, of the Springfield, Massachusetts, Training School, invented the game. Mr. Andrews played on the Y. M. C. A. team of Chicopee, Massachusetts, that year which won the Connecticut Valley Championship.

The 1928 Grand was most unusual in many ways. Only once before, in 1907, when Jeff Blanks of Tennessee won, has this big race been carried off by a man from way down south in Dixie.

The Preliminary Handicap was won by an Ohio shooter, F. B. Hoggatt of Goshen with 97 out of 100 from 17 yards. Mark Arie won the North American Clay Target title with 198 out of 200; C. R. Brand of New York captured the Champ of Champs race with the same score, while Frank Troeh of Oregon took the Doubles competition with 185 out of 200.

Frank Troeh was high on the 1,000 mixed targets with 935; Earl Donahue brought back the professional title to Minneapolis and Ohio won the Team race with 937 out of 1,000.

Win Sale, Denver, Colorado *(right)*, won the World's Professional championship in 1932. Here we catch him leaning on the veteran, O. F. Nigro, of Trinidad, Colorado

Carl Thacker, Sioux City, Iowa, won the World's Open Championship in 1937 with 200 straight

Clyde Mitchell, Milwaukee, copped the Professional Doubles; Casper Hoffman of Denver, the Junior with 97 out of 100; Miss Kitty Boyer of Pennsylvania captured the Ladies' title with 186 out of 200; Steve Crothers won the class AA honors and Walter Warren, then of Chicago, was the winner of the International 100 with 95.

Notes . . . Harry Maginnis, noted Minneapolis gunner, visited his first Grand American and some of the boys recalled the last time (1926) that they saw Harry at Chicago when he gave them a good trimming in the Chicago Handicap. Score 99 out of 100 from the 20-yard mark. Reward—a chest of silverware valued at $1,000. . . . Guy Nichols of Western telling about the first shooting match he saw. Guy, when 14 years of age, with patches on his breeches dropped into a pool hall at Larnard, Kansas, where he heard Ed O'Brien, Fatty Arnold, Bill Heer and Chris Gottleig telling trapshooting stories. Guy visited the shoot the next day and became so excited telling his friends in the pool room that night about the shooters that he broke the cigar case. The proprietor demanded $2.50, but Guy had no money, so Ed O'Brien and the shooters, who were playing pool, came to his rescue and paid the bill. That made Guy a shooter from that day to this.

Harry Maginnis, Minneapolis *(middle, bottom row)*, who won the $1,000 chest of silverware at Chicago, tells Bill Horton *(left)* that he should buy a new gun or learn to shoot the one he has. Fred Lussier is at the right. *(Back row)* George Edvenson and George Berkner, Mayor of Waverly, who would rather shoot live pigeons than eat

1929—MOSE NEWMAN

The 1929 Grand American tourney, the largest held in the history of the sport and one which will be pictured in the minds of the trap world as one of the most spectacular. Six gunners tied for the premier high honors with a score of 98. A Texas gunner, the first to win a Grand American Handicap title, crashed 25 straight in the shoot-off to win the crown. The 98 scores, the yardages of the gunners and the result of the shoot-off ran something like this:

	Yard-age	25 Target Shoot-off	The 100
1. Mose Newman, Sweetwater, Tex.	20	25 x 25	98
2. E. F. Booher, Dayton, Ohio	17	24 x 25	98
3. E. F. Lockwood, Fort Wayne, Ind.	21	23 x 25	98
4. Geo. Slaughter, Benton Harbor, Mich.	22	22 x 25	98
5. E. L. Axtell, Harvard, Ill.	21	22 x 25	98
6. W. J. Englert, Willard, Ohio	19	19 x 25	98

Mose Newman, the winner, was born in Sweetwater, Texas, in the year 1887. March 27, to be exact. He started shooting in his early teens with rifle, pistol and shotgun in the field. He took his first crack at clay targets in 1905.

Mr. Newman once said, "My greatest thrill at the traps, of course, was in winning the Grand American Handicap. I knew I was going to win the Grand, or at least that was my feeling before I left the hotel in Dayton that morning, and I freely told my associates that the Grand was already in the bag, and this was all in earnest on my part, for I felt that I could break the 100, and that should be enough to win. My greatest surprise came to me in missing the two out of the 100, both of which could have been called 'dead' by the referee, for I never saw so much dust come out of two targets as those two that went to the last column."

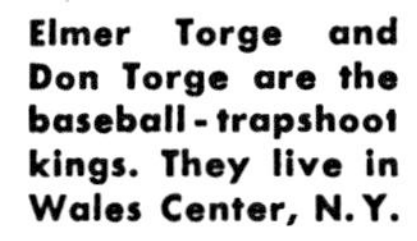
Elmer Torge and Don Torge are the baseball-trapshoot kings. They live in Wales Center, N.Y.

These six gunners broke 98 out of 100 to tie for the 1929 Grand American Handicap title. *(Left to right)* George Slaughter, Benton Harbor, Michigan; E. F. Lockwood, Ft. Wayne, Indiana; Mose Newman, Sweetwater, Texas (the winner of the shoot-off and title); Earl Booher, Dayton; W. L. Englert, Willard, Ohio; Ed L. Axtell, Harvard, Ill.

Newman was a farmer and stockman, having grown up among the pioneers and trail blazers of the west. His father and mother moved west in the late '70's and at that time that section was still infested by raiding Indians. The Newmans raised thoroughbred horses in that section for 20 years, up to 1917, and raced them on the principal tracks in the states, having developed such great sprinters as Burnie Bunten, De Domo and Pan Zareta as well as many others. Mose knew Pancho Villa well in his heyday in the fair land of Mexico and fought many cocks in the pits over which he presided, and acted as judge as they do in that country. Mose has two brothers, A. T. and H. S., and a nephew, H. H. Newman, all of whom have been consistent performers over the traps.

Guy Payne of Oklahoma City, with 199 out of 200, copped the North American Clay Target championship at the 1929 Grand. Sam Jenny, Highland, Illinois, shot a fine race to win the Amateur Doubles, while Earl Donahue of Minneapolis crashed through with another spectacular victory in the Professional race.

Frank Troeh, Portland, Oregon, won the Champion of Champions race, and Rush Razee, Denver, Colorado, copped the Professional Doubles title.

Miss Eunice Haggard of Winchester, Kentucky, led the

Rufus King's victims in the shoot-off for the 1930 Grand American Handicap title were: Lawrence Crampton, Merlen Heights, O.; *(Rufus)*; Dan Casey, Toledo, and J. L. Scott, Toledo

women with 190 out of 200, and Johnny Fontaine, the encyclopedia of trapshooting, who makes his home in Philadelphia when he isn't chasing trapshoots and bow and arrow contests, won the Preliminary Handicap, which attracted 978 gunners.

Bob Hardy, Galesburg, Illinois, won the Junior championship with 99 out of 100, while A. Meiss, of Hazleton, Pennsylvania, paced the Sub-junior shooters. Frank Troeh captured the Jim Day Cup with 477 out of 500.

1930—RUFUS KING

A 14-year old boy, Rufus King of Wichita Falls, Texas, son of the famous Fred King, one of the nation's greatest shots, stunned the shotgun world at the 1930 Grand American by winning the Grand American Handicap with a score of 97 out of 100 in the regular event and then went on to defeat three Ohioans, Dan Casey and J. L. Scott of Toledo and Lawrence Crampton of Merlen Heights. Little Rufus, who looked younger than he was, and who had a carefree air of a boy engaged in a marble game, proved his mettle in the shoot-off before 10,000 fans by breaking 24 out of 25. Casey took

The noted Gus Payne *(second from right)* explains to a group of Oklahoma City shooters how he won the National Clay Target championship in 1929 and 1930. *(Left to right)* Newt Alley, Clarence Lambert, A. W. Wuestenberg, and G. S. Hilly

second place, Scott third and Crampton fourth. Nine hundred sixty-three shooters took part in the big race.

Jean Pope, East Moline, Illinois, scored the most decisive victory ever made in the Preliminary Handicap when he made 100 straight hits from the 22-yard line, defeating this fast field by three targets. It was the first time in Grand American history that this race had been won with 100 straight. Pope, an enthusiastic and popular gunner, had been shooting 15 years. Three 97's followed the great Pope. They were Clarence Orr, East Alton, Illinois, Murrell D. Roberts, Middletown, Connecticut, and Jerry Tanner, Kings Mills, Ohio, who finished in this order after the shoot-off.

Gus Payne, the noted Oklahoma gunner, living in Cleveland, Ohio, that year, retained his North American Clay Target championship when he broke 199 out of 200 in the main event and 25 straight in the shoot-off to defeat A. M. McCrea of Missouri and Eddie Martin of Wisconsin, who had tied him. The Professional championship went to Howard Benson, the popular Lansing, Michigan, gunner, who upset the dope bucket by breaking 197 out of 200 in the regular race and then went on to defeat two of the world's greatest shots, Earl Donahue of Minneapolis and Johnny Jahn of Iowa in the shoot-off.

The Champion of Champions event was captured by E. F. Woodward, Houston, Texas. Woody and H. F. Roberts of East Fultonham, Ohio, tied up with 197's, but the Texas star was too rough in the shoot-off. Shirley Forsgard, Galveston, Texas, scored another victory for the Lone Star state when he copped the Junior title with 95 out of 100. Henry Rosenbrook, Gardnersville, Nevada, and Bud McKinley of Harrisburg, Ohio, fought it out for the Sub-junior championship. Each busted 93 out of 100, with Henry winning the shoot-off.

Mrs. J. S. Murphy, Freehold, New Jersey, and Mrs. Norman Pillot of Houston, Texas, outclassed the Women's field, with Mrs. Murphy breaking 185 out of 200 to win and Mrs. Pillot turned in 184 for second honors.

Ted Renfro, Dell, Montana, proved he was the greatest doubles shooter in the nation when he crashed 191 out of 200 to win the world's Doubles championship. Casper Hoffman, Denver, took second with 188 out of 200.

The AA class title went to Frank Troeh, Portland, who won hands down with 200 straight. Ralph Jenkins, Orleans,

Indiana, took A honors with 196 out of 200 and L. J. Montague, Kansas City, Missouri, paced the B class shooters with 195. It was W. J. Timm, Hammond, Indiana, in the C class scramble with his 190 out of 200 and R. D. Finnell of Coshocton, Ohio, in the D class with 192 out of 200. Nelson Jones, Newark, Ohio, won E class with 188.

Grand notes . . . Frank Troeh had quite a week for himself, taking the All-around championship with 967 out of 1,000. . . . Paul Hiestand, Hillsboro, Ohio, helped himself to the Consolation Handicap trophy when he crashed 99 out of 100 from 18 yards. . . . Billy Beers, Hartford, Connecticut, did a great job in handling the efficient handicap committee. Beers refereed the shoot-offs and Guy Von Schriltz of Kansas and Charlie Greer of South Dakota acted as judges.

Mrs. Norman Pillot of Texas proved she was one of the greatest all-around women gunners in the sport by taking the Women's Doubles race after two shoot-offs and placing second in the National Women's championship. . . . Dave Leahy, the famed New York gunner, placed second in the Consolation Handicap with the great score of 98 out of 100 from 23 yards. Dud Dickenson, Kansas City, Missouri; Henry Abell, Cleveland, Ohio; Fred Wetstein, Springfield, Illinois, and W. C. Brimmer, Sr., Minneapolis, busted 95's in the Consolation competition to share third honors.

Harley Woodward, Houston, Texas, who had been winning shoots since he copped the Texas state title in 1915 when he was 15 years of age, coasted to victory in the International 100 when he broke 98. . . . Ohio won the Team race, with Charlie Bogert, Gus Payne, Mark Hootman, L. P. Cranston and Howard Sullivan in their lineup. They broke 976 out of 1,000. . . . Mrs. Walter Andrews of Atlanta won the Women's All-around and the Preliminary Handicap. . . . F. D. Kelsey of East Aurora, New York, proved he was still a good shot by winning the Veterans' championship with 181 out of 200. . . . Mrs. George Peter, Phoenix, Arizona, was the winner of the Women's Grand American Handicap race with 92 out of 100 from 17 yards.

1931—REV. GARRISON ROEBUCK

The Reverend Garrison Roebuck, a "dark horse" from McClure, Ohio, won the 1931 Grand American with 98 out of a possible 100 from the 17-yard stripe. Roebuck's victory was no walkaway, however, for when the smoke had cleared away in this race of races, it was found that he was tied with the famous Fred Harlow of Newark, Ohio, who won the Grand American in 1908, and R. F. Willbaum, another pretty fair shot from Greenville, Ohio. Harlow was on 22 yards, while Willbaum toed the 19-yard mark.

The shoot-off found Roebuck with the advantage, due to the fact that he was nearer the trap than Harlow or Willbaum. A hush fell over the crowd of 10,000 spectators who had gathered to witness the closing episode of this great event. It was the first time that Ohio had been sure of this championship since Charlie Young presented it to the Buckeye state in 1926.

Harlow was my logical guess to win the shoot-off. He had been in shoot-offs against the greatest shots in the world. However, the yardage disadvantage was there and it told against him with the result that he dropped five targets of the 25 birds in the shoot-off. Willbaum and Roebuck tied with 23's. Then they shot another string and again they tied with 22's.

In the next 25 targets, Willbaum crashed four straight, then stumbled on his fifth and sixth. Roebuck, on the other hand, broke nine straight and then "muffed" his 10th. Roebuck now held a slight advantage. On the next peg they each broke their five targets. That was 15 targets. On the fourth frame Willbaum missed his 16th and 19th, while Roebuck let one go by, his 18th. In the last five to be shot, Roebuck held the upper hand. Willbaum lost his 23rd clay, while Roebuck broke the last five straight, thus definitely making him the winner of the 1931 classic.

Garrison Roebuck and Rufus King

The Remington squad which chalked up the World's squad record at the 1931 Grand American. They broke 497 x 500. *(Left to right)* Art Killam, Rush Razee, Clyde Mitchell, Fred Tomlin and Clyde Wells

Big Karl Maust, the Detroit auto salesman, was the star of the shoot. Maust won the AA class title with 199 out of 200 and the North American Clay Target championship with the same score. The latter race was a scorcher, with three shooters, Frank Troeh, Dr. E. L. Botts of Ohio, who forgot to load his gun in the shoot-off, and George Slaughter of Michigan, tying Karl for the title. Maust broke 150 straight to win the shoot-off.

Gus Payne, the Oklahoma ace, had quite a week for himself, winning the Doubles, International 100 and in addition he was high amateur for the shoot. Jeanette Jay, Waverly, Iowa, won the Women's championship. Tobe Park of Texas carried off the Junior honors while Steve Crothers busted through with another victory in the Champion of Champions race. Earl Donahue of Minneapolis shattered 199 out of 200 to take the Professional title.

Harry Schomerus, Hillsdale, Illinois, was the big noise in the Preliminary Handicap with a 99, and F. D. Kelsey of New York took the Veterans' race hands down. Clyde Mitchell, Milwaukee, did some great shooting in winning the Open championship, with 199 out of 200 after defeating Joe Hiestand in the shoot-off. Mitchell was high professional of the entire tourney with 957 out of 1,000. The Texas team, E. F. Woodward, Harry Hausman, Harley Woodward, Fred King and A. C. Finn, won the Team championship with 975 out of 1,000.

The Remington squad held the spotlight during the week with their great shooting. The squad, composed of Fred Tomlin, Rush Razee, Clyde Wells, Art Killam and Clyde Mitchell,

Ark-La quail hunters take in the Grand American: Dr. J. E. Stevenson, Eddie Alias, H. C. Rogers, L. A. Hummer and Mac Stevenson

broke the world's squad record with 497 out of 500 and another record on 3,000 targets with 2,955 hits. Rush Razee broke the Grand American record on 16-yard targets with 597 out of 600. The Sub-junior winner was Joe Fincel of Dubuque, Iowa, with 89 out of 100.

1932—A. E. SHEFFIELD

Arthur E. Sheffield, Dixon, Illinois, postal clerk, won the 33rd Grand American Handicap title with a score of 98 out of 100 from the 21-yard line. Art was 45 years of age at the time and was shooting his fourth Grand. He had previously shot at the 1912 classic staged at Springfield, Illinois, the 1913 world series of trapdom at Dayton, Ohio, and the year before.

Sheffield broke 25 straight in his first event, but muffed one, his 49th, in his second frame. He went straight in his third event and was tied at 74 out of 75 with L. W. Becker, Canton,

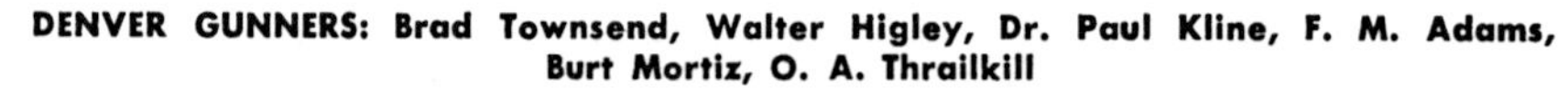

DENVER GUNNERS: Brad Townsend, Walter Higley, Dr. Paul Kline, F. M. Adams, Burt Mortiz, O. A. Thrailkill

Ohio. Becker went to pieces on his final drive for the honors, while Sheffield broke 24 to win.

Sheffield's victory is the story of "the man who came back." After shooting from 1912 until 1917 without showing any great indication of ability, the Dixon gunner gave up the sport temporarily. With 11 years of inactivity behind him, he resumed the clay target sport in 1928. His 1931 average was .9150 on 600 targets. Art still attends the Grand and hopes to repeat some time in the future.

Bobby Olds, 17-year old marksman from Diamondale, Michigan, crashed through to win the Preliminary Handicap with 99 out of 100 from the 21-yard mark. The story of Bobby's victory reads like a Horatio Alger melodrama. Bobby had pulled onions for 75 cents a day to raise enough money to pay his entry in the Preliminary Handicap. Even his striving in the onion patches did not raise enough money, so members of the Lansing Gun Club, headed by Ross Miller and Sam McKinley, made up the difference. Miller took Olds to Vandalia, where the youth justified the Lansing shooters' confidence in his ability. The Olds family rejoiced in Bobby's victory, for only the previous March the mortgage on the old farm was foreclosed. Bobby's win netted him over $1,000.

Fred Etchen, Coffeyville, Kansas, now a shooting instructor, won the International 100 with 98 out of 100 in the main event and 49 out of 50 in the shoot-off to defeat Joe Hiestand and Charlie Bogart, both of Ohio. Fred Tomlin turned in a straight run of 200 to win the open championship.

Five gunners broke 200 straight in the Class championship, with the late Ralph Smoots of Kenton, Ohio, taking the AA class title after the shoot-off. The remaining 200's were Steve Crothers and Walt Beaver of Pennsylvania; George Slaughter of Michigan, who took the A class honors, and Ken Leach of Alberta who won the B class honors. Leach's score was the highest ever turned in by a Canadian at the Grand American.

The National Clay Target Championship went to Monte DeWire, the famous Hamilton Indiana, gunner, but only after a heated shoot-off with Billy Hoon of Iowa. DeWire and Hoon broke 200 straights. Mrs. H. E. Grigsby, Oklahoma City, Oklahoma, won the Women's championship with 191 out of 200, nosing out Mrs. Walter Andrews of Atlanta, Georgia, and Mrs. J. S. Murphy of New Jersey by one bird.

Win Sale, a Colorado trapshooter, won the Professional championship with 199 out of 200. The Champion of Champions race was a thriller, with Steve Crothers on the long end of an interesting shoot-off with Charlie Bogart of Ohio. They broke 199's.

It was a great week for Spencer Olin, the popular East Alton, Illinois, gunner, who led all shooters on mixed targets for the week with 970 out of 1,000 and won the Professional Doubles with 192 out of 200. Ned Lilly, Stanton, Michigan, came through with 99 hits to cop the Junior championship, while Scotty Richards, Hollinsbury, Ohio, a protege of the well known Elmer Harter of Richmond, Indiana, won the Sub-junior honors.

The late Ollie Bottger of Fairfield, Iowa, proved he was one of the greatest doubles shots in the nation when he won the Doubles championship with 191 out of 200. F. D. Kelsey, Aurora, New York, copped the Veterans' championship with 190 out of 200. Sam Jenny, Highland, Illinois, won the Vandalia Open from 25 yards, with 97 out of 100. We can add that the Remington squad turned in outstanding scores in all races. It not only tied the former record of 497 out of 500 for one squad, but went on to break another world's record on 1,000 targets, busting 989.

The trapshooters named John W. Eshelman their president and he served two years.

Grand notes . . . Bill Hoon and Monte DeWire, who tied for the National championship, are both farmers, and, as Bull Pickerel Feitz on the bulletin board remarked, "Hoon shot up 12 bushels of corn in the shoot-off to lose." . . . "What a squad!" whispered Fred Koch from Brookville, Ohio, when Fred Tomlin, Rush Razee, Clyde Mitchell, Art Killam and Clyde Wells, shooting for the green-shirted Remington clan, busted 989 out of 1,000 for a new squad record. . . . Denver sent four crack shots, Brad Townsend, the cartoonist; Win Sale; Rush Razee and Casper Hoffman. . . . Ken Leach, the Calgary gunner who broke 200 straight to win B class, owns a string of race horses and theaters. . . . Popular was Mrs. Walter Andrew's High-over-all championship. . . . Jim Rennick from Columbus, Ohio, handled the Associated Press stories. . . . Spence Olin, the great Western southpaw gunner, who topped all amateurs and professionals, is equally as good at live bird shooting.

TENNESSEEANS AT THE GRAND: Ned Lutz, Bruce Keener, John Noel, Ed Luyben, Bob Campbell

1933—WALTER BEAVER

Beaver, Lilly and Taylor tell the story of the 34th annual Grand American staged at Vandalia field August 21 to 26, 1933. Walt Beaver, an electrician, accomplished what was thought the impossible when he shattered 98 out of 100 in the main event and 25 straight in the shoot-off, from the 25-yard line, to win the Grand American Handicap race. It marked the first time in history that a shooter had won the roaring Grand from 25 yards.

But Ned Lilly, 17-year old Stanton, Michigan, boy, was the star of the shoot. No other youngster in shotgun history, before or since, has even come close to Ned's achievements, such as he turned in at the 1933 Grand American. Let's get them straight. He won the Junior title with 100 straight, the National Clay Target championship with 199 out of 200, the

Texas stars: *(Left to right)* E. F. Woodward, Houston, who holds the world's High Average record of .9950 on 1,000 registered targets in 1933; Harry Hausman, J. T. Caldwell, C. L. Dupuis and Forest McNeir. McNeir won the National Clay Target championship with 200 straight in 1940

All-around championship with 964 out of 1,000 and tied Walt Beaver for the Grand American Handicap title when he broke 98 from the 24-yard stripe.

Here is the picture of the 1933 Grand American shoot-off.

Beaver is 36, plain looking, wears no tie, needs a shave, is beginning to look stoutish. He looks like your next door neighbor, just come home from his labors in the shop, who goes out in the back yard to manipulate a lawn mower, for a before-supper workout. He is a man of the salt of the earth.

Lilly stands at 24 yards and Beaver at 25. No Grand American king has ever stood back more than 23 yards. Neither look very happy. Both look very determined. They do not smile or speak, it's strictly business.

Lilly shoots first, calls "Pull!" bravely and without a quiver in his voice. He gets his target and it falls apart as if hit with a sledge hammer. Beaver shoots and gets his with just as clean a shot. At No. 4, Lilly shoots over the clay and misses. At No. 8 the same thing happens. Beaver goes on about his shooting, steadily and without restraint. He gets his 25. Lilly gets 23. Youth for once has not been served.

John Taylor, Newark, Ohio, attending his 30th Grand American, did everything possible in the professional ranks by winning four titles: The Professional championship, with 197 out of 200; the Doubles, with 187 out of 200; the Pro Handicap with 97 out of 100 from 25 yards, and the Professional All-around.

Herschel Cheek, the well liked Clinton, Indiana, trapshooting star, captured the Champion of Champions race with 197 out of 200, while Frank Lightner made it two straight Iowa victories in the Doubles contest when he scored 187. You will recall that Ollie Bottger of Iowa won this title in 1932. The Veterans' championship went to T. G. Cathan of Chagrin Falls, Ohio, who rung up 87 out of 100.

Alice Crothers, daughter of the famed Steve, showed the women how to point a shotgun when she led this field with 183 out of 200. Elmer Torge, Wales Center, New York, came through with colors flying to take the class AA honors with 199 out of 200, while H. S. Shellito, Ames, Iowa, took the Preliminary Handicap with 98 from 20 yards, but only after a heated shoot-off with one C. E. Roecher of Pomeroy, Ohio, who stood on 17 yards.

The Open championship went to E. F. Woodward, Houston, Texas, who rounded out 199 out of 200. It was a fitting victory, because Woody had won the yearly Amateur High-average title with .9950, a world's record mark that still stands.

E. C. McQuitty, a Danville, Illinois, cigar salesman, pounded out a 99 from 19 yards to win the Vandalia Open, and Bobby Poore, Butte, Montana, took the Sub-junior with 94 out of 100.

Grand notes . . . Four 100 straights were chalked up in the first 100 targets of the Amateur Championship race: Joe Hiestand, Lewis Slocum, J. W. Alston and Ned Lilly. . . . H. H. Smith from Troy, Ohio, is plenty tough on clay targets and the pasteboards. . . . "Just 30 years ago I went to my first Grand American," recalled Count Smyth, the Missouri champion. Count and Art McCrea went together. . . . H. F. Bullock was the only hunter who killed a bear in New Jersey the past year. . . . Watching the amateurs and professionals shoot, Henry P. Davis, editor of the National Sportsman, said, "I'll bet the amateurs will win by six targets." A good bet, because that was exactly the way it ended.

George Peck, of "Peck's Bad Boy" fame, conducted a page in Outdoors, a new Chicago publication. . . . That grand old veteran of the game, Henry Brown of Milwaukee and Harry N. Kirby of Ohio had a reunion. . . . J. M. Hawkins, the New Haven professional, has written several interesting books on trapshooting. . . . Pop Heikes, the 1900 Grand American winner, was on hand selling Sports Afield magazine. . . . From Long Beach came Bill Parker, Gus Smith, Bill Cree, Belle McCord Roberts, who is a fine shot, and Joe Steed. . . . Jimmy Napier of Pittsburgh was busy showing his new trap.

1934—L. G. DANA

Lawrence G. Dana, Derrick City, Pennsylvania, won the 1934 Grand American Handicap title with 98 out of 100 from the 17-yard line. The 58-year old Pennsylvanian, father of five children, was attending his first Grand American. He came only because Al Mulhaupt and some of his cronies in Bradford, of which Derrick City is a suburb, told him it would be a swell way to spend a vacation. Dana had been shooting at clay targets 10 years, but his average was never over 88 per cent.

BIM CASTLE WINS A "GRAND" AT THE IOWA STATE SHOOT: Jones, Radloff, Wagner, Boardman, Finch, (Castle), Robinson, Cooper, Chapman pay up

Shooting in one of the late squads, he went into his final event of 25 targets knowing that he had to break every one to beat five 97's that were chalked up on Professor Earl Feitz' bulletin board. And he broke them, one and all. But Lawrence Dana's job wasn't completed as yet. Shooting in the 101st squad, near the end, was H. F. Pace, another unknown from Mansfield, Ohio. Pace also broke 98 targets, and that meant a shoot-off.

The 47-year old Ohio plumber might have won, just as well as Dana. Like his opponent, he never had captured a trap-shooting title before and his 98 in the Grand American was his best score. This was only his second Grand, and his first since 1920.

But fate is a cruel mistress, as well as a fickle one. She escorted H. F. Pace almost to the throne and then deserted him. She cast eyes instead on Lawrence George Dana and it

New Jersey gunners are always among the leaders at the Grand American. *(Left to right)* William Kurtz, 1927 Grand American All-around champion; D. M. Roselle, L. R. Slocum, G. C. Tilton and E. B. Springer

was Lawrence George Dana who was the man of the hour and the day, the man of destiny.

As they lined up in the shoot-off, Dana at 17 yards and Pace at 19, most of the big crowd that banked themselves around the trap would probably have picked the short, stocky Pace as the winner. He seemed calm, while Dana seemed nervous. The bespectacled Pennsylvanian wiped his hands on his jacket, rubbed them on the muzzle of his gun, fidgeted around, before almost every shot. But Dana was to win the Grand American Handicap and he won it. With all his apparent nervousness, he broke 24 out of 25. The cool and collected Pace shattered only 23. So trapshooting had a new Grand American Handicap champion.

Walter Beaver, the Keystone ace, won the North American Clay Target championship with 199 out of 200 in the main event and 75 straight in the shoot-off to defeat Forest McNeir of Texas, Hale Jones of Illinois and Joe Hiestand of Ohio. The Doubles crown went to Mark Arie of Illinois, while Bunny Sanders of West Virginia turned in 191 out of 200 to lead the women gunners. Bunny defeated Mrs. D. S. McClain of Atlanta in the shoot-off.

Homer Clark, Alton, Illinois, then 15 years of age, bagged the Sub-junior title while 17-year old John Dick of Minneapolis took the Junior crown. They each busted 95's.

Johnny Jahn, the great Spirit Lake, Iowa, trapshooter, who is still going strong, won the Professional championship, but only after a shoot-off with Clyde Mitchell of Milwaukee. Mark Arie scored a victory in the Champion of Champions race in which he broke 197 out of 200 and W. A. Tabor, Union City, Oklahoma, found the targets to his liking and won the Veterans' honors with ease when he broke 191 out of 200.

Walt Beaver again came to the front with a victory in the class AA competition with 199 out of 200 in the regular event and 25 straight in the shoot-off to erase Gerald Batten, mighty Chicago gunner.

A strong Illinois quintette, Mark Arie, Hale Jones, Gerald Baten, W. A. Stephenson, Hillsdale, and C. Fehringer of Dupo copped the Team race with 959 out of 1,000.

Shooting from the 19-yard mark, Henry Holbrook, a banker from Sorento, Illinois, led a strong field of nearly 600 gunners to capture the Grand American Preliminary race.

Holbrook defeated W. L. Yeaman of Iowa and Harry Trimmer of Michigan in the shoot-off, after breaking 96 out of 100 from the 19-yard line. Joe Hiestand won the All-around championship with 878 out of 900.

Grand notes . . . Jim Bottomley, star first sacker of the Cincy Reds, took Tuesday off and watched the gunners in action. . . . Billy Beers was the best dressed man on the grounds. . . . Larry Duke, the tobacco gent from Fort Myers, Florida, broke 100 straight the same day as his picture hit the first page of the Daily news. We had arranged the story, so Larry helped us out with the first 100 straight he had ever broken at the Grand. . . . Charlie Green is the president of the McCrory stores. Lives in New York City and is a great guy. . . . Joe Cherry amused thousands with his movies in the Remington tent. . . . It was Guy Chiesman's first trip from Washington, where he is one of the leaders. And Guy lost his double gun.

Coley Coleman was in charge of the fine DuPont MX magazine and I wrote a daily column for it. . . . "Spain" Spainhour, Chicago, was the boss of the handicap committee. . . . Henry Holbrook, Illinois, and A. J. Boeder, South Dakota, are both bankers in their home towns. . . . Ansil Miller came all the way from Eustis, Florida, to tell the boys about his Winter Vandalia. . . . Otto Radloff, the pickle king from Iowa and Billy Finch kept up the interest with side bets on the shoot-offs—they ran all the way from a "fin" to three figures.

Ralph Marano, the New York wine merchant, is quite a skeet shot. . . . Charlie Phellis, New York City, owns the famous Emily Stokes, one of the greatest trotters of the year, a favorite in the recent Hambletonian. . . . We photographed the three 100 straight gunners from 25 yards: Phil Miller, 1924, with 118 straight; Clyde Wells, 1931, with 101 straight, and Mark Arie, this year, with 125 straight from the 25-yard line. . . . Popular Jim Skelly, one of the old guard, shot the Handicap race. . . . That fine gentleman from the south, C. B. Stickley, represented Virginia in the Champ of Champs race. . . . Harry Thoens from New York was very happy when he copped the Vandalia Open. . . . Mrs. Don McClain of Atlanta, who tied for the Women's crown, is one of the sweetest personalities in the game. . . . Homer Dick, that good shot out of Illinois, crashed 94 from 22 yards in the big race. . . . John Eshelman didn't run out of chewing tobacco. . . . Mrs. Paddock, well known New York shooter, broke 94 out of 100 in the Preliminary, 95 in the Grand. . . . "Carp" Carpenter, the big game hunter from New Hampshire, is planning another Alaskan trip. . . . Charlie Hymer, Hercules, stands ace high with all of his men.

Ralph Boorde of Hoopeston, Illinois, fished at Calvert's on Lake of the Woods after the Grand. . . . The Knoxville gunners were Ned Lutz, Junior Lutz, Joe and Mrs. Chilton. All are trapshooting bugs. . . . Dud Dickenson's manager is Big Heinie Sievert from Toledo. . . . Bob Coffey, Prairie City, Iowa, served as president of the Amateur Trapshooting Association in 1934 and 1935.

1935—J. B. ROYALL

A train conductor, widely known in southern trapshooting circles, J. B. Royall of Tallahassee, Florida, won the 1935 Grand American Handicap. Royall won the Grand that year but only after one of the most colorful shoot-offs of all times. Here was the picture. Royall and Sam Vance, Tillsonburg, Ontario, one of the most popular gunners in the game, were locked in tie after the regular event with 98's. Each stood on 20 yards. It was truly the deep south against the north, something that never had happened before in the trapshooting sport.

About four o'clock, after all the yardage shoot-offs had been held, the husky, grim-visaged railroad conductor and the steady, methodical Canadian stepped up to the firing line to decide the greatest prize in trapshooting.

At the Mid-West International at Grand Forks were: Lee Hughes of North Dakota; Russ Bordson, Minnesota; Vic Reinders, Wisconsin; Bert and Tom Brodie, Winnipeg

Awaiting their turn for the Women's Champion of Champions race at the 1941 Grand American. *(Left to right)* Bunny Sanders (the winner) of West Virginia; Mrs. H. J. Williams, Margaret Flewelling, Mrs. George Cameron, Mrs. Geo. Peters (standing), D. M. Legg and Frances Lee

Vance was the first to miss, dropping his 14th bird. Then Royall faltered on the 19th and they finished the string of 25 without another miss to leave the issue deadlocked. In the second event of 25, Royall fell behind when he muffed his seventh bird. On and on they churned the clays to dust. It looked like a cinch for the Canuck. He had broken his 14th bird and just 11 were between him and victory. And victory meant the first Canadian triumph in the annals of shotgun history. Up went his gun for No. 15, but fate played its role and the referee called "Lost." Again they were deadlocked. Then the Canadian faltered badly, missing his 20th and 21st, virtually assuring the championship for Royall. The pressure was still terrific, the man from the far south failed on his 24th, leaving the outcome in doubt until the final target, but he got that one, and the crown was his.

It was Ben Butts of Ferndale, Michigan, who upset the dope bucket when he defeated the heavily backed Steve Crothers and Russell Elliott in a heated shoot-off for the class AA title. They had broken 200 straights in the regular event. The Illinois squad, made up of Batten, Arie, Jones, Dick and Stifal, won the Team race with 985 out of 1,000. Elmer Torge, Wales Center, New York, the former baseball catcher, copped the Champion of Champions tilt with 200 straight.

Freddy Tomlin crashed another of his famous 200 straights to cop the Professional championship. Charlie Young, Springfield, Ohio, finally admitted he was old enough to enter the

Veterans' race and won it with 196 out of 200. Otto B. Kiehl, 14-year old from Pittsburg, Kansas, pupil of the noted Guy Von Schriltz, broke the fine score of 98 to cop the Sub-junior crown. Homer Clark, Jr., East Alton, Illinois, won the Junior competition with 99 out of 100.

Joe Hiestand, Hillsboro, Ohio, and Lela Hall of East Lynne, Missouri, were crowned king and queen of trapshooting. Joe won the National Amateur championship with 199 out of 200, while Lela led the women's field by four targets, breaking 191 out of 200. Hiestand had a big week for himself, copping the Doubles as well with 93 out of 100 and the All-around with 880 out of 900.

Ray Zweiner, the fast stepping Gopher gunner, won the Preliminary Handicap with 99 out of 100 from the 21-yard mark, nosing out "peerless" Steve Crothers in the shoot-off. A Grand American squad record was equalled when Hale Jones, Sam Jenny, Mark Arie, Frank Troeh and Gerald Batten broke 497 out of 500.

Bunny Sanders, Keyser, West Virginia, set a new Grand American Handicap women's long run record—114 straight, while Fred Tomlin made a new Grand American Handicap Professional record—430 straight. Walt Beaver won the Vandalia Open championship with 200 straight. C. F. Mitchell, Roco, Nebraska, copped the Vandalia Open Handicap with 98 out of 100 from 17 yards. Again Clyde Mitchell, Milwaukee, showed his stuff by winning the Professional All-around with 856 out of 900.

Grand notes . . . Popular Ben Butts from Michigan turned in the long run at the Grand American, 515 straight, a record. Gus Peret, busy with his camera as usual, said that he has hunted big game in Africa and has invaded Alaska 13 times for Kodiak. . . . Attractive Mrs. Don McClain from Atlanta showed them how it was done in the Preliminary race when she broke 94.

It was a triple tie in C class with Buck Eye B. I. Hughes "the winnah," but he had to eliminate W. R. Smith from Indiana and J. E. Monegan of LaCrosse, Wisconsin.

At Uncle Clarence Marshall's shoot at Yorklyn, Delaware, just before the Grand, Bill Eldred, Joe Hiestand, Hale Jones, Ned Lilly and Art Cuscaden broke 498 out of 500, a new squad record. . . . Paul Earle, Starr, South Carolina, one of the greatest shots in the south, took third position in the Grand American Preliminary when he coasted in with 98 from 23 yards. . . . The East was too tough in the East-West Team race, winning by seven targets, with Ben Butts, Steve Crothers, John Taylor, J. W. Napier, Joe Hiestand, T. K. Lee, Capt. J. B. Grier, Walt Beaver, Monte DeWire and Fred Routledge in the lineup. . . . Hale Jones led the Western team with 200 straight and was followed by Homer Dick, George Jewett, H. Brown, Gerald Batten, Frank Troeh, Mrs. Lela Hall, Count Smyth, Oscar Franz and Russ Elliott.

1936—BEN F. CHEEK

Benjamin F. Cheek, 59-year old garage owner and automobile mechanic, was the winner of the 1936 Grand American Handicap, but only after one of the most dramatic shoot-offs in the history of Grand American shoots. Here is the way it happened. Cheek, after the regular 100 targets, in which he broke 98 out of 100 from 16 yards, was tied up with Herb Bush, a shooting "fool" when it comes to handicaps, and Ed Buckwalter of Springfield, Ohio. Buckwalter stood on 16 yards, while Bush toed the 21-yard stripe.

Buckwalter fired the first shot in the shoot-off and broke his target. Cheek shot and scored. So did Bush. With monotonous regularity, they all cracked in a row. But things began to happen with the 25th bird. Buckwalter, a 32-year old

Joe Latimer *(left)* of Butte, Montana, broke 200 straight in the AA Class championship race at the 1941 Grand American. The other shooters are Cal Ray, noted Oregon shooter; Herman Peterson, Montana, vice president of the A. T. A., and Johnny Gray, Idaho

Ben Cheek *(left)*, winner of the shoot-off; Ed Buckwalter and Herb Bush

printer, missed. When Cheek and Bush got their targets, the Ohian was relegated to third place.

A second 25-bird event thus was necessary. Bush blew first, missing his 30th target, and then ran out. Cheek made 18 more in a row, but erred on his 44th attempt, only seven targets away from the promised land. That gave them 49 out of 50.

So a third shoot-off was ordered. This time Cheek missed first, dropping his 66th pigeon, but matters became even when Bush fell down on the 69th. Cheek immediately followed with a miss on the 70th, but the score was level again when the Illinois gunner failed on his 73rd. They got their remaining clays to stand even, 71 out of 75.

So a fourth shoot-off was demanded. In the fourth and fatal shoot-off, Bush failed on his 80th bird, but Cheek missed on his 83rd. Cheek went one up when his opponent lost his 88th,

Pacific coast gunners: George Porter, E. W. Pease, T. E. "Dan" Daniels, Charlie Dockendorf, Charlie Leith and Al Riehl. Dockendorf, one of the best trapshoot cashiers in the nation, is secretary-treasurer and manager of the Pacific International Trapshooting Association. He lives in Stanwood, Washington

but they were again even after the 94th, which Cheek missed. Here the crowd moaned.

With the groans still piercing the air, Bush, instead of waiting for the noise to subside, hurriedly called for his pull and his 95th target fell to the ground unharmed by any pellets from his shell. Cheek ran out, and with his run went the Grand American Handicap glory.

Hale Jones, Wood River, Illinois, stole the show Monday when he copped the Champion of Champions race with 197 out of 200 in the main event and 25 straight in the shoot-off to defeat Ralph Jenkins, the Orleans, Indiana, star. Jones had won the Vandalia Open Handicap on the day before with 97 out of 100 from the 24-yard mark.

Homer Clark and Rudy Etchen were the shooting stars in the Junior events. Homer again tucked away the Junior honors with 97 out of 100, while 13-year old Rudy, from Wichita, Kansas, first stepped into the clay target limelight by grabbing off the Sub-junior with 96.

The Professional championship went to that great shot, Captain J. B. Grier, Rockland, Delaware, who blasted out 199 out of 200. Joe Hiestand, Hillsboro, Ohio, was the star of the week, winning the Amateur Clay Target championship with 199 out of 200, the Doubles with 96 out of 100, the Vandalia Open with 198 out of 200, the class AA with 200 out of 200, the Grand American Handicap 16-yard championship with 595 out of 600, and was High-over-all with 881 out of 900.

Lela Hall, Strasburg, Missouri, with 196 out of 200, repeated in the Women's championship, but only after a terrific competition with Marie Kautzky Grant of Ft. Dodge, Iowa. Marie, in an early squad, broke 195 out of 200 and Lela had to break her last 50 straight later in a heavy wind and rain to cop the title. Hiestand had a battle on his hands in winning the National Clay Target championship, being tied with Hale Jones, Walter Beaver and Chummy Plummer from Flin Flon, Manitoba, all of whom had broken 199's. Joe broke 75 straight to cop the laurels.

The Grand American Preliminary Handicap went to E. L. "Red" Hawkins, the popular Ft. Wayne, Indiana, gunner, who broke 97 out of 100 from 21 yards. Charlie Young, Springfield, Ohio, won the Veterans' race with 194 out of 200. Roy Meadows and his wife from Des Moines garnered the Husband and Wife title with 374 out of 400. Mrs. Meadows, I might mention, won the Women's Grand American Handicap and Preliminary titles with a 93 and a 96 out of 100 from 18 yards.

Grand notes... Doc Alexander, Vermont, and New York's Wild Howard Akin lay claim to being the greatest two-man grouse team in the world. . . . "Bubber" Alford, genial manager of the Charlotte Harbor Hotel, Punta Gordo, Florida, took time out to tell the boys about his big shoot in January. . . . Henry Jones, Syracuse, attracted much attention with that fine dog of his, more than Detroit's Van Studdiford did with his brightly colored shooting jacket. . . . Just wouldn't be a Grand American without genial Fred Baskett, the cafe gent and Jailor Dud Veal from the Blue Grass state.

Dr. P. C. Banghart, London, Ontario, came back with a bang that year. . . . F. E. Shaw, Joliet, would rather attend a shooting match than to make out his income tax. . . . If you can tell the Sanmann boys apart, you're a wizard. Yes, both were there. "Doc" from New York City and J. F. from Lincoln, Nebraska. . . . They don't come any better than L. C. Turnock, and his A class victory was popular with everybody. . . . The big league squad of Cuscaden, Eldred, Lilly, Hiestand and Hale Jones, who busted 499 out of 500 at Yorklyn, were there. . . . The pleasant little chap, Harvey Carlisle from Salt Lake City is a real shot.

Johnny Rowland, the New Jersey state champ, broke 193 out of 200 in the Champ of Champs race. It was Johnny's first Grand and he brought along Miles Ross, S. B. Carpenter and W. T. Case, all former New Jersey state champs one way or another. . . . C. S. Bailes, popular Long Beach gunner, didn't bring along Bill Cree this year and Eddie Newburg was in the "dumps." . . . For good old fried chicken, we didn't overlook Connie Stumph's car. . . . Homer Dick, the famed Illinois gunner, has a real youngster. . . . Curly headed Frank Kahrs of Remington dropped in on his way to Camp Perry. . . . Ed Hammond, 67-year old Oakland gunner, was the happiest man on the grounds when he churned out 98 out of 100 Tuesday. . . . M. J. Bell, President of Sports Afield, again attended the Grand and got a great kick out of meeting the boys and talking "lumber jack."

"Noisy" A. D. Day from Assumption, Illinois, practiced

pointing his new gun around the house before the Grand, didn't know it was loaded, and it went off and killed their pet canary. . . . Mr. and Mrs. R. A. Paddock of New York met with an auto accident on the way to the big shoot. Mrs. Paddock had won the New York state women's championship with 195 out of 200 a few weeks before. . . . Otto Keihl, popular Pittsburg, Kansas, youngster, gave his dad quite a thrill when he won the D class laurels. . . . Pretty Suzy Jackson has quit changing guns and is on the way to recovery. Suzy and Jack have shot a carload of shells. . . . This fellow Hinklin from Marion, Ohio, who busted 97 out of 100 in the Grand American Handicap race, shot 6,000 registered targets in 1935. . . . J. A. Poore, Montana's great attorney, brought his boys to the Grand. . . . It was Joe Cotant's first visit from Idaho and he had a great time.

If you want to know anything about fly fishing, ask "Hink" Hinkle from Texas. . . . Carl Koeffler, who tied Turnock for the A class championship, is an aviator and hotel proprietor in Milwaukee. . . . D. L. McDonald, Amarillo, Texas, broke the first 100 straight of the tourney. It brought him the John Philip Sousa trophy. . . . J. A. Imes, Chicago, had a tough fight to win the E class title from M. J. Swanick of Brooklyn, New York. . . . Margaret Loring, the A.T.A. statistician, knows every shooter by his first name. . . . The boys talking about the world's record shoot-off between Ned Lilly and Kurt Heide for the 1936 Michigan State title. . . . Lilly, 225 straight . . . Heide, 224 x 225. Ohio won the Team Championship with 966 x 1,000, with Hiestand, Young, Turnock, Ross and Voss in their line-up.

1937—FRANK G. CARROLL

Frank G. Carroll, 35-year old hardware merchant of Brecksville, Ohio, emerged from the greatest scoring spree in trapshooting history to win the 38th annual Grand American Handicap title, but he was forced to break 100 straight

Kurt Heide

For more than 25 years, John Clay *(left)* has run the wealthy Houston Gun Club. Gillette Hill, a swell guy, is at his right

Lynn Hunt, Bronx, N. Y., is a member of New York City Baseball Federation and a fine trapshot as well

THEY KNOW THEIR POWDER. Mrs. H. M. Hollyfield of Portland and Mrs. Eddie Bauer of Seattle. Probably you have heard of Eddie Bauer's famous sporting goods store in Seattle. If not—visit him some time

Ted Renfro, Dell, Montana, won the world's live pigeon championship at Monte Carlo in 1933. Ted sent me this picture from Monte Carlo just after he won the championship. *(Left to right)* Tony Masten, Walter Warren, who won several world's live pigeon championships, Gene Springer and Ted Renfro

1924 CANADIAN OLYMPIC TEAM: *(Top row)* Johnny Black, Tom Harland, Sam Vance, S. Newton, George Beattle, W. Barnes, J. Montgomery, Herb Moody

from the 19-yard mark to win. Barking at Carroll's heels with 99 out of 100 were 11 gunners, a lone target keeping each from the hall of fame. They were Don Shelton (second place after the shoot-off), A. B. Springer, that Herb Bush guy again, and Ray Falcon from Illinois, Fred King and Forest McNeir from Texas, Bruce Sloan from Kentucky, F. J. Snider from Ohio, Harry Kretschmann, a Canadian, Charlie Huntington from Missouri, and young Stanley Meadows from Iowa.

Carroll's victory, which came as a complete surprise to more than 15,000 spectators, was worth more than $3,000 to our "dark horse" friend. The new champion was the huskiest man ever to take the crown. He was six feet, four inches tall and weighed 215 pounds. After the big race Carroll said, "I didn't think I had a chance to win anything here. When I entered the big race I didn't even play the (money) optionals."

Carroll is a member of the Brecksville Gun Club, which has

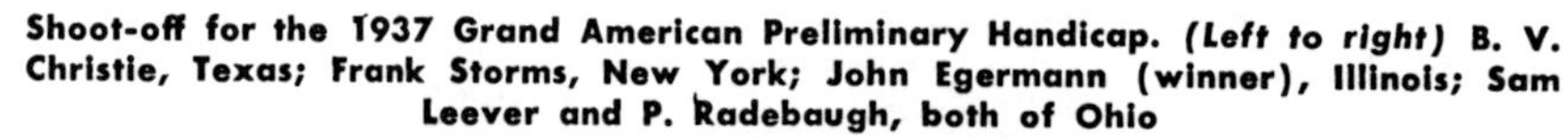

Shoot-off for the 1937 Grand American Preliminary Handicap. *(Left to right)* B. V. Christie, Texas; Frank Storms, New York; John Egermann (winner), Illinois; Sam Leever and P. Radebaugh, both of Ohio

only two members, John Q. Markin and Carroll. He doesn't smoke or drink, has been married for 11 years, but has no children.

Everybody, it seems, had a slice at Grand American championships that year. Phil Miller won the Amateur championship with 200 straight and Hale Jones copped the Champion of Champions tilt with 100 straight. John Egermann, Naperville, Illinois, captured the Preliminary Handicap with 99 from 19 yards, while Ned Lilly came through with a victory in the Doubles, scoring 98. Lela Hall repeated in the Women's event with 194 and Stan Meadows took the Junior with 98.

Fred King scored 881 out of 900 to carry the All-around back to Wichita Falls, Texas. Clyde Wells came through with a neat 200 straight for the Professional crown. The Sub-junior went to Rudy Etchen and the Veterans' title to E. E. Daniels, Birmingham, Michigan. Charlie Bogert, Sandusky, Ohio, the gun man, copped the AA class honors with 200 straight, and C. E. Heaton of Fairfax, Iowa, lifted the Vandalia Open from 21 yards with 99. Carl Thacker, Sioux City, scored another Iowa victory in the Open championship with 200 straight, and Mr. and Mrs. Fred Hess of Philadelphia took charge of the Husband and Wife event with 383 out of 400.

Wisconsin came through with a smashing victory in the Team championship, scoring 982 out of 1,000 with Vic Reinders, Dr. O. B. Hinz, Carl Schroeder, Claude Olney and Harry Billett in their lineup. Carl Stevens, Zanesville, Ohio, won the Pro All-around with 874 out of 900 and Stanley Meadows won A class; Bill Horton, Moose Lake, Minnesota, B class; R. V. Polen, Dayton, Ohio, C class; M. J. Swanick, Brooklyn, New York, D class, and J. C. Baker, Highland, Ohio, the E class laurels. That was the picture of the 1937 Grand.

Grand notes . . . O. N. Ford, Del Monte, wasn't talking through his hat when he wrote me to watch Dorothy Morrison of Long Beach. She's a fine shot. Big George Jewett and John Derdoski from Minnesota shot out a dozen 198's and then settled down to a dog fight of their own. . . . Jack Guenveur, Emmett Hines, Henry Winchester and Al Riehl did a bangup job running the office.

Captain Mel Hicks from Georgia did some fancy shooting for the crowd and was good. . . . Bill Moore was on hand as usual for the Sportsmen's Review, "grubbing," as Bill calls it, out the news. . . . Charlie Hopkins, Western maestro, flashed a big smile when Hale Jones won the Champion of Champions race. They hunt geese together at Cairo, Illinois. . . . Doc Ashby and Logan Harbican were very much there from the Windy City. "Hap" fed half the crowd at his trailer. . . . Walter Peacock's trophies were the finest I had seen at the Grand. . . . Adolph Nelson, sponsor of the Detroit shoot in July, took the boys in the handicap race Saturday.

It just wouldn't be a Grand without the Dana-Mulhaupt combine. Understand "Mul" was giving a few free lunches at the Biltmore again that year. . . . Carrick Mustion looked as fine as ever, despite his recent ptomaine attack while at Detroit. . . . Ad Topperwein and Mrs. Ad put on one of their famous exhibitions. Ad has been shooting for 60 years and Mrs. Top started at the St. Louis world's fair.

Jim Hanley from Stamford, Connecticut, annexed another 100 friends at the Grand. . . . What Maryland lacked in quantity she made up in quality with the great D. Franklin Beck on hand. . . . Emmett Simmons, state champ, G. H. Kries, the elk hunter, and T. T. McMahan came from Montana and enjoyed every minute of the shoot. . . . E. E. Daniels, the Veterans' champ, has been shooting just 47 years. . . . Bill Cree, who won the C class doubles, is a prominent Long Beach attorney and a high grade fellow.

Bill Parker, a real Amateur Trapshooting Association booster, from Long Beach, never misses a Grand. . . . J. R. Carson from Uhricsville, Ohio, doesn't set the world afire with his shotgun, but he does really enjoy the big shoot. . . . The Polens from Dayton are good shooters, evidenced by R. V.'s C class title and the fact that his wife finished fourth among the women in the Grand, with 94. . . . Harold Russell, in charge of the Federal tent, is an all around skeet and trap shooter, holds five pistol championships. . . . Bernice Billet was the apple's eye of the photographers. Bernice hails from Wisconsin. . . . F. D. Hawkins, of Recoil Pad fame, was among the 13 South Dakota shooters. . . . Charlie Greer fired the first shot of the tourney, as usual.

The famous Johnstown, Pennsylvania, trio, Dr. E. C. Boyer, big game hunter, Frank Pentrach and Dr. J. D. Kieper, were very much on hand. . . . Jack Condrey made the team for the first time. . . . Eddie Coe of Mississippi and Al Ivins, former Grand American victor, have been chasing shoots since

VETERANS' CHAMPIONS

E. E. Daniels (1937)

E. E. Bush (1938)

F. D. Kelsey (1930-31-32)

W. A. Tabor (1934)

T. G. Cathan (1933)

A CALIFORNIA SQUAD AT THE GRAND: Bill Parker, Belle McCord Roberts, Bill Cree, Joe Steed, Gus Smith

1895. . . . Dan Cauley, the big Crystal Lake gunner, was the happiest man on the grounds when Carroll came through. Lawrence Bird, Cauley, Bill Akers and Aaron Bird all belong to the Crystal Lake Gun club. . . . Walter Winteringham broke a 200 straight on Monday and another 200 straight on Tuesday. His long run of 414 straight on registered targets was the high run of the week.

1938—TED WEST

Ortello William "Ted" West, a 45-year old district highway superintendent from Coshocton, gave the Buckeye state another Grand American Handicap champion in 1938. Ted, who had been shooting targets for 17 years, defeated Parr Rhines, another of Ray Loring's colts from Marseilles, Illinois, in a thrilling shoot-off by one target. This is the way it happened.

Rhines finished with a 99 out of 100 in one of the early

1938 Pennsylvania Team champions. *(Left to right)* M. McBrayne, C. D. Wolfe, Jimmy Stinson, W. Beaver, and Johnny Rigg. Rigg won the Grand American Doubles championship the following year

WASHINGTON, D. C. TRAPSHOOTING STARS: Dr. W. D. Monroe, C. C. Fawsett, W. F. Burrows, Dr. J. C. Wynkoop, R. D. Morgan

squads while West came up with the same count a couple of hours later. West took the crown with a score of 22 out of 25, missing his first two targets late in the event after he seemingly had the crown in the bag.

It was a battle royal for third place on the 98's. Dr. J. W. Stanton, the popular Chicago gunner, took the prize when he crashed 100 straight from the 19-yard line, after breaking 98 out of 100 in the main event. If I were to pick the most outstanding performance of all Grand American shoot-offs, before or since, that I have witnessed, Doc's brilliant victory would stand tops.

Herb Bush, Eaton, Illinois, the hard luck Grand American gunner, came next, in fourth place. The same Bush broke 98 out of 100 to tie for the title several years before, and you may recall that he broke 99 out of 100 the previous year. Fifth place went to T. R. Vail, Industry, Illinois, while Walter Sams of Athens, Georgia, cornered sixth position. Then came T. Birch, Louisville, Kentucky; A. B. Springer, Metropolis, Illinois; the great Paul Earle from Starr, South Carolina, and A. M. Feltus from Mobile, Alabama, who took 10th place.

Joe Hiestand, Hillsboro, Ohio, turned in the greatest shooting ever witnessed at a Grand, that year. Let's follow the Buckeye bullet down the trapline. Saturday he crashed 100 straight in the Preliminary, Sunday he won the Open championship with 200 straight, Monday it was another 200 straight, Tuesday he made ink spots out of another 200, which gave him the Amateur Clay Target championship, and a long run of 766 which erased Fred Tomlin's world's record run which Fred had just completed that week. (Fred finished with 714, breaking Boyd Duncan's run which he hung up in 1923 when he scored 621 straight.)

Wednesday Joe kept right on going, breaking another 200 straight to tie Phil Miller for the class AA honors, which Phil won in the shoot-off. That gave Hiestand a long run of 900 straight at the Grand American, with 66 more that he brought from Yorklyn, Delaware. We might also add that Hiestand visited several other shoots, later, running his string up to 1,179, which still stands as a world's record. Joe also won the All-around that year with 881 out of 900.

There were other victors at the 1938 Grand. Mark Hootman, Ohio, won the Champion of Champions with 100 straight and L. R. Slagle, South Charleston, Ohio, copped the Preliminary Handicap with 98 out of 100 from 19 yards. Then there was Fred Etchen with his Doubles victory, 96 out of 100; Lela Hall with another championship in the Women's division, with 195 out of 200; Rudy Etchen, the Junior; E. E. Bush, Tallahassee, Florida, the Veterans'; Karl Maust, the Professional, with 199 out of 200; Ray Fienup, St. Louis, the Subjunior, with 98; John and Bunny Sanders, Keyser, West Virginia, the Husband and Wife. Pennsylvania won the Team championship with Beaver, Wolfe, Riggs, McBrayne and Stinson in their lineup. They broke 983 out of 1,000.

Grand notes . . . For tough luck, we'll take Doc Hagerty for running into that airplane and Phil Miller for doubling his gun on his last pair of doubles that would have given him a tie with Fred Etchen. . . . B. V. Christie of Texas came to the Grand with a $20,000 streamlined trailer. . . . H. E. Nickum, O. E. Spangler and J. T. Irick of Wyoming attended their first Grand American and vowed they would be back next year.

Charlie Greer fired the first shot and C. F. Bliss, Bob Oster, Jr., D. B. Berkley and Dick Shroyer shot in his squad. . . . Both Fred Etchen, the Doubles champ, and L. R. Slagle, new Preliminary king, are southpaws. . . . Glad to see Guy Housley, outdoor editor of the "Chicago Daily News," win the C class Doubles; and Ren Heaton, popular Terre Haute gunner, win the B class title with his 198 out of 200. . . . Hiestand's long run on registered, practice and shoot-offs was 1,191. . . . Never saw a more enthusiastic gunner than big Ed

They bring their wives and children to the Grand American. Some stop at hotels and others stay in tents and rest camps. Here's a happy-go-lucky group of sportsmen from Illinois. Chris Bunn is wearing his usual smile and A. B. Springer's thoughts seem to be with those quail back in southern Illinois. Do you recognize Roy Kentfield, C. E. Hay, C. Orr, Ed Willers, Phil Sudendorf, Jack Bruns, who won the Vandalia Open last fall, Herb Longden, Dr. R. N. Canaday, Joe Kellerman, Homer Clark, Sr., Sy Durham, Bobby Stifal, E. L. Pennington, Ray Fienup, J. L. Kleeschulte, Herb Bush, R. Y. Champion, "Hap" Harbican, Bob Burress, Art Stifal, E. F. Best and Bill Fienup?

Here they are—the guys that give you your classification and yardage at the Grand American. The 1941 Grand American Handicap committee: *(Left to right)* Parr Rhines, Illinois; Joe Chilton, Tennessee; Bill Parker, California; Walter Johnson, New Jersey, and E. B. Chamberlin, New York

Team shoots are popular in trapshooting. Some years ago Chicago and Dayton, Ohio staged several real shoulder to shoulder battles. *Top row, left to right:* Graham Grosvener (Chicago), Bud Talbott (Dayton), Fred Rike (D), Jim Markham (D), Ed Swift (C), Doc Herrman (D), S. G. Allyn (D), Walter Johnson (C), Ford Carter (C), F. C. Letts (C), W. W. Sunderland (D); *Bottom row:* O. L. Harrison (D), Dr. W. A. Ewing (D), Bob Dickey (D), George Henneberry (C), John Drake (C), John Huffman (D), Bob King (D), George Greene (D)

Chase from Wisconsin. . . . Hod Brown, Oklahoma City, Ray Zweiner, Minnesota, and O. W. Witt, Broadland, Indiana, busted 198's Wednesday and tangled up in a shoot-off for A class honors with Ray the "winnah."

Ralph Leist, Pataskala, Ohio, was quite pleased with his 198 out of 200 for B class honors. . . . So was Frank Mazanet of Madison, Wisconsin, with his 196 for the C class title. . . . One target from the Preliminary Handicap title were Sam Vance, Tilsonburg, Ontario; Charlie Heaton, Fairfax, Iowa; George Proctor, former Massachusetts champ; Captain I. G. Hay of the Panama Canal; Jim Vinckel from Illinois, and Al Chalfant, who hails from Somerset, Ohio. . . . And last but not least, the great Western team broke the world's squad record with 993 out of 1,000, with F. H. Woodock, 199; Karl Maust, 199; Captain J. B. Grier, 200; Joe Davison, 199, and Homer Clark, 196, in their lineup.

1939—D. L. RITCHIE

Dwight L. Ritchie, Goshen, Ohio, a shooting pupil of Sam Leever's, the former Pittsburgh baseball star, won the 1939 Grand American Handicap title, but only after the screwiest shoot-off in Grand American history. He had tied up with George Wagner of Dayton in the main event, each breaking 99's, Ritchie at 22 yards, Wagner at 23. Here is the picture of the shoot-off.

Mr. Ritchie was first to shoot. He muffed his first target. "That," said Mr. Ritchie in his soft spoken way, "was due to tension. I was a little too careful, I guess." Mr. Wagner, as cool as a cucumber, broke his first seven targets. Ritchie blew another, his eighth. Then another, which placed him three targets down in nine. Wagner didn't seem to mind the pressure. As far as I was concerned, the race was over. Victory appeared certain for the Dayton shooter.

Then things began to happen. Wagner, a smiling, likeable, darn good fellow and one helluva worker around a gun club, began to weaken. You have seen a pitcher go haywire in the last inning of a tight baseball game; you have seen a fighter get knocked out in the last round after he had the fight cinched; that happened to George Wagner, the pride of the Cash Register City.

Wagner missed his 14th target. He still had a big lead and nobody gave it a thought. Surely he wouldn't miss two more birds in the final 10 after breaking 99 out of 100 in the main event. He broke his 15th target. Just 10 to go for the Grand American Handicap crown—the greatest event in the clay target sport.

And then, in less time than it takes to pen this line, George Wagner lost the Grand American laurels. You have seen a pitcher on the verge of a no-hit game—then suddenly singles, doubles and home runs rain off of the opposing bats like hail stones. Well, that's what happened to George. Boom! Boom! Boom! He dropped his 16th, 17th and 18th targets. That 18th target won Ritchie the shotgun crown. Wagner finished his 25 targets with four misses, while Ritchie didn't miss after his 9th target.

P. O. Harbage, West Jefferson, Ohio, won both the Open championship and National Clay Target titles with 200 straights, which stamped him as star of the week. Walter Peterson, Lynn, Massachusetts, came up with 100 straight to win the Champion of Champions race, while Fred Tomlin took the Professional honors with 199 out of 200.

Mrs. Wm. Gilbert, a newcomer from Madison, Wisconsin, scored an impressive victory in the Women's race with a 98 and then went on to break her last 100 straight. H. S. Shellito, Ames, Iowa, captured the Open Handicap with 99 out of 100 and John and Bunny Sanders again carried back the Husband and Wife championship to dear old West Virginia.

Rudy Etchen again won the Junior title with 97 out of 100 and Ray Fienup repeated in the Sub-junior with 98. Ohio, with P. O. Harbage, Charlie Morgan, E. V. Ross, George Cady and Joe Hiestand in their lineup, won the Team championship with 984 out of 1,000.

Johnny Rigg of Conshohocken, Pennsylvania, topped the Doubles gunners with 97 out of 100 and Walter Wintering-

NEW YORK A. C. STARS: Frank Scola, Tony Masten, A. F. MacNicol, Harry Thoens, Zammie Simmons

HERCULES BOYS AT THE GRAND: Charlie Hymer (the boss), Henry Winchester, Jay Graham, J. R. Hinkle, John Jahn, Art Cuscaden, Norman Wright

ham of Barrington, Illinois, captured the Preliminary Handicap with 99 out of 100 from the 22-yard mark. Walt, you may recall, won the B class title in 1937 with 200 straight and crashed another 200 to tie Phil Miller and Bob Coffey for the National championship. Joe Hiestand and Homer Clark each broke 594 out of 600 to tie for high guns on 16-yard targets and Phil Miller took the All-around with 880 out of 900.

A pair of 200's were scored in the Class races. Jack Lindsay, Okmulgee, Oklahoma, the skeet shooter, was one of them, winning AA class, and Fred King of Texas was the other, copping the A class laurels. E. H. Schmidt, Xenia, Ohio, won B class; Roy Miller, Grove City, Minnesota, won C class and Gene Adrian, Monroeville, Indiana, snared the D class title.

OHIO TEAM CHAMPS (1939): Charlie Morgan, Joe Hiestand, George Cady, E. V. Ross, P. O. Harbage. Ray Loring holding the Sports Afield Team Trophy

George Wagner, who tied Ritchie, shot in this squad. *(Left to right)* George Peters, Alvin Hextell, Dr. Fred Schuster, George Wagner and M. Schwar

Grand notes . . . When I asked P. O. Harbage how it felt to win the National championship with 200 straight he replied, "I paid for 200 targets. I thought I might as well break 'em." . . . The other sensation of the Grand was Mrs. Wm. Gilbert, who started shooting the last August 16th, on her husband Bill's birthday. She broke 12 out of 25. . . . Just wouldn't be a Grand without the "Show me" twins, Harry Davis and his pal, O. E. Grecian. . . . Lute Gambell, a rabid Cincy Red fan, brought Willard Hergsberger, catcher of the Reds, down for a few shots. . . . Doc Lilly's famous Chi Cubs were not doing so well and Doc was in the dumps. . . . Bart Saxbe spent most of his time telling the boys about his Canadian fishing trip. One 40- and two 30-pound lake trout.

Joe Hiestand and Homer Clark high on 16-yard targets, 594 out of 600. Florence Mos, Ohio, and Mrs. W. D. Treadway, Maryland, gave Mrs. Gilbert quite a chase in the Women's championship race with their 97's. . . . Dad C. J. Mos won the Professional Doubles with 94. . . . John Rigg, new Doubles champ, is a confirmed bachelor and is 52. . . . Lawrence Kreig, Newark, Ohio, was at his old post, watching the cash. . . . Houston Johnny Clay and Walter Peacock talked ponies instead of trapshooting.

Tiny Blair from Kansas wasn't a bit smaller and was just as jovial. . . . Dave Henry flew in from Kansas City for the Champ of Champs race. Flew back next day. . . . Tom Hale from Mt. Pleasant, Tennessee, busted his shotgun. . . . Phil Miller, Clyde Mitchell, Chummey Plummer, Junior Johnston and Ed Luyben ran 472 straight, a Grand American squad record. . . . That 199 was a nice piece of work on the part of C. H. Sears, the Harpster, Ohio, expert, in the Open championship tussle. . . . It was Hercules' Jimmy O'Neil's first

HUSBAND AND WIFE CHAMPIONS

John and Bunny Sanders (1935-38-39)

Mr. and Mrs. Roy Meadows (1936)

Mr. and Mrs. Fred Hess (1937)

Mr. and Mrs. Van Marker (1940)

Dr. and Mrs. E. Roose (1941)

Grand and he liked it. . . . George Dillon, who hails from Maysville, Kentucky, banged out the C class championship Wednesday. . . . Popular Joe Chilton from Knoxville would rather lose an eye than miss the roaring Grand. . . . When Dan Bittinger, Ferd Kahler and Bill Waldock get together, things begin to happen fast. . . . George Gillette from the Badger state always takes home a trophy. . . . Nic Huck, the Kansasville, Wisconsin, mayor, was on hand. . . . Jimmy O'Hanlon of the New York Athletic Club was in charge of the firing line, and there is no better handler.

H. P. "Hap" Nicklas of Durand spent most of his time telling the boys about the 1940 Wisconsin state shoot. . . . Dud Dickenson and Frank Kachelhoffer took care of the bulletin board and Dud was as noisy as ever. . . . One of these days I'm going to take up A. B. Springer on one of his quail promises. . . . Handicap committee, Eddie Dygert, Bill Parker, Logan Harbican, Jimmy Stinson and Gordon Hight, did a swell job. . . . W. B. Belz, the shooting glass expert, and Gus Alexander, the jacket man, shared a tent. . . . Remington's Dunny Reynolds was all smiles when Freddy Tomlin crashed through with the Professional victory. . . . Charlie Bogert, the famed Sandusky trader and trapshot, had more guns than usual. . . . Tom Deen was the busiest man on the grounds, promoting the winter shoots in Florida.

1940—E. H. WOLFE

Ernest H. Wolfe, a popular and well known gunner out of Charleston, West Virginia, defeated 820 of the nation's greatest trapshooters to win the 1940 Grand American Handicap.

Before noon, Wolfe had recorded a 98 out of 100 from 23 yards. He had missed his 49th and 91st targets. Wolfe entertained only a slim hope that his score would stand up. As a matter of fact, I talked with him a few minutes after he had shot his 98. I told him that his score might stand up and that a photo of him, right then and there, might bring him luck.

"I don't think my score will stand up, Jimmy," he said. "Good luck to the rest of the shooters, and it won't bother me whether or not my 98 stands up—98 is still a good score." To those who know him personally, it was a typical Wolfe answer. A very good shot, that you know by his 23-yard average—but plain modest.

There was a wee bit of tension as the long day wore on. It must have been the longest afternoon that Mr. Wolfe ever put in. He did eat lunch—but I don't know how much. He must have had nervous indigestion all afternoon until finally at 4:30 it was obsolutely discovered that no one else had a chance to beat his score. Thus, a new champion was crowned.

Ernie is just another fellow, but one of the most likeable shooters on the ground. He has been married 18 years, has a son, Bob, and a daughter, Betty. The $1,750 he won went into the bank for a nest egg to help send the youngsters to college. He is an accountant by trade. He didn't think he would win the Grand, so didn't play the optional money.

Roy Miller, Grove City, Minnesota, a "dark horse," won the Preliminary Handicap with 100 straight from 20 yards. Miller had been shooting so poorly that Horace Aldritt and the Minnesota boys had to coax him to shoot the Preliminary that day.

Forest McNeir, the colorful Houston, Texas, gunner, won the North American Clay Target championship with 200 straight. Mr. McNeir is 65.

Fred Tomlin, Glassboro, New Jersey, opened the shooting Sunday with a victory in the Open championship when he scored 199 out of a possible 200. The Vandalia Open Handicap was won by E. M. Young of Zanesville, Ohio, who scored 95.

Lela Hall, Strasburg, Missouri, hung up another championship in the Women's race when she shattered 97. Florence Mos of Cincinnati was next with 95. Fred Tomlin took his second championship of the week when he won the Professional

At the Utah State shoot: *(Top row)* F. J. McGanney, Mrs. Wiley Coleman, Gus Becker; *(Bottom row)* Harry Todd, Sam Sharman and C. B. Higgins. Sharman won the Champion of Champions race at the 1940 Grand

Chummey Plummer, from the little, northern Manitoba gold mine town, Flin Flon, was among the high all-around leaders at the 1940 classic

honors with 196 out of 200 in the regular event and 75 straight in the shoot-off, defeated Mitchell, Mos, Flewelling and Davison. The "vet" Sam Sharman of Salt Lake City took the Champion of Champions tussle, but only after a stubborn shoot-off with the famed Charlie Gunning of Colorado and J. E. McFadden of Maryland. They broke 99's.

E. L. Hawkins, Ft. Wayne, Indiana, was the victor in the Doubles race, with 98 out of 100, while John Martin of Providence copped the Junior title with 99 out of 100. E. C. Colosky, Jr., of Minneapolis took the Sub-junior with 88. The Husband and Wife event went to Mr. and Mrs. Van Marker of Evanston, Illinois, who shattered 189 out of 200. The Father and Son victory went to Ned Lilly and his father, Stanton, Michigan, who turned in 193 out of 200, but they had to outshoot Elmer and Don Torge of New York, who had tied them.

Famous Western Professionals at Del Monte: *(Left to right)* Harvey Bostick, Charlie Knight, Nels Dunn, Dave Flannigan, Charlie Plank; *(Kneeling)* Fred Grewell, E. L. Ilgner, C. B. McDowell

SOUTHERN SPORTSMEN WHO NEVER OVERLOOK THE VANDALIA SHOW: ***(Left to right)*** **Larry Grant, Mrs. Don McClain, Jack Tway, Mrs. Grant, Gordon Hight, Mrs. Hight, Walter Sams, Jr.**

Johnny Fontaine, Philadelphia, wasn't so old—he copped the Veterans' race with 98 out of 100, a creditable score for anybody.

The Hoosiers showed they could shoot when they took the Team championship with 981 out of 1,000. Their quintet included Phil Miller, Ralph Jenkins, L. C. Wise, Herschel Cheek and Junior Johnston.

Horace Aldritt of Excelsior, Minnesota, grabbed off the class AA honors with 198 out of 200, while the A class laurels went to Ralph Jenkins, of Orleans, Indiana, who broke 199. Eddie Alias, the fast stepping Shreveport, Louisiana, gunner, took B with 196, and T. J. Webb was awarded the C class crown with another 196. Webb lives in Towanda, Pennsylvania. L. C. Jepson, Dwight, Illinois, captured the D class with 197, a great score for this class. It was number one Grand American for both Jepson and Alias.

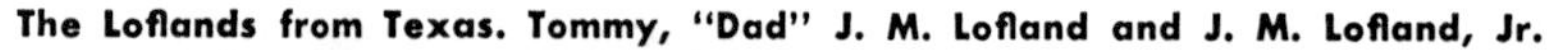

The Loflands from Texas. Tommy, "Dad" J. M. Lofland and J. M. Lofland, Jr.

H. L. Cheek, Clinton, Indiana, won the Amateur All-around honors with 1,131 out of 1,200, while Clyde Mitchell, Minneapolis, scored again when he led the Professionals with the marvelous score of 1,137, six targets in front of the entire field. Other winners were: Glenn Oswald, Columbus, Ohio, the Professional Grand American Handicap title, 97 from 22 yards; Ralph Jenkins, the Jim Markham Trophy, with 100 straight; Stan Meadows, Grimes, Iowa, the Jim Day Cup, with 385 out of 400; Don Flewelling, Harvey, Illinois, the Pro Preliminary Handicap, with 96 from 22 yards; Lela Hall, the Women's Grand American Handicap, and Sheverly Jean Nusom of Quincy, Oregon, the Women's Preliminary Handicap. Lela busted a 95, while Sheverly turned in 93. The Van Cleve Trophy went to Mrs. George Cameron of Houston, Texas.

Grand notes . . . Two years ago Glenn Oswald was selling Sports Afield magazines to buy a shotgun. Today he is the Professional Handicap title holder. . . . Big Bill Drennen of Utica, Illinois, didn't do a thing but bust 99 out of 100 from the 23-yard mark in the Preliminary Handicap, which would have brought him a couple of thousand bucks if Roy Miller hadn't changed his mind and shot the Handicap. . . . Junior Johnston added $500 to his bankroll when he won one of the 50 target specials. . . . During the Grand American, A. Y. Yenowine, secretary of the Terre Haute gun club, dropped dead after he had broken 24 out of 25 in the Grand American Handicap race. Yenowine was loved by every trapshooter in Indiana and he left a big gap in trapshooting.

Big Ed Brown was on hand from Toledo looking up his many friends. . . . Jimmy "Pop" Atkinson came all the way from New Castle, Pennsylvania, and it was his first Grand American since 1906. Pop won a horse and buggy in the Consolation race that year and sold it to Mal Hawkins for $150. . . . Attractive Mrs. Cameron from Houston, Texas, won the Women's Doubles crown. . . . Mrs. Wm. Lassen, Kansas women's champ, took third place in the Women's race with 93. . . . M. M. Marcussen, Rock Island, Illinois, is the only registered trapshooter there, but is one of the nation's toughest all around gunners in my book.

Old Bill Crum, the engraver, was very much there. Bill covers the big skeet, trap and pistol meets from coast to coast.

Highest priced gun he ever engraved belonged to Billy Hunter of Kansas City. It cost 3,600 berries without a recoil pad. . . . Rod Cooper from Louisville broke 49 out of 50 doubles Wednesday, missed his last target, which was really a gold target. "That's nothing," said Rod. "Several years ago at the Kentucky state shoot I broke 96 out of 100 doubles, was low in my squad." That squad was made up of the vet Homer Clark, who reeled off 100 straight, Bill Eldred and John Kreis, 98's, and Ralph Jenkins, 97. . . . Skipper, aged 17, and Odd Williams, 13, came all the way from Lawrence, Kansas, with their Dad. Skipper attends Culver.

Big Elmer Harter from Richmond, Indiana, is as tough as ever, evidenced by his 97 out of 100 in the Grand American Preliminary. . . . Ralph Jenkins was the reason that Indiana pulled through in the Team race. Ralph broke 199 out of 200, and they needed it. . . . George Gault, well known New York shooter, who hadn't attended a Grand American for some years, said, "It hain't the same old place without Ben Field." . . . A. B. Tucker, Dayton, Ohio, had a few minutes of glory Thursday morning in the Grand American Preliminary with his leading 98. Ten minutes later he was second.

Don McClelland, the good looking New York champ and old Sioux Indian "Chew Tobacco" A. F. Jones from Minnesota busted 198's in the Class championships. . . . Ed Alias escaped a lot of hard work when he busted 196 out of 200 to lead the B class gunners. Right on his heels, with 195's, were: Doc Springton, Evansville, Indiana; John Lofland, Ft. Worth, Texas; H. E. Bloomenrader, Highmore, South Dakota, and Tommy Herr, Jr., of Syracuse. . . . When it comes to congenial shooters, you can't beat the Loflands from Texas, Dad, John and Tommy. They are oil well diggers on a big scale. . . . The Van Cleve Trophy went to Mrs. George Cameron of Houston. . . . Captain Pablo Cruz led a big contingent of Cuban shooters. . . . Ernie Maetzold, Minneapolis, was elected president of the Amateur Trapshooting Association, replacing Fred King of Texas.

For many years, M. M. Marcussen was the only registered trapshooter in Rock Island, but always very tough on all kinds of targets

1941—WALTER TULBERT

Walter Tulbert, 52-year old furnace salesman from Detroit, Michigan, was the winner of the 1941 Grand American. Tulbert, a distinctive new trapshot, came to the Grand with an average of 88 per cent, so he was stationed on the 18-yard line by the handicap committee. Two weeks before, I had watched Tulbert in action at the National Skeet shoot at Indianapolis. He is a good skeet shot. A fair trapshot, he had never broken more than 90 out of 100 at trapshooting before.

When the smoke had cleared away in the Grand American Handicap race Friday, Tulbert and one Del Bundschuh, of Fremont, Ohio, another unknown, who shot from 17 yards, were high guns over the 1,091 shooters, with 99's.

The shoot-off was one of the most spectacular in Grand American history. Both had shot their bolts in the championship race and the big crowd of more than 10,000 shotgun fans sat in for the kill.

The Ohioan started out like a house on fire and he looked like a winner when he crashed his first 10 targets. Tulbert was apparently nervous and "blew" his fifth and sixth targets. Bundschuh appeared to have the famous classic safely won when something happened. He missed his 12th target, then his 14th. That made it even.

Then each broke the next four targets. The Fremont gunner muffed his next bird, the fatal 19th, and that cost him the championship. Tulbert finished straight for the title.

Tulbert's companion at the traps was a 25-year-old pump gun which he had bought for $40. Born in Phoenix, Arizona, the new trapshot king later moved to Cleveland, where he spent 15 years before going to Detroit, where he has lived for the past six years.

He was a lieutenant in World War I, serving as an

Russell Elliott

South Dakota shooters at the 1941 Grand: *(Top row, left to right)* F. D. Hawkins, George Sullivan, Ben Mescher, W. McLaughlin and Ed Boetcher; *(Bottom row)* Don Swanson, S. N. Noyes, H. Bloomenrader and H. Rierson

ammunition dump inspector. He has hunted all his life and goes south for quail each winter.

Neither one of these shooters played the optionals. However, each shooter won about $1,400, which wasn't bad.

Three gunners scored 98's. They were F. B. Noble, Newton Falls, Ohio; Percy Harbage, West Jefferson, Ohio, and M. D. Roberts, Middletown, Connecticut. Miss W. Marie Hill, Kansas City, Missouri, attending her first Grand, broke the remarkable score of 96 from 17 yards to cop the Women's Grand American Handicap trophy, while Herman Ehler, San Antonio, Texas, came up with 97 from 22 yards to win the Professional Handicap laurels.

Big Karl Maust of Columbus, Ohio, and Vic Reinders of Waukesha, Wisconsin, were the stars of the shoot. Karl won both the Open championship with 200 straight and the Cham-

Minnesota won the 1941 State Team championship: *(Left to right)* Art Finney, Ray Zweiner, Horace Aldritt, (Ray Loring, Mgr. A. T. A.), George Zweiner and Otto Nelson

pion of Champions with 100 straight, while Vic cleaned up the Doubles with 96 out of 100 and the All-around with 874 out of 900.

The Preliminary Handicap went to Elmer Lucas, Peebles, Ohio, who scored 99 from 18 yards. Russell Elliott of Kansas City, Missouri, and Ted Ross of Millersport, Ohio, fought it out for the National Amateur championship, after each had broken 199 out of 200 in the main event. Elliott, a hard luck gunner at the Grand, won the shoot-off and championship.

Clyde Wells, hard shooting Bridgeport, Connecticut shooter, took the Professional honors with 199 out of 200, while Jack Bruns of Wood River, Illinois, came through with a victory in the Vandalia Open with 98.

The Junior winners were Ray Fienup of St. Louis, Missouri, with 98 out of 100, and Bobby Stifal of Casey, Illinois, in the Sub-junior, with 97. Clyde Mitchell, Minneapolis, again showed his prowess as an all-around gunner by taking the

Several years ago Bob Coffey, Ned Lilly and Joe Hiestand invaded the Pacific coast trapshoots. Here they line up with five western stars. *(Left to right)* George Young, Guy Chiesman, O. N. Ford, (Ned Lillly), (Bob Coffey), Frank Troeh, (Joe Hiestand) and Ted Renfro

Minnesota gunners at the 1941 Grand American: ***(Back row, left to right)*** **G. A. Graham, Bill Horton, R. C. Whepley, Ed Honer, Ernie Maetzold, E. C. Colosky, Sr., E. C. Colosky, Jr., J. J. Richardson, Bill Souba, P. B. Otness, Walter McLeod, L. H. Otness, Art Holm, Dan McInnis, George Johnson, Eddie Long, Elmer Carlson, Dick Guptill;** ***(Seated)*** **H. Forslund, John Derdoski, Kenneth Nelson, Archie Peterson, Otto Nelson, Ray Zweiner, George Zweiner, Art Finney, Roy Miller**

Professional All-around with 862 out of 900; Charlie Young copped the Veterans' again with 99 out of 100, and Dr. G. and Katherine Roose of Salem, Ohio, took home the Husband and Wife event with 194 out of 200.

A couple of 200 straights were registered in the class championships—one by Joe Hiestand for AA class and the other by Art Finney of Mankato, Minnesota, for A class. Horace Aldritt of Excelsior had won the class A for Minnesota the previous day with 198 out of 200.

Dr. O. T. Dean of Seattle was the winner of the B class honors when he pushed over 199 out of 200. W. S. Barnes of Sykesville, Maine, took the C class laurels with 197 out of 200, and J. A. Cox of Munhall, Pennsylvania, edged out the D class gunners when he scored 191 out of 200.

Minnesota captured its first state Team victory when they scored 984 out of 1,000. Their lineup included Art Finney, the two Zweiner boys, Ray and George, Otto Nelson and Horace Aldritt. Bunny Sanders was the victor in the newly dedicated Women's Champion of Champions race, which attracted a large entry. She scored 98.

The Women's race was a thriller from start to finish with the famous Marie Kautzky Grant on the long end of the score, but only after a heated shoot-off with Mrs. C. A. Thomas, the Dayton skeet shooter, and Mrs. George Cameron, the dangerous Houston gun pointer. They broke 97's.

The Father and Son event was won by Ray Fienup and his dad. Dad crashed a 99, Ray a 98.

The big shoot attracted 1,334 shooters, a new all time record.

Net Lutz, Knoxville, Tennessee, gunner, was elected president of the Amateur Trapshooting Association, replacing Ernie Maetzold of Minneapolis.

Grand notes . . . Ted Ross, Ohio, who tied Russ Elliott for the National championship, says he's a better duck hunter than he is a target shot. Must be some shot, Ted. . . . Happiest man on the grounds was Frank Smythe, the Tennessee champ, who broke 100 straight in the Champion of Champions race. . . . George Gray left his razor blade business long enough to run the bulletin board. . . . Jack Mitchell, Remington, and Fred Etchen had charge of the Sports Writers shoot. . . . We didn't overlook Roger Fawcett, the magazine gent, taking third place on the All-around list, either.

It was E. L. King's first Grand American. He broke enough targets to get an Amateur Trapshooting Association check and will have it framed for his Seattle office. . . . Mac Allen, ad man for Western, would rather fish for smallmouth bass than shoot or eat. . . . Popular Lucy and Margaret Jenkins had charge of the bridge games. . . . Pretty Blanche Wolf from New York City led women gunners in the Open championship with 197 out of 200, averaged .9720 on her Grand American targets. Not bad.

Gail Evans, ad maestro for Remington, can't wait for the opening of the duck season. . . . Roscoe Turner, famed aviator, who took the first aerial view of the grounds back in 1925, was a visitor and took me for a high ride. . . . Joe Latimer, who busted 200 straight in the class championship race, is the Montana state champ. . . . J. D. Collins, Jr., from the Canal Zone, was the first man on the grounds. . . . J. R. Strauss has made five trips to the Grand from the Canal Zone. . . . P. A. Romig, Ohio, who came in a wheel chair two years ago, looked as fit as a fiddle.

Homer Collins, Verne Miller, Gil Hartley, and C. Hartley flew in from Duluth. . . . E. A. Schupbach, Wyoming state champ, and Lester Stecher drove to the Grand together. Les lives in Nebraska, but they live only 65 miles apart. . . . Fred Ford from Detroit is a natural 99'er. Broke 10 consecutive 99's at Sunday shoots that year. Fred broke 200 straight to win the 1941 Michigan state championship, only 200 of the season. . . . Attractive Mrs. Sam Noyes from South Dakota shot the Grand for the first time. . . . Eddie Alias and Mercer Tennille from Shreveport, Louisiana, are both great shots and grand sportsmen.

Big Springs, Nebraska, 500 population, sent five shooters: Glenn and Wayne Bailey, Dayton Dorn, Leo Atkinson and Ralph Zimmerman. . . . Looked like Tim and Joe Carson in the Father and Son race when they shattered their first 50 straight. . . . Mack Frazier from Frankfort, Indiana, looked like the Preliminary Handicap winner when he broke his first 75 straight, then missed two. . . . Everybody and his dog likes Net Lutz, the new Amateur Trapshooting Association president from Knoxville. . . . Don Torge, 17 years of age, broke 96 out of 100 from 22 yards in the Preliminary race. Don is a ball player, a southpaw, first sacker. . . . Paul E. Davis, the New Jersey state champ, brought along his old duck gun with sights made from bicycle spokes.

Bernie Ellsesser, compiler of scores, has attended 35 Grand Americans. Bernie is managing editor of the York, Pennsylvania "Gazette." . . . A la Jack Dempsey, Herman Peterson, the Montana rancher, refused to shave. . . . "Just came down to shoot," said Larry Grant, the Atlanta sportsman. Larry and Gordon Height blew in Sunday. . . . Casper Hoffman, Denver, won the Colorado state championship when he was 15 and has had 22 yards or more in the handicap since. . . . Don Mihills, Fond du Lac, Wisconsin, has been coming to the Grand for years. Sunday he broke 99 out of 100, his greatest score. . . . C. G. Wehr, the Hamilton, Ohio, creamery man, would rather lock up his business than to miss a Grand.

The press tent and Grand American office were on the receiving end of Sheriff Charlie Miller's famous peaches. Here is the Michigan peach tent. *(Seated left to right)* E. M. Young, Fred Briegel and Jay Graham. *(Standing)* Carl Madan, Frank Vignoe, Bob Porritt, Howard Furnace and Charlie Miller, on the right

SPORTS EDITORS TRAPSHOOT AT THE 1941 GRAND AMERICAN: ***(Top, left to right)*** **Bill Mayfield, Don Mack, Johnny Mock, Ben Garlicov, Jimmy Robinson, (Winner—48x50) Frank Harris;** ***(Bottom)*** **Alvin Rosensweet, Jim Stuber, Bob Smith, Fritz Howell, Fred Etchen (Referee)**

GRAND AMERICAN AT LIVE PIGEONS

The first Grand American Handicap at live pigeons was held in March, 1893, at Dexter Park, New York. There were only 21 entries. This small entrance was probably due to the severe conditions governing the competition, which included an entrance fee of $25, with birds extra. Money was divided among the three high guns, and that a bird must fall within 21 yards of the trap from which it came in order to be scored "dead."

This last condition and the money division were changed at subsequent handicaps, the number of "high guns" being based upon the number of entries. R. A. Welch of New York was the winner with 23 out of 25.

1894—The second tournament was held at Dexter Park, April 5, and there was a decided increase in the number of entries, 54 shooters taking part. This is quite a contrast, however, from the 1,334 gunners who took part in the Grand American at Vandalia in 1941. Two shooters killed 25 straight pigeons to tie for first place, T. W. Morfey of New York and Captain A. W. Money, the famous English shooter of that time. Morfey won the shoot-off.

1895—The third tournament was held at Willard Park, N. Y., April 4th, with 61 entries and 58 starters. Three tied for first place with 25 straights. The winner was J. G. Messner of New York.

1896—O. R. Dickey of Boston won the fourth annual Grand American with 24 out of 25. The entries increased to 109, and 105 shooters started in the competition. The shoot was staged at Elkwood Park, near Long Beach, N. J., on March 25th.

1897—Tom Marshall, Keithsburg, Ill., one of the most famous shooters of all times, won the fifth annual live pigeon Grand American at Elkwood Park, March 25th, with the only 25 straight kills among the 146 shooters.

1898—Ed Fulford, Utica, N. Y., captured the sixth annual shoot at which nine 25 straights were recorded for first place. There were 207 entries, 187 taking part in the big race. The shoot was held March 23 on the same grounds as in the previous two years.

1899—Tom Marshall again proved his superiority with his shotgun by winning the event that year with another 25 straight in the main event and the title by defeating five other gunners in a thrilling shoot-off. The tourney was again held at Elkwood Park, on April 12th, with 278 entries, 262 starting in the event.

1900—The eighth tournament was held at Interstate Park, Queens, Long Island, N. Y., April 4. There was a slight falling off of attendance, 244 entering and 211 starting in the event. Eight 25 straights were scored for first place. The falling off in the number of shooters was not because of the failing interest, but due to the experience of the contestants last year, when there were only three sets of traps and so many shooters, that the wait between rounds was very trying; two days and a half were required to finish the event. A Canadian, Howard D. Bates of St. Thomas, attending his first American shoot, won the shoot-off and title. Bates, a duck hunter, was 25 years of age and had been shooting only four years.

1901—E. C. Griffith, Pascoag, R. I., who still shoots, won the ninth annual tournament held at Interstate Park, April 3. There were 222 entries and 201 starters. Twenty-two gunners killed the 25 straight that year. Griffith won the Grand American at clay targets the same year. He is the only shooter, dead or alive who has won both the Grand American at Live Birds and the Grand American at clay targets.

1902—The tenth annual live pigeon Grand American was

shifted to Kansas City, Mo., where the big meet was held at the Blue River Shooting Park. The attendance established a record, 493 entries being received, and 456 shooters participating in the event. The winner was Herman Hirschy of Minneapolis, who killed 25 straight in the main event, and defeated 32 other world known gunners, Charlie Spencer (who took second place), Rollo Heikes, J. D. Pollard, L. H. Owen, George Roll, Guy Dering, S. Snyder, Don Morrison, G. W. Clay, Luther Squier, Fred Gilbert, Russell Cool, G. V. D. Darby, H. E. Boltenstern, Tom Nichols, Ed Bingham, T. F. Dockson, Ed Troeh, J. H. Boisseau, Hood Waters, J. H. Holmes, H. B. Hill, Bill Crosby, Pat Adams, J. E. Avery, Slim Glover, W. H. Herman, Ed Banks, W. W. Turner, R. Eugenia and J. Kaintuck, who had tied him. This was the last Grand American at Live Pigeons. Fred Whitney of Des Moines, Iowa, was the cashier of the shoot.

INTERNATIONAL TEAM MATCHES AND OLYMPIC GAMES

The proposition that a team of America's best in the trapshooting game should visit England and try conclusions with the British cracks, began to be agitated in 1901. Paul North, of Cleveland, O., took an active part in the preliminary work and started a campaign to raise $4,000 for the team's expenses. The trapshooters of the country responded generously and the amount was soon pledged, and a team was sent over in June.

The matches were staged on the Middlesex Gun Club's grounds, six miles northeast of London. The American team easily defeated the British, 866 out of 1,000 to 801 in the first race, June 11. In the winning lineup were Bill Crosby with high score, 93 out of 100, C. W. Budd, Ernie Tripp, Pop

1920 AMERICAN OLYMPIC TEAM: *(Top row, left to right)* **Mark Arie, H. Bonser, Ben Donnelly, Fred Plum;** *(Lower row)* **Frank Wright, Frank Troeh, Jay Clarke, Jr., Forest McNeir**

1924 AMERICAN OLYMPIC TEAM: Clarence Platt, John Noel, Sam Sharman, Frank Hughes, Fred Etchen; *(Kneeling)* Captain W. H. Fawcett, Bill Silkworth

Heikes, T. S. Parmalee, R. Merrill, J. A. R. Elliott, Jack Fanning, Fred Gilbert and Tom Marshall. Bill Crosby again led the American team to victory with a 95 on the second day—score, Americans, 877—British, 794.

The third match was held on June 13th, and it also proved to be the last, as the purse of $5,000 was to go to the winner of three out of five contests, and the Americans won for the third consecutive day. Bill Crosby again led the American team with 90 out of 100, a good score considering the fact that the weather was bad. The Americans, 843—British, 749. Then the Yanks shot a team race with Scotland in Glasgow and Fred Gilbert and R. Merrill broke 100 straights, followed by Bill Crosby's 99 which was too much for the Scotties. Score—Americans, 969—Scotland, 882. Two barrels were used in these matches.

1908 OLYMPIC GAMES

The Americans were not represented at the Olympic games held in London in 1908. The Canadians sent over a team that took second place, just two targets behind the winning English first team. Walter H. Ewing, Westmount, Canada, won the Individual Olympic Championship with 72 out of 80 targets while George Beattie, Hamilton, Ont., was next high scorer.

1912 OLYMPIC GAMES

In 1912 the trapshooters of the United States woke up to the fact that it might be well to go to Stockholm, Sweden, and see what could be done toward scoring a few points for Uncle Sam in the clay bird competition.

The Americans had easy sailing and copped the title with 532 out of 600. Jay Graham, Ingleside, Ill., still going strong, topped the Yanks with 94 out of 100. In the American lineup were C. W. Billings, D. F. McMahon, Ralph Spotts, John Hendrickson, George Lyon, Frank Hall and Dr. E. F. Gleason. England took second place with 511 x 600, and Charlie Palmer of London had to break his last target or they would have finished in a tie with Germany.

In the Individual Championship race, each country was allowed at least seven entries. There were 83 entries in all, representing thirteen nations, and 68 of these took part in the competition.

Jay Graham again took charge of affairs when he cracked the great score of 96 out of 100 to win. Remember, the "position of the gun" made the conditions extra hard for the Americans, as they were not accustomed to "holding the gun below the elbow."

Alfred Goeldel, of a prominent German family, was second with 94 out of 100, and Henry Blau of Russia was third with 91. There was a tie for fourth place between H. R. Humby of Great Britain and Albert Preuss of Germany, who scored a pair of 88's.

1920 OLYMPIC GAMES

The Americans staged a walk-away at the 1920 Olympic games staged at Antwerp, Belgium. Mark Arie and Frank Troeh led the winners with 94's and were followed by Forest McNeir, 93, Horace Bonser, 93, Frank Wright, 89, and Jay Clarke, Jr., the Captain of the team, who scored 84. The Belgium team was next with 503 out of 600, forty-four targets behind the Yanks. Then came Sweden, England and the Canadian teams. Eight teams entered the championship races. Fred Plum and Ben Donnelly were also members of the team.

Mark Arie won the Individual Championship with 95 out of a possible 100. Frank Troeh was second with 93, but was handicapped by shooting in a heavy shower. Ed Winans, East Alton, Ill., was coach of the team.

THE CHICAGO DAILY NEWS CHARITY SHOOT: ***(Left to right)*** **Walter Peacock, Gerald Batten, Frank Huseman, Logan Harbican, Scotty Campbell. Scotty was the manager. Over 1,000 shooters entered**

1924 OLYMPIC GAMES

The Americans again won the 1924 Olympic Championship in Paris, France. The team sailed from New York on May 28th, on the Minnewaska for London. They shot there for three weeks. Captain Fred Etchen of the Americans won the British Open with 100 straight in the main event and 100 straight in the shoot-off to defeat Frank Hughes, of the American team, and George Beattie and S. Newton of the Canadian teams, who had tied him.

Mrs. Fred Etchen won the Women's Open race. The Americans won the Olympic Championship in France with 363 out of 400, edging out the Canadians and Finland by three targets. Halsey of Hungary won the Individual Championship with 98 out of 100. Frank Hughes of the Yanks took second place with 97 out of 100, but only after shooting out J. Montgomery of the Canadians and Huber of Finland who had tied him. On all targets, Hughes led the American team with .9750, with Fred Etchen in second place with .9701. Captain Billy Fawcett, manager of the American team, was next with .9626. Other members of the American team were Bill Silkworth, Sam Sharman, Clarence Platt and Johnny Noel.

HOW TO ORGANIZE A GUN CLUB

In every neighborhood there are a certain number of outdoor lovers who would welcome the idea of a gun club. We have found that every sportsmen's club should have a Gun Club, which not only affords practice and sport, but will build up the financial standing of your club.

First, get a leading spirit in your community, a fellow with a lot of push and Bang! Get them together. Spring the Big Idea—and talk it over. The first step is to appoint a good live wire committee and your campaign for members is simplified. No need for large annual dues—better to have a large group of shooters and keep your club alive by throwing more clay targets, of which there is a profit.

Contact your newspaper sports or outdoor editor. Invite him to the first meeting. Get the sporting goods dealers interested. Officers should be elected: President, Vice-President,

The first step in organizing a Hunters' Special is to get the business men interested. Here are a group who donated to the first shoot at Minneapolis. *(Bottom row, left)* Joe Brush, Anglesey Cafe; Bill Buchen, Murphy Insurance Agency and Jack Connors, outdoor editor, Times Tribune. *(Top row, left)* Ray Ewald, Golden Guernsey Milk; Jerry Gerow, President Cafe, and Hugo Benson, Covered Wagon.

Second step is publicity. Here's Charlie Johnson, genial sports editor of the Star-Journal, pounding out a story on the Hunters' Special

Secretary, Treasurer, Field Captain and Board of Directors. I have always found it a good idea to give everybody a "title." Draw up a set of By-Laws. Be sure that you appoint a popular secretary and he will go a long ways to making your club—a grouch can easily spoil one. A date should be set for the next meeting. Some clubs start out by having a dance or social, sell tickets and get some money in the treasury.

This not only applies to trapshooting, but skeet as well. But here is a little advice. Your shooters will be enthusiastic. Don't let them shoot too many targets. Make your programs short so that they will fit all pocketbooks. For information on holding shoots, write Ray E. Loring, Amateur Trapshooting Association, Vandalia, Ohio, or Henry Ahlin, National Skeet Association, 275 Newbury Street, Boston, Mass. For information on gun clubs, write the Western Cartridge Company, East Alton, Ill., the Federal Cartridge Company, Foshay Tower, Minneapolis, or the Remington Arms Company, Bridgeport, Connecticut.

THE HUNTERS' SPECIAL

Hunters' Special trapshoots were introduced by this writer and a few friends in Minneapolis in 1938. I had attended a meeting of the gun and ammunition manufacturers' meeting in New York City and at that meeting plans were discussed for beginners' shoots—how could we get the novice interested?

We recall that General Elliott Dill, President of the Institute, Charles Hymer, Ted Doremus, Major John Hession, Frank Byrne, Clarence Hutt, Bill Shadel of the National Rifle Association, sports editor Si Burick, Frank Kahrs and Stewart Commeaux, secretary of the Arms and Ammunition Institute, were present at this meeting.

On the way home to Minneapolis the thought occurred to me that a beginner shoot with the name "hunter" attached in some way should bring out the shooters. I suggested "Hunters'

Special" as a good name to Guy Nichols, Harold Russell, Clyde Mitchell and a few of the local professionals and they thought it was worth a try.

We tied up our first shoot with the Northwest Sportsmen's Show, at the St. Anthony Gun Club, Minneapolis, managed by Dan McInnis. The officers of the club, Ted Culbertson, President; Charles Murphy, Vice-President, and a few of us got together and planned our first shoot.

Sports editor Charlie Johnson, the Star, Dick Cullum, the Journal and George Barton and Bob Beebe, Tribune, gave valuable assistance in their columns, with plugs and stories, while radio announcers, George Higgins, WTCN, Stu Mann, WDGY, Rollie Johnson, WCCO, Bennett Orfield, WTCN, Cedric Adams, WCCO, and Halsey Hall, KSTP, also gave us some wonderful co-operation.

The event called for 50 targets, open to the novice or hunter who had never shot at registered targets before. We had decided to register the shoot with the Amateur Trapshooting Association, for the reason that they would take care of our scores and give us valuable information at all times. From the very start, I was convinced that this form of shooting would go over with a bang.

Picking out the trophies: *(Left)* Ernie Maetzold, President of the Twin Cities Gun Club, who believes in merchandise prizes which he examines; *(Center)* Mel Corrie, manager of Corrie Sporting Goods Store and Jay Laidlaw, secretary of the club

Team races are popular. Here is the Rock Spring (Shakopee, Minnesota) team: *(Left to right)* Tony Leitte, George Hart, Hart Motor Express; Mike Droney, Art Holm and Ted Culbertson, President of the St. Anthony club, who put on the first Hunters' Special

The shoot, which was cashiered by Jack and Clyde Mitchell, was a 50 target program, divided Lewis Class system, which gave every novice shooter a chance, regardless of his score.

Prizes had been donated by business firms. The Champion Outboard Motor Company, thanks to Ralph Herrington, put up five Champion outboard motors. Other trophies were donated by the Northwest Sportsmen's Show. The shoot attracted 231 registered shooters, a new world's record for a one-day shoot.

The winner was Sherm Brooks, a Minneapolis duck hunter who broke 49 out of 50. He won the Hart Motor Express Trophy. Curt Davis, an airmail pilot, won Chuck Saunders' Cafe Exceptionale B class Trophy with 39 x 50. Dick Olson, salesman, won the C class Kip Hale Buckhorn Trophy with 33 out of 50 and Mort Hastings, in winning Lyle Wright's Minneapolis Arena Trophy, broke 25 out of 50 to win D class.

The shooters' scores ran all the way from 49 to 4 out of 50. A woman, Mrs. C. R. Norton from Marshall, Minnesota, broke 48 out of 50, tied Art Holm, Ralph Herrington and C. McClure for second prize. More than 20,000 targets were trapped during the day and the gun club made a nice profit and everybody went home satisfied. So concluded the first Hunters' Special trapshoot in history.

Hunters' Special shoots are being held in all parts of the country. The Detroit Times, under the leadership of Don

Gillis, outdoor editor, staged the Times-Montgomery Ward Hunters' Special at Detroit recently and it attracted more than 2,000 shooters. Johnny Mock of the Pittsburgh Press staged a shoot that had more than 1,000 gunners on the firing line; Si Burick, sports editor of the Dayton Daily News, put on a record breaker at the A. T. A. trapshooting grounds, with over 1,000 shooters; Ernie Bihler, Omaha, set a new record at their club and similar shoots have been held in all parts of the country. For added information on how to hold a Hunters' Special, write Jimmy Robinson, Phoenix Bldg., Minneapolis.

HOW TO CLASSIFY SHOOTERS AND DETERMINE WINNERS

(Lewis Class System)

After the shoot is over, the thing to do is to classify your shooters. The men who work for the ammunition and gun companies, the professional shooters, are experienced in handling this job, and they will cooperate with speed and precision, both of which are necessary in order that the news of the shoot may be prepared for the newspapers. When the winners have been determined, type out your story, and furnish lists of the shooters and their scores.

There are several ways of classifying the novice shooters to determine the winners in each class. The Lewis class system is very popular and is used at the majority of Hunters' Special shoots. This method gives each shooter an equal chance at the awards, regardless of whether he has shot a high or a low score. In case of a tie, reverse system is used to find out which shooter takes precedence.

Here are the hunters lining up for the shoot: *(Left to right)* Vic Buchanan, Frank Schultz, Buck Buchanan, Metz Leiderbach, Art Holm, Eileen Boyes and Cashier Fred Lussier

These boys ran the Detroit Times-Montgomery-Ward shoot which attracted a world's record entry of over 2,000 shooters: *(Left to right)* Grant Ilseng, Charles B. Lord, Detroit Times; Russell Hunsinger, general manager of the Montgomery-Ward stores and Don Gillis, outdoor editor of the Detroit Times.

An explanation of the Lewis class system follows:

This system does not modify the conditions of the contest or the scores of the contestants in any way. It does not come into action until the shoot is over, when it takes the scores made as a basis for the equitable distribution of the trophies, its awards being automatic.

All the scores are arranged in numerical order, from the highest to the lowest in the entire event or program, and are then divided into from two to five equal groups, or classes, which, beginning with the class containing the highest scores, are designated consecutively as Class 1, 2, etc., according to number of classes.

In making up these classes the following rules must be adopted:

1. Where a short class is necessary, due to odd entry list, the short class shall head the list.
2. Where the line of division falls in a number of tie scores, the contestants are assigned to the class in which the majority of the scores appear.
3. Where an equal number of tie scores appear on either side of the line, contestants shall be assigned to the head of the lower class.
4. Where the original division is changed, due to tie scores, this change shall apply only to the classes directly affected and the original division shall continue in the other classes.

We submit an example which shows the operation of Lewis Class where there are a considerable number of tie scores.

Example: In a program covering a 50-target race, advertising a trophy distribution by Lewis Class—four classes—we have twenty shooters participating. This would mean a division of five shooters to each class. With twenty-three shooters, the division would be Class 1, five—and Classes 2, 3 and 4, six shooters each, as per Rule No. 1.

Compilation of winners with the following hypothetical scores in the field of twenty shooters with four classes would be as follows:

Scores		Class 1
49	........................Winner	49x50
48		
48		Class 2
47	Since equal number of ties appear on	47x50
47	each side of dividing line, two 47's	47x50
—	above line are assigned to head of	
47	class below line and the four 47's tie.	47x50
47		47x50
46		
45		
43		
—		Class 3
43	Here the class below line has majority	43x50
43	of tie scores; therefore, the score above	43x50
43	line is assigned to majority class and	43x50
42	heads lower class, with four 43's winning.	43x50
42		
—		Class 4
42	In this class majority of tie scores	41x50
41	are above line and the 42 below line	
40	is assigned to upper class, the 41 win-	
39	ning trophy.	
38		

The prizes are then divided into as many equal parts as there are classes; and the high man or men in each class are the winners of the prizes allotted to that class. The above system can be used at skeet or trapshoots.

ROY SWAN
Father of the Lordship Shoot

AL KOYEN, Fremont, Nebr.
1916 G.A.H. Preliminary King

H. E. L. Timm, Chicago, helped Illinois win the G. A. Team Championship in 1927

P. E. Morris, Wichita, won 1934 Kansas State with 200 straight

J. G. ROE, Paris, Tenn. (100 Straight—1938 State Skeet)

GLENN C. LINDSLEY (200 Straight—New York State —1937)

EDDIE NEWBURG *(left)* seems quite pleased because his friend Homer Dick *(right)* helped Illinois win the 1935 team championship

TRAPSHOOTING
RECORDS

TRAPSHOOTING RECORDS

Grand American Handicap

Year	Entries	Name	Residence	Yd.	Sc.
1941	1091	Walter Tulbert	Detroit, Mich.	18	99
1940	850	E. H. Wolfe	Chstn., W. Va.	23	98
1939	750	D. L. Ritchie	Goshen, Ohio	22	99
1938	814	O. W. West	Coshocton, Ohio	20	99
1937	932	F. G. Carroll	Brecksville, Ohio	19	100
1936	704	B. F. Cheek	Clinton, Ind.	16	98
1935	608	J. B. Royall	Tallahassee, Fla.	20	98
1934	612	L. G. Dana	Derrick City, Pa.	17	98
1933	597	Walter Beaver	Berwyn, Pa.	25	98
1932	722	A. E. Sheffield	Dixon, Ill.	21	98
1931	938	Gar. Roebuck	McClure, Ohio	17	96
1930	966	R. King, Jr.	Wichita Falls, Tex.	16	97
1929	1100	M. Newman	Sweetwater, Tex.	20	98
1928	891	I. Andrews	Spartansburg, S. C.	20	95
1927	873	Otto Newlin	Georgetown, Ill.	20	98
1926	932	C. A. Young	Springfield, Ohio	23	100
1925	710	E. C. Starner	Ithaca, N. Y.	17	98
1924	528	H. C. Deck	Plymouth, Ohio	16	97
1923	513	Mark Arie	Champaign, Ill.	23	96
1922	588	J. S. Frink	Worthington, Minn.	22	96
1921	637	E. F. Haak	Canton, Ohio	21	97
1920	715	A. L. Ivins	Red Bank, N. J.	19	99
1919	848	G. W. Lorimer	Piqua, Ohio	18	98
1918	620	J. D. Henry	Elkhart, Ind.	16	97
1917	808	C. H. Larson	Waupaca, Wis.	20	98
1916	683	J. F. Wulf	Milwaukee, Wis.	19	99
1915	884	L. B. Clarke	Chicago, Ill.	18	96
1914	515	W. Henderson	Lexington, Ky.	22	98
1913	501	M. S. Hootman	Edgerton, Ohio.	17	97
1912	377	W. E. Phillips	Chicago, Ill.	19	96
1911	418	Harvey Dixon	Oronogo, Mo.	20	99
1910	383	R. Thompson	Cainsville, Mo.	19	100
1909	457	Fred Shattuck	Columbus, Ohio.	18	96
1908	362	Fred Harlow	Newark, Ohio	16	92
1907	495	J. J. Blanks	Trezevant, Tenn.	17	96
1906	290	F. E. Rogers	St. Louis, Mo.	17	94
1905	352	R. R. Barber	Paulina, Ia.	16	99
1904	336	R. Guptill	Minneapolis, Minn.	19	96
1903	192	M. Diefenderfer	Wood River, Neb.	16	94
1902	91	C. W. Floyd	New York, N. Y.	18	94
1901	75	E. C. Griffith	Pascoag, R. I.	19	95
1900	74	R. O. Heikes	Dayton, Ohio	22	91

North American Clay Target Champ.

Year	Name	Residence	S.	A.	Bk.
1941	Russ Elliott	Raytown, Mo.	16	200	199
1940	F. W. McNeir	Houston, Tex.	16	200	200
1939	P. O. Harbage	West Jefferson, O.	16	200	200

North Am. Clay Target Champ. (Cont.)

Year	Name	Residence	S.	A.	Bk.
1938	Joe Hiestand	Hillsboro, Ohio	16	200	200
1937	Phil R. Miller	French Lick, Ind.	16	200	200
1936	Joe Hiestand	Hillsboro, Ohio	16	200	199
1935	Joe Hiestand	Hillsboro, Ohio	16	200	199
1934	Walter Beaver	Berwyn, Pa.	16	200	199
1933	Ned Lilly	Stanton, Mich.	16	200	199
1932	M. E. DeWire	Hamilton, Ind.	16	200	200
1931	Karl Maust	Detroit, Mich.	16	200	199
1930	Gust Payne	Cleveland, Ohio	16	200	199
1929	Gus Payne	Oklahoma City, Okla.	16	200	199
1928	Mark Arie	Champaign, Ill.	16	200	198
1927	Guy V. Dering	Columbus, Wis.	16	200	200
1926	S. L. Jenny	Highland, Ill.	16	200	199
1925	S. M. Crothers	Philadelphia, Pa.	16	200	200
1924	Frank Hughes	Chicago, Ill.	16	200	199
1923	Phil R. Miller	Dallas, Tex.	16	200	199
1922	D. Fauskee	Worthington, Minn.	16	200	197
1921	Nick Arie	Dallas, Tex.	16	200	198
1920	F. S. Wright	Buffalo, N. Y.	16	200	197
1919	F. S. Wright	Buffalo, N. Y.	16	200	199
1918	W. H. Heer	Guthrie, Okla.	16	100	99
1917	Mark Arie	Champaign, Ill.	16	100	99
1916	F. M. Troeh	Portland, Ore.	16	100	99
1915	C. Newcomb	Philadelphia, Pa.	16	100	99
1914	W. Henderson	Lexington, Ky.	16	100	99
1913	Bart Lewis	Auburn, Ill.	18	200	195
1912	E. W. Varner	Adams, Neb.	18	200	192
1911	C. C. Collins	Kankakee, Ill.	18	200	196
1910	Guy V. Dering	Columbus, Wis.	18	200	189
1909	D. A. Upson	Cleveland, Ohio	18	200	188
1908	George Roll	Blue Island, Ill.	18	200	183
1907	H. M. Clark	Urbana, Ill.	18	200	188
1906	Guy Ward	Walnut Log, Tenn.	18	150	144

North American Doubles Champ.

Year	Name	Residence		Bk.
1941	Vic Reinders	Waukesha, Wis.	100	96
1940	E. L. Hawkins	Fort Wayne, Ind.	100	98
1939	John D. Rigg	Conshohocken, Pa.	100	97
1938	Fred R. Etchen	Wichita, Kan.	100	96
1937	Ned Lilly	Stanton, Mich.	100	98
1936	Joe Hiestand	Hillsboro, Ohio	100	96
1935	Joe Hiestand	Hillsboro, Ohio	100	93
1934	Mark Arie	Champaign, Ill.	100	94
1933	F. J. Lightner	Cedar Rapids, Ia.	200	187
1932	O. C. Bottger	Fairfield, Ia.	200	191
1931	Gus Payne	Oklahoma City, Okla.	200	185
1930	E. W. Renfro	Dell, Mont.	200	191

THE VETERAN SUMNER JOHNSON Presents FOREST SAUNDERS with Minnesota diamond badge. Saunders is an Exhibition shooter

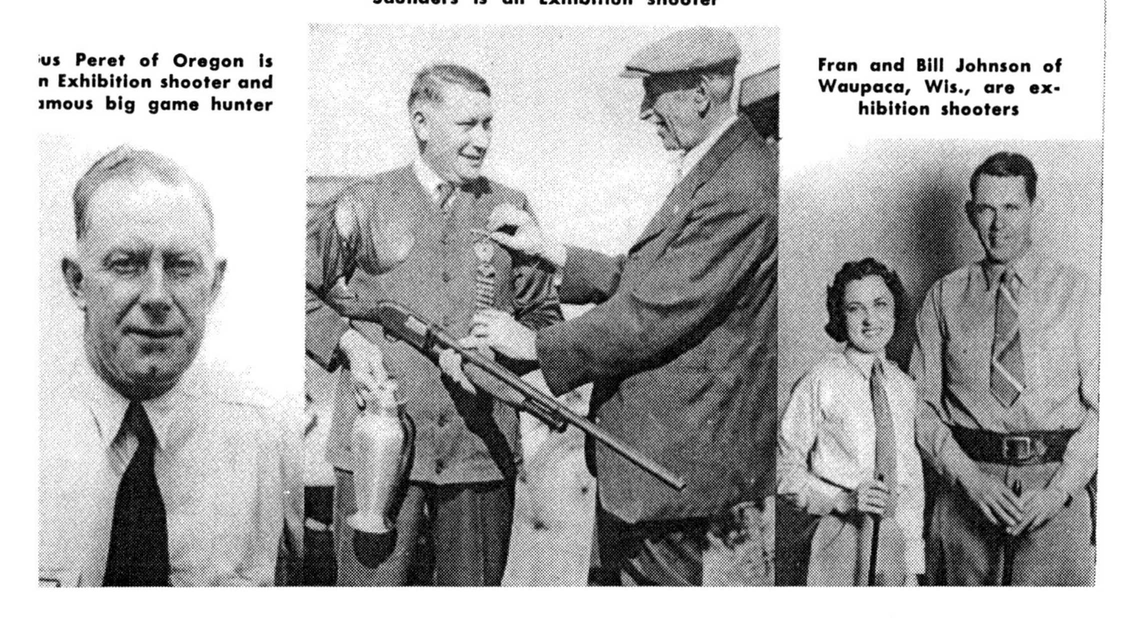

...us Peret of Oregon is ...n Exhibition shooter and ...amous big game hunter

Fran and Bill Johnson of Waupaca, Wis., are exhibition shooters

North American Doubles Champ. (Cont.)

Year	Name	Residence	S. A.	Bk.
1929	Sam Jenny, Highland, Ill.		200	191
1928	F. M. Troeh, Portland, Ore.		200	185
1927	F. M. Troeh, Portland, Ore.		200	188
1926	Bart Lewis, Auburn, Ill.		200	192
1925	C. W. Olney, West Allis, Wis.		200	191
1924	P. R. Miller, Dallas, Tex.		200	191
1923	P. R. Miller, Dallas, Tex.		200	181
1922	R. A. King, Delta, Colo.		200	170
1921	R. A. King, Delta, Colo.		100	94
1920	P. H. O'Brien, Helena, Mont.		100	92
1919	Nic. Arie, Dallas, Tex.		100	91
1918	Frank M. Troeh, Portland, Ore.		100	90
1917	C. B. Platt, Bridgeton, N. J.		100	96
1916	Allen Heil, Allentown, Pa.		100	89
1915	Guy V. Dering, Columbus, Wis.		100	91
1914	W. Henderson, Lexington, Ky.		100	90
1913	George Lyon, Durham, N. C.		100	94
1912	Mark Arie, Champaign, Ill.		100	89

North American Clay Target Champ.

WOMEN

Year	Name, Residence	S. A.	Bk.
1941	Marie Kautzky Grant, Ft. Dodge, Ia.	100	97
1940	Mrs. Lela Hall, Strasburg, Mo.	100	97
1939	Mrs. Wm. Gilbert, Madison, Wis.	100	98
1938	Mrs. Lela Hall, Strasburg, Mo.	200	195
1937	Mrs. Lela Hall, Strasburg, Mo.	200	194
1936	Mrs. Lela Hall, Strasburg, Mo.	200	196
1935	Mrs. Lela Hall, E. Lynne, Mo.	200	191
1934	Mrs. "Bunny" Sanders, Keyser, W. Va.	200	191
1933	Alice Crothers, Philadelphia, Pa.	200	183
1932	Mrs. H. E. Grigsby, Oklahoma City	200	191
1931	Jeanette Jay, Waverly, Ia.	200	191
1930	Mrs. J. Murphy, Freehold, N. J.	200	185
1929	Miss E. Haggard, Winchester, Ky.	200	190
1928	Miss K. Boyer, Mt. Carmel, Pa.	200	186
1927	Mrs. H. Harrison, Rochester, N. Y.	200	192
1926	Mrs. J. C. Wright, Atlanta, Ga.	200	190
1925	Miss G. Reid, Portland, Ore.	200	185
1924	Miss G. Hobson, Bowling Green, Ky.	200	185
1923	Mrs. E. L. King, Winona, Minn.	200	186
1922	Mrs. E. L. King, Winona, Minn.	200	187
1921	Mrs. T. Randall, New York, N. Y.	100	98
1920	Mrs. J. H. Bruff, Pittsburgh, Pa.	100	85
1919	Mrs. A. H. Winkler, Chicago, Ill.	100	90
1918	Mrs. H. Almert, Chicago, Ill.	100	89

Junior 16-Yard Champ. of North America

Year	Name, Residence	Score
1941	Ray Fienup, St. Louis, Mo.	98x100
1940	John S. Martin, Providence, Ky.	99x100
1939	Rudy Etchen, Wichita, Kan.	97x100
1938	Rudy Etchen, Wichita, Kan.	98x100
1937	Stanley Meadows, Des Moines, Ia.	98x100
1936	Homer Clark, Jr., Alton, Ill.	97x100
1935	Homer Clark, Jr., Alton, Ill.	99x100
1934	J. S. Dick, Jr., Minneapolis, Minn.	95x100
1933	Ned Lilly, Stanton, Mich.	100x100
1932	Ned Lilly, Stanton, Mich.	99x100
1931	Tobe Park, Houston, Tex.	99x100
1930	S. Forsgard, Galveston, Tex.	95x100
1929	Bob Hardy, Galesburg, Ill.	99x100
1928	C. Hofman, 3rd, Denver, Colo.	97x100
1927	W. P. Jenkins, Orleans, Ind.	98x100
1926	James Bonner, New York City	97x100
1925	James Bonner, New York City	197x200
1924	D. Shallcross, S. Seekonk, Mass.	98x100
1923	J. F. Bonner, New York City	88x100
1922	D. Shallcross, S. Seekonk, Mass.	96x100
1921	Elmer Herrold, Ashkum, Ill.	48x 50
1920	T. Beam, Jr., W. Frankfort, Ill.	48x 50
1919	G. A. Miller, Brewton, Ala.	49x 50

Preliminary Handicap Winners

100 Targets

Year	Ent.	Winner	Yds.	Bk.
1900	..	H. C. Bridges "Tarheel"	19	89
1901	..	E. D. Fulford	18	95
1902	..	Dr. O. F. Britton "Partington"	17	92
1903	..	M. E. Hensler	17	91
1904	..	L. A. Cummings	18	98
1905	..	R. R. Barber	16	98
1906	..	C. M. Powers	20	93
1907	..	Geo. L. Lyon	19	96
1908	..	C. H. Ditto	18	95
1909	..	Frank Fisher	18	94
1910	..	W. J. Raup	16	99
1911	..	C. B. Eaton	18	99
1912	..	W. S. Hoon	19	94
1913	..	A. B. Richardson	20	96
1914	..	C. F. Riffe	17	96
1915	689	R. H. Morse	18	95
1916	515	Al Koyen	19	97
1917	666	John Peterson	18	99
1918	543	E. J. Buck	18	96
1919		No preliminary held		
1920	594	H. K. Mitton	19	99
1921	485	M. L. Fox	19	99
1922	465	H. C. Taylor	16	97
1923	425	D. C. Hayward	20	99
1924	530	H. L. Weisman	16	99
1925	708	S. A. Green	19	99
1926	835	O. H. Nutt	19	99
1927	761	C. E. Leek	19	98
1928	764	F. B. Hoggatt	17	97
1929	978	J. B. Fontaine	21	99
1930	945	Jean Pope	22	100
1931	863	H. B. Schomerus	21	99
1932	718	Bobby Olds	21	99
1933	602	H. S. Shellito	20	98
1934	572	H. H. Holbrook	19	96
1935	602	Ray Zweiner	21	99
1936	693	E. L. Hawkins	21	97
1937	820	J. W. Egermann	19	99
1938	733	L. R. Slagle	19	98
1939	689	W. Winteringham	22	99
1940	739	Roy W. Miller	20	100
1941	964	Elmer Lucas	18	99

Where Past Grand American Tournaments Have Been Held

Year	Place	Year	Place
1941	Vandalia, O.	1920	Cleveland, O.
1940	Vandalia, O.	1919	Chicago, Ill.
1939	Vandalia, O.	1918	Chicago, Ill.
1938	Vandalia, O.	1917	Chicago, Ill.
1937	Vandalia, O.	1916	St. Louis, Mo.
1936	Vandalia, O.	1915	Chicago, Ill.
1935	Vandalia, O.	1914	Dayton, O.
1934	Vandalia, O.	1913	Dayton, O.
1933	Vandalia, O.	1912	Springfield, Ill.
1932	Vandalia, O.	1911	Columbus, O.
1931	Vandalia, O.	1910	Chicago, Ill.
1930	Vandalia, O.	1909	Chicago, Ill.
1929	Vandalia, O.	1908	Columbus, O.
1928	Vandalia, O.	1907	Chicago, Ill.
1927	Vandalia, O.	1906	Indianapolis, Ind.
1926	Vandalia, O.	1905	Indianapolis, Ind.
1925	Vandalia, O.	1904	Indianapolis, Ind.
1924	Vandalia, O.	1903	Kansas City, Mo.
1923	Chicago, Ill.	1902	New York
1922	Atlantic City, N. J.	1901	New York
1921	Chicago, Ill.	1900	New York

Sub-Junior Champions

Year	Name, Residence	Score
1941	Bobby Stifal, Casey, Ill.	97x100
1940	E. C. Colosky, Minneapolis, Minn.	88x100
1939	Ray Fienup, St. Louis, Mo.	98x100
1938	Ray Fienup, St. Louis, Mo.	98x100
1937	Rudy Etchen, Wichita, Kans.	95x100
1936	Rudy Etchen, Wichita, Kans.	96x100
1935	Otto Kiehl, Pittsburg, Kans.	99x100
1934	Homer Clark, Jr., Alton, Ill.	95x100

Sub-Junior Champions (Cont.)

1933	Robert Poore, Butte, Mont	94x100
1932	Scottie Richards, Hollansburg, Ohio	87x100
1931	Joe Fincel, Dubuque, Iowa	89x100
1930	H. Rosenbrook, Gardnerville, Nev	93x100
1929	A. Meiss, Hazelton, Pa	97x100
1928	John Corkery, Yonkers, N. Y	89x100
1927	Howard Kieffer, Orrville, O	95x100
1926	Howard Kieffer, Orrville, O	96x100

Jim Day Cup

1941	Vic Reinders, Waukesha, Wis	400	390
1940	Paul Holloway, Pine Valley, N. J	400	387
1939	Phil Miller, French Lick, Ind	400	387
1938	Phil Miller, French Lick, Ind	400	388
1938	Ned Lilly, Stanton, Mich	400	388
1937	Phil Miller, French Lick, Ind	400	390
1937	R. A. King, Wichita Falls, Tex	400	390
1936	Joe Hiestand, Hillsboro, O	400	389
1935	Joe Hiestand, Hillsboro, O	400	388
1934	Joe Hiestand, Hillsboro, O	400	388
1933	Ned Lilly, Stanton, Mich	500	474
1932	Russell Elliott, Kansas City, Mo	500	476
1931	Gus Payne, Oklahoma City, Okla	500	471
1930	E. W. Renfro, Dell, Mont	500	481
1929	F. M. Troeh, Portland, Ore	500	477
1928	F. M. Troeh, Portland, Ore	500	462
1927	F. M. Troeh, Portland, Ore	500	472
1926	F. M. Troeh, Portland, Ore	500	475
1925	C. W. Olney, West Allis, Wis	500	479
1924	Phil R. Miller, Dallas, Texas	500	477
1923	Phil R. Miller, Dallas, Texas	500	471

Gates Trophy

1941	Walter Tulbert, Detroit, Mich	100	99
1940	E. H. Wolfe, Charleston, W. Va	100	98
1939	D. L. Ritchie, Goshen, O	100	99
1938	O. W. West	100	99
1937	F. G. Carroll, Brecksville, O	100	100
1936	B. F. Cheek, Clinton, Ind	100	98
1935	J. B. Royall, Tallahassee, Fla	100	98
1934	L. G. Dana, Derrick City, Pa	100	98
1933	Walter Beaver, Berwyn, Pa	100	98
1932	A. E. Sheffield, Dixon, Ill	100	98
1931	Garrison Roebuck, McClure, O	100	96
1930	R. King, Jr., Wichita Falls, Texas	100	97
1929	Mose Newman, Sweetwater, Teas	100	98
1928	Isaac Andrews, Spartanburg, S. C	100	95
1927	Otto Newlin, Georgetown, Ill	100	98
1926	C. A. Young, Springfield, O	100	100

Grand American Handicap at 25 Live Birds

First Held in 1893, Last in 1902

Year	Winner	Yds.	Kd.
1893	R. A. Welch	28	23
1894	T. W. Morfey	28	25

Grand American Handicap (Cont.)

1895	J. G. Messner	25	25
1896	O. R. Dickey	29	24
1897	Tom A. Marshall	28	25
1898	E. D. Fulford	29	25
1899	Tom A. Marshall	29	25
1900	H. D. Bates	28	25
1901	E. C. Griffith	28	25
1902	H. C. Hirschy	29	25

G.A.H. Champion of Champions Race

1923	Mark Arie, Champaign, Ill	196
1924	Claude Olney, West Allis, Wis	198
1925	Steve Crothers, Philadelphia, Pa	200
1926	Mark Arie, Champaign, Ill	199
1927	Oscar Hanson, Fremont, Nebr	197
1928	C. R. Brand, Buffalo, N. Y	198
1929	Frank Troeh, Portland, Ore	199
1930	E. F. Woodward, Houston, Texas	197
1931	Steve Crothers, Philadelphia, Pa	200
1932	Steve Crothers, Philadelphia, Pa	199
1933	H. L. Cheek, Clinton, Ind	197
1934	Mark Arie, Champaign, Ill	197
1935	Elmer Torge, Wales Center, N. Y	200
1936	Hale Jones, Wood River, Ill	196
1937	Hale Jones, Wood River, Ill	100x
1938	Mark Hootman, Hicksville, O	100x
1939	Walter Peterson, Lynn, Mass	100x
1940	Sam Sharman, Salt Lake City, Utah	99x
1941	Karl Maust, Columbus, O	100x

(x denotes 100 target program. The rest are 200 target programs.)

Professional Champions

1906	Walter Huff, Macon, Ga	145x150
1907	W. R. Crosby, O'Fallon, Ill	192x200
1908	Fred Gilbert, Spirit Lake, Iowa	188x200
1909	Fred Gilbert, Spirit Lake, Iowa	193x200
1910	Charlie Spencer, St. Louis, Mo	190x200
1911	Les German, Aberdeen, Md	198x200
1912	W. R. Crosby, O'Fallon, Ill	198x200
1913	Charlie Young, Springfield, O	197x200
1914	No Contest	
1915	No Contest	
1916	Phil Miller, Dallas, Texas	99x100
1917	Homer Clark, Alton, Ill	94x100
1918	Homer Clark, Alton, Ill	194x200
1919	Bart Lewis, Auburn, Ill	200x200
1920	Charlie Spencer, St. Louis, Mo	195x200
1921	Art Killam, St. Louis, Mo	198x200
1922	Art Killam, St. Louis, Mo	197x200
1923	Johnny Jahn, Spirit Lake, Iowa	198x200
1924	Art Killam, St. Louis, Mo	197x200
1925	Homer Clark, Alton, Ill	199x200
1926	Fred Tomlin, Glassboro, N. J	200x200
1927	Fred Tomlin, Glassboro, N. J	198x200
1928	Earl Donahue, Minneapolis, Minn	197x200
1929	Earl Donahue, Minneapolis, Minn	200x200

CANAL ZONE GUNNERS: *(Right to left)* P. M. Disharoon, Sr., Bernice Hunter, Mrs. P. M. Disharoon, Sr., L. B. Carr, P. J. Jones, Captain I. G. Hay, B. W, Stephenson, Paul Disharoon, Dr. A. E. Gerrans

CUBAN TEAM at the Grand American: George Miranda, Dr. Seafin Tuesada, Frank Steinhart, Carlos Quinteros, Major P. Cruz

Professional Champions (Cont.)

Year	Champion	Score
1930	Howard Benson, Lansing, Mich.	197x200
1931	Earl Donahue, Minneapolis, Minn.	199x200
1932	Win Sale, Denver, Colo.	199x200
1933	John Taylor, Newark, O.	197x200
1934	Johnny Jahn, Spirit Lake, Iowa	196x200
1935	Fred Tomlin, Glassboro, N. J.	200x200
1936	Cap. J. B. Grier, Rockland, Dela.	199x200
1937	Clyde Wells, Bridgeport, Conn.	200x200
1938	Karl Maust, Columbus, O.	199x200
1939	Fred Tomlin, Glassboro, N. J.	199x200
1940	Fred Tomlin, Glassboro, N. J.	196x200
1941	Clyde Wells, Bridgeport, Conn.	199x200

Grand American All-Around Champions

Year	Champion	Score
1916	Frank Troeh, Portland, Ore.	664x 700
1917	Mark Arie, Champaign, Ill.	676x 700
1918	Mark Arie, Champaign, Ill.	562x 600
1919	Frank Troeh, Portland, Ore.	673x 700
1920	R. H. Bungay, Ocean Park, Calif.	760x 800
1921	R. A. King, Wichita Falls, Texas	938x1000
1922	Phil Miller, Dallas, Texas	939x1000
1923	Mark Arie, Champaign, Ill.	957x1000
1924	Mark Arie, Champaign, Ill.	957x1000
1925	Steve Crothers, Philadelphia, Pa.	956x1000
1926	Frank Troeh, Portland, Ore.	968x1000
1927	Wm. Kurtz, Monroeville, N. J.	957x1000
1928	Frank Troeh, Portland, Ore.	935x1000
1929	Frank Troeh, Portland, Ore.	958x1000
1930	Frank Troeh, Portland, Ore.	967x1000
1931	Gus Payne, Tulsa, Okla.	952x1000
1932	Mark Arie, Champaign, Ill.	969x1000
1933	Ned Lilly, Stanton, Mich.	964x1000
1934	Joe Hiestand, Hillsboro, O.	878x 900
1935	Joe Hiestand, Hillsboro, O.	880x 900
1936	Joe Hiestand, Hillsboro, O.	881x 900
1937	R. A. King, Wichita Falls, Texas	881x 900
1938	Joe Hiestand, Hillsboro, O.	881x 900
1939	Phil Miller, French Lick, Ind.	880x 900
1940	H. L. Cheek, Clinton, Ind.	1131x1200
1941	Vic Reinders, Waukesha, Wis.	874x 900

Veterans Race

Year	Champion	Score
1930	F. D. Kelsey, East Aurora, N. Y.	181
1931	F. D. Kelsey, East Aurora, N. Y.	182
1932	F. D. Kelsey, East Aurora, N. Y.	190
1933	T. G. Cathan, Chagrin Falls, O.	187
1934	W. A. Tabor, Union City, Okla.	191
1935	Charlie Young, Springfield, O.	196
1936	Charlie Young, Springfield, O.	194
1937	E. E. Daniels, Birmingham, Mich.	195
1938	E. E. Bush, Tallahassee, Fla.	192
1939	John Peterson, Randall, Iowa	96x
1940	Johnny Fontaine, Philadelphia, Pa.	98x
1941	Charlie Young, Springfield, O.	99x

(Note: x denotes 100 target program. Other years are 200 targets.)

Husband and Wife Event

Year	Champions	Score
1935	John and Bunny Sanders, Keyser, W. Va.	382
1936	Roy and Mrs. Meadows, Des Moines, Iowa	374
1937	Mr. and Mrs. Fred Hess, Philadelphia, Pa.	383
1938	John and Bunny Sanders, Keyser, W. Va.	379
1939	John and Bunny Sanders, Keyser, W. Va.	382
1940	Mr. and Mrs. Van Marker, Chicago, Ill.	189x
1941	Dr. G. A. Roose and wife, Salem, O.	194x

(Note: x denotes 200 target program. Other years are 400 targets.)

High Average Trapshooters

Year	Shooter	Shot at	Broke	Average
1908	Chan Powers, Decatur, Ill.	5690	5383	.9460
1909	J. S. Young, Chicago, Ill.	4730	4498	.9509
1910	J. S. Day, Midland, Texas	4280	4164	.9728
1911	W. S. Spencer, St. Louis, Mo.	2100	2022	.9623
1912	Bill Ridley, What Cheer, Iowa.	800	767	.9587
1913	Bart Lewis, Auburn, Ill.	6080	5811	.9557
1914	W. Henderson, Lexington, Ky.	2050	1981	.9663
1915	W. Henderson, Lexington, Ky.	2800	2731	.9753
1916	Fred Harlow, Newark, O.	2010	1964	.9771
1917	W. H. Heer, Guthrie, Okla.	2050	1997	.9741
1918	Frank Troeh, Portland, Ore.	6845	6665	.9722
1919	Mark Arie, Champaign, Ill.	2920	2856	.9780
1920	Frank Troeh, Portland, Ore.	8880	8660	.9752
1921	Art Risser, Paris, Ill.	2150	2104	.9786
1922	Frank Troeh, Portland, Ore.	6260	6159	.9838
1923	Phil Miller, French Lick, Ind.	2550	2505	.9823
1924	Frank Hughes, Mobridge, S. D.	1000	983	.9830
1925	A. B. Harris, Louisville, Ky.	1350	1325	.9814
1926	A. J. Stauber, Los Angeles	1500	1473	.9820
1927	A. J. Stauber, Los Angeles	1475	1461	.9905
1928	A. J. Stauber, Los Angeles	1250	1239	.9912
1929	T. D. Hackett, Atlantic City	1100	1080	.9818
1930	E. F. Woodward, Houston, Tex.	1800	1783	.9905
1931	E. F. Woodward, Houston, Tex.	2200	2174	.9881
1932	A. J. Stauber, Los Angeles	1000	994	.9940
1933	E. F. Woodward, Houston, Tex.	1000	995	.9950

Bill Moore, Editor Sportsmen's Review

High Average Trapshooters (Cont.)

Year	Name	Shot at	Broke	Average
1934	Cal Waggoner, Diller, Nebr.	1000	989	.9890
1935	Walter Beaver, Berwyn, Pa.	5100	5033	.9868
1936	Hale Jones, Wood River, Ill.	2550	2519	.9878
1937	Hale Jones, Wood River, Ill.	1800	1783	.9905
1938	Phil Miller, French Lick, Ind.	3050	3019	.9898
1939	Tommy Lovett, Houston, Tex.	1000	989	.9890
1940	W. F. Harder, Lincoln, Nebr.	2300	2279	.9908
1941	Walter Beaver, Berwyn, Pa.	3050	3017	.9891

High Average Professionals

Year	Name	Shot at	Broke	Average
1916	Homer Clark, Alton, Ill.	2100	2055	.9800
1917	Les German, Aberdeen, Md.	6285	6137	.9764
1918	Homer Clark, Alton, Ill.	2310	2228	.9752
1919	Rush Razee, Curtis, Nebr.	2120	2078	.9801
1920	Guy Ward, Lake Charles, La.	6425	6249	.9726
1921	Rush Razee, Curtis, Nebr.	1875	1838	.9802
1922	Bart Lewis, Auburn, Ill.	2250	2209	.9817
1923	John R. Taylor, Newark, O.	2000	1969	.9845
1924	Guy Ward, Lake Charles, La.	1050	1027	.9780
1925	Fred Tomlin, Glassboro, N. J.	2825	2784	.9854
1926	Art Killam, St. Louis, Mo.	1200	1180	.9833
1927	Clyde Wells, Memphis, Tenn.	1350	1332	.9866
1928	Earl Donahue, Minneapolis	2650	2591	.9777
1929	Earl Donahue, Minneapolis	1620	1596	.9851
1930	Fred Tomlin, Glassboro, N. J.	3710	3631	.9787
1931	Earl Donahue, Minneapolis	3500	3445	.9842
1932	Fred Tomlin, Glassboro, N. J.	2100	2078	.9895
1933	Fred Tomlin, Glassboro, N. J.	2975	2935	.9865
1934	Rush Razee, Denver, Colo.	2350	2303	.9800
1935	Fred Tomlin, Glassboro, N. J.	3925	3843	.9791
1936	Fred Tomlin, Glassboro, N. J.	1900	1863	.9805
1937	Capt. J. B. Grier, Rockland, Dela.	3300	3262	.9884
1938	Fred Tomlin, Glassboro, N. J.	2200	2183	.9922
1939	Fred Tomlin, Glassboro, N. J.	2450	2433	.9930
1940	Joe Davison, Kansas City, Mo.	2050	2023	.9868
1941	Cap. J. B. Grier, Rockland, Dela.	2200	2170	.9863

N.Y.A.C. Amateur Trapshooting Champions

Year	Name	Score
1905	John Hendrickson	94
1906	William Foord	94
1907	Edward F. Gleason	95
1908	George S. McCarty	96
1909	George S. McCarty	98
1910	No competition.	
1911	Henry Kahler	173
1912	B. M. Higginson, Jr.	185
1913	Charlie Newcomb	179
1914	Ralph L. Spotts	188
1915	George L. Lyon	192
1916	Ralph L. Spotts	196
1917	Charlie Newcomb	191
1918	Fred Plum	197
1919	Joe E. Jennings	197
1920	Jay Clark, Jr.	197
1921	George S. McCarty	198
1922	George S. McCarty	195
1923	Leon Davis	195
1924	H. W. Voorhies	193

N.Y.A.C. Amateur Champions (Cont.)

Year	Name	Score
1925	Steve Crothers	197
1926	Frank Wright	199
1927	Steve Crothers	198
1928	Steve Crothers	196
1929	J. H. Wantling	194
1930	Steve Crothers	193
1931	Tracey Lewis	194
1932	Walter Beaver	194
1933	J. H. Kretschman	192
1934	E. C. Lamerson	198
1935	Joe Hiestand	199
1936	Joe Hiestand	198
1937	Walter Beaver	198
1938	Roger Fawcett	199
1939	Steve Crothers	197
1940	D. Frank Beck	197
1941	Walter Beaver	197

Yorklyn, Delaware 500 Target Championship

Year	Name	Score
1921	Isaac Turner	492
1925	James L. Luke	461
1925	Steve Crothers	496
1926	Fred W. Hess	486
1927	Steve Crothers	496
1928	Steve Crothers	489
1929	Mark Arie	492
1930	Walter Warren	496
1931	Steve Crothers	499
1932	Steve Crothers	497
1933	Joe Hiestand	497
1934	Frank M. Troeh	496
1935	Joe Hiestand	499
1936	Ned Lilly	496
1937	Phil Miller	498
1938	Roger Fawcett	497
1939	Walter Beaver	494
1940	Joe Hiestand	498
1941	Joe Hiestand	498

International Flyer Championship Kansas City

Year	Name	Score
1917	George Nicolai	95x100
1918	H. E. Snyder	93x100
1919	George Nicolai	98x100
1920	Frank Troeh	94x100
1921	H. E. Snyder	96x100
1922	Fred Etchen, Frank Troeh, Walter Warren	94x100
1923	C. J. Mos, Frank Troeh, J. E. Crawford	91x100
1924	Claude Olney	96x100
1925	Claude Olney, C. J. Mos	97x100
1926	Fred Etchen	98x100
1927	Sam Jenny, Fred Etchen	79x 80
1928	Ted Renfro	79x 80
1929	Frank Troeh	96x100
1930	Mark Arie	99x100
1931	N. V. Pillot	97x100
1932	Frank Troeh	99x100
1933	Spencer Olin	95x100
1934	H. E. Woodward	95x100

E. B. Chamberlin, Jimmy O'Hanlon and Tom Lawrence at the N. Y. A. C. shoot

Lawrence Krieg, Secretary A. T. A.

Dr. F. E. Butler, Bellefontaine, Ohio, is treasurer of the Amateur Trapshooting Association

International Flyer Championship (Cont.)

1935 E. B. Melrath....79x 85
1936 Sam Jenny....94x100
1937 Sam Jenny....90x100
1938 Phil Miller....92x100
1939 Ted Renfro....92x100
1940 Phil Miller....95x100
1941 Ted Renfro....92x100

STATE TRAPSHOOTING CHAMPIONS

Alabama

1914 J. K. Warren, Birmingham.... 97
1915 J. K. Warren, Birmingham.... 99
1916 H. C. Ryding, Birmingham.... 98
1917 A. Lawson, Greensboro.... 99
1918 W. A. Leach, Gadsden.... 98
1919 W. E. Gordon, Bessemer.... 288
1920 J. K. Warren, Birmingham.... 292
1921 Lee Moody, Bessemer.... 195
1922 E. R. Alexander, Tuskegee.... 189
1923 O. L. Garl, Birmingham.... 195
1924 T. K. Lee, Birmingham.... 199
1925 T. K. Lee, Birmingham.... 189
1926 Walton Hill, Birmingham.... 195
1927 H. R. Marriott, Mobile.... 197
1928 T. K. Lee, Birmingham.... 198
1929 E. D. Flynn, Mobile.... 191
1930 H. R. Marriott, Mobile.... 198
1931 Walton Hill, Birmingham.... 198
1932 T. K. Lee, Birmingham.... 199
1933 H. C. Ricks, Tuscumbia.... 198
1934 T. K. Lee, Birmingham.... 196
1935 T. K. Lee, Birmingham.... 198
1936 H. C. Ricks, Tuscumbia.... 197
1937 T. K. Lee, Birmingham.... 198
1938 T. K. Lee, Birmingham.... 196
1939 A. M. Feltus, Mobile.... 199
1940 T. K. Lee, Birmingham.... 196
1941 A. M. Feltus, Mobile.... 197

Arizona

1914 Tom Edens, Phoenix.... 99
1915 H. P. De Mund, Phoenix.... 98
1916 C. P. Cooley, Holbrook.... 87
1917 R. P. De Mund, Phoenix.... 98
1918 D. E. Morrell, Phoenix.... 99
1919 T. L. Edens, Phoenix.... 292
1920 T. L. Edens, Phoenix.... 285
1921 Nic Arie, Kingman.... 194
1922 Joe Steed, Kingman.... 189
1924 B. A. Gillespie, Phoenix.... 196
1925 W. M. Cady, Flagstaff.... 197
1926 T. L. Edens, Phoenix.... 199
1927 Geo. Peter, Phoenix....199
1928 Geo. Peter, Phoenix.... 197
1929 Geo. Peter, Phoenix.... 198
1930 Geo. Peter, Phoenix.... 197
1931 Geo. Peter, Phoenix.... 197
1932 Geo. Peter, Phoenix.... 194

Arkansas

1914 T. R. Tansil, Blytheville.... 92
1915 T. R. Tansil, Blytheville.... 99
1916 T. R. Tansil, Blytheville.... 97
1917 J. E. Chatfield, Texarkana.... 96
1918 J. E. Chatfield, Texarkana.... 97
1919 J. E. Chatfield, Texarkana.... 288
1920 C. M. Farrell, Little Rock.... 282
1921 Fred Shauver, Nettleton.... 197
1922 J. E. Chatfield, Texarkana.... 197
1923 J. E. Chatfield, Texarkana.... 189
1924 G. W. Kausler, Brickeyes.... 191
1925 G. W. Kausler, Brickeyes.... 191
1926 G. W. Kausler, Brickeyes.... 191
1927 G. W. Kausler, Brickeyes.... 191
1928 Fred Shauver, Nettleton.... 192
1929 H. T. Shipper, Osceola.... 193
1930 B. E. Cooper, Hot Springs.... 194
1931 B. E. Cooper, Hot Springs.... 196
1933 Julius Petty, England.... 194

Arkansas (Cont.)

1934 W. P. Smead, Osceola.... 191
1935 W. P. Smead, Osceola.... 193
1936 M. C. Stevenson, Fort Smith.... 194
1937 M. C. Stevenson, Fort Smith.... 197
1939 M. C. Stevenson, Fort Smith.... 196
1940 M. C. Stevenson, Fort Smith.... 196
1941 Julius Petty, England.... 197

California

1914 M. T. Leffler, Los Angeles.... 96
1915 J. F. Couts, Los Angeles.... 96
1916 H. Pfirrmann, Los Angeles.... 100
1917 F. H. Mellus, Los Angeles.... 99
1918 Fred S. Bair, Eureka.... 100
1919 J. F. Dodds, Los Angeles.... 291
1920 Walter Warren, Yerington, Nev.... 293
1921 Walter Warren, Yerington, Nev.... 197
1922 H. Pfirrmann, Los Angeles.... 195
1923 W. E. Staunton, San Francisco.... 193
1924 J. B. Lewis, San Francisco.... 197
1925 Tony Prior, San Francisco.... 194
1926 Dr. H. W. Armstrong, Los Angeles.... 195
1927 W. P. Sears, Martinez.... 198
1928 Fred Griffin, Santa Cruz....200
1929 O. N. Ford, Del Monte.... 197
1930 L. B. Marsh, Long Beach.... 197
1931 A. J. Stauber, Los Angeles.... 193
1932 A. J. Stauber, Los Angeles.... 200
1933 A. J. Stauber, Los Angeles.... 198
1934 Dr. H. W. Armstrong, Los Angeles.... 199
1935 H. M. Hubbard, San Diego.... 195
1936 A. J. Stauber, Los Angeles.... 197
1937 Grant Ilseng, Fresno.... 197
1938 Grant Ilseng, Fresno.... 198
1939 Grant Ilseng, Los Angeles.... 198
1940 R. E. Fergason, Los Angeles.... 197
1941 R. E. Fergason, Los Angeles.... 196

Colorado

1914 Jas. Higgins (New Mex. & Wyo.) La Junta.. 100
1915 R. A. King, Delta (New Mex. & Wyo.).... 98
1916 R. A. King, Delta (New Mex. & Wyo.).... 100
1917 R. A. King, Delta (New Mex. & Wyo.).... 99
1918 R. A. King, Delta (New Mex. & Wyo.).... 93
1919 W. R. Thomas, Denver.... 285
1920 C. A. Gunning, Longmont.... 292
1921 R. W. Christopher, Greeley.... 198
1922 Hugh M. Smith, Berthoud.... 198
1923 Hugh M. Smith, Berthoud.... 198
1924 Brad Townsend, Denver.... 198
1925 John Nicolai, Denver.... 195
1926 C. A. Gunning, Longmont.... 191
1927 Casper Hoffman, Denver.... 186
1928 D. L. McAffree, Pueblo.... 198
1929 O. E. McIntyre, Colorado Springs.... 199
1930 O. E. McIntyre, Colorado Springs.... 197
1931 O. E. McIntyre, Colorado Springs.... 199
1932 O. E. McIntyre, Colorado Springs.... 196
1933 F. W. Kukuk, Burlington.... 197
1934 C. A. Gunning, Longmont.... 198
1935 C. A. Gunning, Longmont.... 197
1936 Homer Braddock, Denver.... 197
1937 C. A. Gunning, Longmont.... 194
1938 Leroy Scheer, Wray....197
1939 C. A. Gunning, Longmont.... 199
1940 C. A. Gunning, Longmont.... 197
1941 C. A. Gunning, Longmont.... 198

Connecticut

1915 Chas. Vanstone, Bridgeport.... 94
1916 A. L. Chamberlin, New Haven.... 94
1917 W. A. Flinn, Greenwich.... 98
1918 B. F. Bishop, New Haven.... 95
1919 Herb Barstow, Rockville.... 293
1920 F. E. Watkins, Hartford.... 293
1921 J. H. Finch, Greenwich.... 194
1922 George Sivers, Bridgeport.... 193
1923 Herb Barstow, Rockville.... 196
1924 Herb Barstow, Rockville.... 191

Connecticut (Cont.)

1925 A. M. Tull, Waterbury 194
1926 Herb Barstow, Rockville 196
1927 W. G. Beswick, West Haven 198
1928 C. P. Walters, Hartford 190
1929 E. H. Raymond, Danbury 197
1930 E. H. Raymond, Danbury 194
1931 E. H. Raymond, Danbury 199
1932 I. Iron, Waterbury 195
1933 M. D. Roberts, Middletown 195
1934 M. D. Roberts, Middletown 193
1935 W. C. Capewell, Bridgeport 195
1936 W. C. Capewell, Bridgeport 193
1937 M. D. Clark, Woodbury 197
1938 W. C. Capewell, Bridgeport 197
1940 W. R. Patrick, Hartford 197
1941 M. D. Clark, Woodbury 195

Delaware

1914 A. B. Richardson, Dover 96
1915 A. B. Richardson, Dover 100
1916 Wm. Edmanson, Newport 95
1917 L. B. Beauchamp, Harrington 94
1918 Wm. Foord, Wilmington 98
1919 Wm. Foord, Wilmington 277
1920 Wm. Foord, Wilmington 294
1921 H. L. Morgan, Wilmington 196
1922 E. E. Dupont, Greenville 186
1923 L. D. Willis, Wilmington 190
1924 Dr. H. Lendeman, Wilmington 196
1925 L. D. Willis, Wilmington 195
1926 W. L. Luke, Talleyville 195
1927 L. D. Willis, Wilmington 189
1928 G. Sylvester, Wilmington 195
1929 G. Sylvester, Wilmington 196
1930 Isaac Turner, Wilmington 195
1931 Dr. W. R. Pierce, Milford 192
1932 Wm. Foord, Milton 195
1933 Wm. Foord, Milton 196
1934 J. B. Grier, Rockland 192
1935 J. B. Grier, Rockland 191
1936 Wm. Foord, Milton 193
1937 Chas. W. Jenkins 195
1938 C. E. Simon, Wilmington 198
1939 Dr. W. R. Pierce, Milford 196
1940 Isador Keil, Wilmington 195
1941 T. C. Marshall, Jr., Yorklyn 192

District of Columbia

1931 C. C. Fawsett, Washington 184
1932 W. F. Burrough, Washington 191
1933 R. D. Morgan, Washington 192
1934 C. C. Fawsett, Washington 187
1935 Parker Cook, Washington 194
1936 Walter Wilson, Washington 192
1937 R. D. Morgan, Washington 193
1938 Parker Cook, Washington 193
1939 W. S. Wilson, Washington 190
1940 T. K. Wynkoop, Bethesday 191
1941 Walter Wilson, Washington 196

Florida

1916 T. H. Evans, Orlando 91
1917 G. W. Ball, Miami 97
1918 J. A. Hansbrough, Tampa 91
1919 W. N. Boylston, Leesburg 291
1920 W. N. Boylston, Leesburg 293
1921 George Williams, Miami 192
1922 T. J. Aycock, Jacksonville 195
1923 George D. Williams, Miami 195
1924 T. J. Aycock, Jacksonville 192
1925 G. D. Williams, Miami 197
1926 O. J. Cook, Haines City 195
1927 Frank Shull, Hollywood 194
1928 T. B. Sherrill, Tampa 198
1929 Harry Johnson, Haines City 199
1930 P. P. Schutt, Punta Gorda 195
1931 J. B. Royal, Tallahassee 191
1932 H. E. Johnson, Haines City 198
1933 H. E. Johnson, Haines City 197

Florida (Cont.)

1934 J. B. Royal, Tallahassee 184
1935 J. B. Royal, Tallahassee 192
1936 T. B. Deen, Jacksonville 193
1937 John R. Taylor, Astor 194
1938 John R. Taylor, Astor 197
1939 Harry Messlor, Astor 194
1940 Tom Deen, Jacksonville 195
1941 E. R. Pratte, Miami 198

Georgia

1914 J. M. Barrett, Augusta 93
1915 J. M. Barrett, Augusta 97
1916 Brad Timms, Atlanta 98
1917 W. H. Jones, Macon 97
1918 J. M. Barrett, Augusta 99
1919 H. D. Freeman, Atlanta 272
1920 H. D. Freeman, Atlanta 287
1921 W. C. Carpenter, Atlanta 188
1922 H. J. Foster, Atlanta 195
1923 W. H. Lanier, Augusta 194
1924 W. H. Lanier, Augusta 194
1925 H. D. Freeman, Atlanta 199
1926 W. H. Lanier, Augusta 195
1927 W. H. Lanier, Augusta 195
1928 H. C. McKenzie, Atlanta 196
1929 H. C. McKenzie, Atlanta 196
1930 Vassa Cates, Brunswick 193
1931 W. H. Lanier, Augusta 196
1932 J. P. Pullen, McDonough 190
1933 H. C. McKenzie, Atlanta 196
1934 Jack Tway, Atlanta 189
1935 J. P. Pullin, McDonough 197
1936 H. N. Alford, Atlanta 195
1937 J. P. Pullin, McDonough 197
1938 Chas. Tway, Atlanta 187
1939 J. P. Pullin, McDonough 194
1940 J. P. Pullin, McDonough 196
1941 Clyde King, Jr., Atlanta 191

Idaho

1914 F. D. Wade, Wendell 98
1915 E. C. Grice, Boise 98
1916 E. M. Sweeley, Twin Falls 98
1917 D. J. Holohan, Burley 96
1918 Guy Chiesman, Lewiston 99
1919 Chas. Hahn, Lewiston 283
1920 H. R. Seckel, Boise 293
1921 E. C. Grice, Boise 193
1922 A. E. Sherman, Boise 189
1923 Harry Seckel, Boise 189
1924 Guy Chiesman, Lewiston 198
1925 M. M. Wright, Lewiston 198
1926 F. P. Porter, Kellogg 192
1927 F. R. McCabe, Boise 189
1928 W. D. Bush, Boise 193
1929 F. R. McCabe, Boise 199
1930 Guy Chiesman, Lewiston 197
1935 C. A. Galloway, Greer 197
1936 J. C. Gray, Nampa 195
1937 C. A. Galloway, Greer 189
1940 Joe Cotant, Pocatello 195
1941 Joe Cotant, Pocatello 198

Illinois

1914 G. H. Reitz, Gilman 96
1915 C. H. Ditto, Keithsburg 99
1916 Chas. Burmeister, Chicago 100
1917 Mark Arie, Thomasboro 98
1918 Chan Powers, Decatur 98
1919 Mark Arie, Thomasboro 295
1920 Mark Arie, Thomasboro 294
1921 Chan Powers, Decatur 198
1922 M. E. Jenny, Lexington 197
1923 Mark Arie, Champaign 197
1924 Barney Ashe, Harrisburg 200
1925 Dr. A. M. Aszman, E. St. Louis 188
1926 Mark Arie, Champaign 197
1927 Frank Hughes, Chicago 198
1928 R. B. Rosensteil, Freeport 197

THESE TRAPSHOOTERS BROKE 200 STRAIGHTS TO WIN THEIR STATE TITLES

Dr. N. G. Riggins—Bruce Sloan (Kentucky)

H. P. Messlor (New Jersey) Cal Waggoner (Nebraska) A. J. Stauber (California)

Guy Von Schriltz (Kansas) Waldo Seavey (Maine) John Milne (Ontario)

L. B. Smith (New York)

C. O. Free (Indiana)

Fred Ford (Michigan)

Hank Pendergast (New York)

Frank Lightner (Iowa)

Fred Menth (Minnesota)

Dean Hurd (Utah)

Illinois (Continued)

1929 W. G. Warren, Chicago 198
1930 S. D. Pierce, Geneseo 196
1931 Mark Arie, Champaign 198
1932 J. N. LeLievre, Elgin 198
1933 Walter Gries, Benson 198
1934 Mark Arie, Champaign 199
1935 Gerald Batten, Chicago 196
1936 Hale Jones, Wood River 196
1937 Hale Jones, Wood River 198
1938 Hale Jones, Wood River 198
1939 H. Longden, Taylorville 199
1940 O. J. Gillett, Dwight 197
1941 Bert West, S. Pekin 199

Indiana

1914 W. A. Roach, Terre Haute 94
1915 R. H. Bruns, Brookville 98
1916 Leroy Pickett, Frankfort 99
1917 W. L. Straughan, Waveland 99
1918 G. R. Shuck, Kempton 98
1919 Monte De Wire, Hamilton 294
1920 Monte De Wire, Hamilton 296
1921 G H. Ford, Indianapolis 198
1922 F. D. Thompson, Frankfort 193
1923 Monte De Wire, Hamilton 198
1924 Monte De Wire, Hamilton 196
1925 Monte De Wire, Hamilton 196
1926 J. Wilcoxson, Hammond 193
1927 D. C. Rogers, Logansport 198
1928 D. M. Hudson, Hammond 196
1929 Cra Ax, Jasonville 197
1930 S. W. Cook, Jr., Evansville 198
1931 M. E. De Wire, Hamilton 196
1932 Geo. Wendling, No. Salem 199
1933 H. L. Cheek, Clinton 200
1934 Monte De Wire, Hamilton 198
1935 Monte De Wire, Hamilton 195
1936 R. M. Jenkins, Orleans 195
1937 C. O. Free, Indianapolis 200
1938 Phil Miller, French Lick 200
1939 H. L. Cheek, Clinton 198
1940 L. C. Wise, Carmel 198
1941 H. L. Cheek, Clinton 198

Iowa

1914 J. R. Jahn, Spirit Lake 97
1915 J. R. Jahn, Spirit Lake 98
1916 W. M. Ridley, What Cheer 100
1917 J. R. Jahn, Spirit Lake 98
1918 Chas. Hummell, La Porte City 99
1919 B. F. Elbert, Des Moines 294
1920 W. S. Hoon, Jewell 291
1921 W. S. Hoon, Jewell 197
1922 Geo. Nunn, Jefferson 197
1923 A. H. Luke, Hampton 195
1924 G. H. Anderson, Estherville 195
1925 J. F. Fisher, Titonka 189
1926 Geo. Nunn, Jefferson 196
1927 H. M. Jones, Sioux City 193
1928 Bim Castle, Charles City 195
1929 J. F. Fisher, Titonka 198
1930 W. J. Scourick, Ackley 199
1931 B. H. Grimm, Humeston 199
1932 Chas. Forrett, Waukee 197
1933 Frank J. Lightner, Cedar Rapids 200
1934 Dr. John Patterson, Des Moines 197
1935 W. S. Hoon, Jewell 199
1936 Dr. J. Patterson, Des Moines 194
1937 W. S. Hoon, Jewell 197
1938 W. S. Hoon, Jewell 197
1939 Stanley Meadows, Grimes 199
1940 W. S. Hoon, Jewell 196
1941 L. O. Harris, Marshalltown 197

Kansas

1914 E. W. Arnold, Larned 93
1915 H. C. Hood, Pittsburg 95
1916 Geo. Grubb, Wetmore 99

Kansas (Cont.)

1917 Steve Hoyne, Salina 97
1918 E. W. Arnold, Larned 97
1919 F. J. Cairns, Tampa 285
1920 Fred Etchen, Coffeyville 283
1921 R. E. Ainsworth, Larned 197
1922 F. J. Cairns, Tampa 197
1923 W. H. Stephenson, Pittsburg 198
1924 Rex Hill, Eldorado 187
1925 Roy Govenius, Augusta 195
1926 J. W. Lloyd, Wichita 196
1927 Joe Burns, Salina 198
1928 Joe Davison, Ottawa 196
1929 Fred Etchen, Wichita 197
1930 Guy Von Schriltz, Pittsburg 197
1931 Fred Etchen, Wichita 197
1932 Guy Von Schriltz, Pittsburg 200
1933 Guy Von Schriltz, Pittsburg 200
1934 P. E. Morris, Wichita 200
1935 A. H. Rose, Hutchinson 193
1936 C. B. McDowell, Phillipsburg 197
1937 Fred Etchen, Wichita 196
1938 Rudy Etchen, Wichita 196
1939 Rudy Etchen, Wichita 198
1940 A. H. Rose, Hutchinson 198
1941 Jim Andrews, Anthony 199

Kentucky

1914 W. Henderson, Lexington 97
1916 J. D. Gay, Pine Grove 98
1917 Zach Offutt, Louisville 95
1918 W. Hall, Maysville 99
1919 W. Henderson, Lexington 298
1920 F. B. Hillis, Lexington 288
1921 W. Henderson, Lexington 196
1922 W. Henderson, Lexington 199
1923 A. B. Harris, Louisville 197
1924 W. H. Hall, Maysville 196
1925 A. B. Harris, Louisville 197
1926 J. W. Manning, Louisville 196
1927 W. E. Gladstone, Louisville 196
1928 W. E. Gladstone, Louisville 198
1929 J. W. Manning, Louisville 198
1930 Herman Keen, Newport 197
1931 Dr. W. E. Fallis, Louisville 197
1932 Rod Cooper, Louisville 197
1933 Frank N. Dailey, Frankfort 196
1934 Rod Cooper Louisville 196
1935 F. E. Boone, Lexington 196
1936 W. H. Hall, Maysville 198
1937 Dr. N. G. Riggins, Hazard 198
1938 J. Brown, Lexington 195
1939 Bruce Sloan, Albany 200
1940 Dille Craig, Berry 199
1941 W. T. Jonas, Lexington 195

Louisiana

1914 J. T. Austin, Monroe 98
1915 J. E. Ribb, Shreveport 94
1916 W. T. Wadley, Alexandria 95
1923 L. J. Davis, Bethany 195
1924 J. C. Lewis, Baton Rouge 193
1925 A. M. Perkins, Baton Rouge 193
1926 A. M. Perkins, Baton Rouge 194
1927 L. J. Davis, Bethany 196
1928 W. F. Taylor, Shreveport 196
1929 A. M. Perkins, Baton Rouge 197
1930 A. M. Perkins, Baton Rouge 195
1931 Fred Wappler, Shreveport 192
1932 A. M. Perkins, Baton Rouge 199
1933 J. P. Towery, Shreveport 196
1934 E. Robson, Cupples 198
1935 Fred Wappler, Shreveport 196
1936 H. C. Rogers, Shreveport 199
1937 T. O. Bancroft, Monroe 185
1938 H. C. Rogers, Shreveport 190
1941 M. Tinnelle, Shreveport 197

Maine

1915 E. A. Randall, Portland 99
1916 E. A. Randall, Portland 93
1917 E. A. Randall, Portland 95
1918 O. P. Weymouth, Portland 99
1919 A. H. Waldron, Richmond 286
1920 E. A. Randall, Portland 285
1925 W. G. Hill, Portland 192
1926 Dr. E. Paine, Waterville 188
1927 C. R. Blaisdell, Oakland 191
1928 C. W. Getchell, Waterville 191
1929 W. N. Seavey, Lovell 173
1930 W. N. Seavey, Lovell 196
1931 W. N. Seavey, Lovell 196
1932 W. N. Seavey, Lovell 196
1933 W. N. Seavey, Lovell 195
1934 F. K. Cole, Dover Foxcroft 192
1935 W. N, Seavey, Lovell 200
1936 J. H. Whitney, Portland 186
1937 C. R. Blaisdell, Oakland 191
1938 W. N. Seavey, Lovell 194
1939 W. N. Seavey, Lovell 196
1940 James E. Cousins, Salisbury Cove 192
1941 Dr. E. W. Paine, Waterville 192

Maryland

1914 D. F. Mallory, Baltimore (& D.C.) 97
1915 E. W. Ford, Baltimore (& D.C.) 97
1916 M. G. Gill, Baltimore (& D.C.) 98
1917 J. S. Michael, Aberdeen (& D.C.) 97
1918 R. D. Morgan, Washington (& D.C.) 97
1919 R. D. Morgan, Washington (& D.C.) 293
1920 E. L. Bartlett, Baltimore (& D.C.) 276
1921 R. M. Lee, Monkton (& D.C.) 191
1922 C. C. Fawsett, Washington (& D.C.) 188
1924 W. H. Hogarth, Baltimore (& D.C.) 189
1925 Frank Roseberry, Baltimore (& D.C.) 194
1926 C. C. Fawsett, Washington (& D.C.) 192
1927 C. M. Lanahan, Glencoe (& D.C.) 195
1928 R. M. Lee, Monkton (& D.C.) 197
1929 J. H. Hunter, Washington (& D.C.) 187
1930 C. W. Osborne, Aberdeen (& D.C.) 196
1931 R. M. Lee, Monkton 194
1932 Geo. Clark, Annapolis 198
1933 H. C. Krout, Maryland Line 197
1934 D. F. Beck, Havre De Grace 198
1935 D. F. Beck, Havre De Grace 194
1936 D. F. Beck, Havre De Grace 198
1937 D. F. Beck, Havre De Grace 198
1938 D. F. Beck, Havre De Grace 198
1939 J. C. Michael, Aberdeen 196
1940 J. F. McFadden, Pylesville 198
1941 J. F. McFadden, Pylesville 198

Massachusetts

1914 G. L. Osborn, Brookline 96
1915 E. A. Staples, Boston 98
1916 G. L. Osborn, Brookline 97
1917 S. W. Putnam, Fitchburg 98
1918 G. L. Osborn, Brookline 100
1919 G. L. Osborn, Brookline 287
1920 L. F. Curtis, Newton Highlands 272
1921 Jay Clarke, Jr., Worcester 193
1922 Leon H. Davis, Boston 197
1923 Leon H. Davis, Boston 197
1924 Jay Clarke, Jr., Worcester 191
1925 Leon Davis, Boston 194
1926 L. A. Gridley, Huntington 196
1927 Dud Shallcross, S. Seekonk 195
1928 Dud Shallcross, S. Seekonk 195
1929 W. A. Peterson, Lynn 198
1930 H. E. Lancey, Leominster 196
1931 W. A. Peterson, Lynn 193
1932 W. A. Peterson, Lynn 197
1933 G. M. Proctor, Lynn 193
1934 E. A. Staples, Framingham 186
1935 G. M. Proctor, Allston 199
1936 W. A. Peterson, Lynn 197
1937 G. M. Proctor, Allston 197

Massachusetts (Cont.)

1938 E. T. Rogers, Byfield 198
1939 W. A. Peterson, Lynn 198
1940 W. A. Peterson, Lynn 196
1941 G. M. Proctor, Greenwood 197

Michigan

1914 W. L. Stonehouse, Pontiac 96
1915 B. S. Gaylord, Owosso 93
1916 J. L. Bryant, Ceresco 98
1917 C. A. Galbraith, Bay City 100
1918 J. L. Bryant, Ceresco 93
1919 J. A. Skinner, Cedar Springs 296
1920 G. H. Slaughter, Benton Harbor 287
1921 J. A. Fesler, Detroit 198
1922 J. W. McLaughlin, Detroit 198
1923 Howard Benson, Lansing 195
1924 R. C. Miller, Lansing 199
1925 Karl Maust, Detroit 197
1926 Karl Maust, Detroit 197
1927 H. A. Bauknecht, Muskegon 197
1928 G. Slaughter, Benton Harbor 195
1929 Karl Maust, Detroit 197
1930 Sam Parker, Kalamazoo 199
1931 Karl Maust, Detroit 197
1932 Ned Lilly, Stanton 197
1933 Karl Maust, Detroit 197
1934 Karl Maust, Detroit 199
1935 Kurt Heide, Utica 198
1936 Ned Lilly, Stanton 199
1937 Fred Ford, Detroit 198
1938 Ned Lilly, Stanton 199
1939 Ned Lilly, Stanton 199
1940 Ned Lilly, Stanton 193
1941 Fred Ford, Detroit 200

Minnesota

1914 F. A. Richter, Minneapolis 98
1915 F. S. Novotney, St. Paul 96
1916 S. W. Hamilton, St. Paul 96
1917 C. A. Mason, Thief River Falls 99
1918 Dr. F. H. Allen, Staples 97
1919 J. Harker, Minneapolis 287
1920 F. A. Richter, Minneapolis 293
1921 L. Hezzelwood, Minneapolis 198
1922 Dave Fauskee, Worthington 194
1923 Dave Fauskee, Worthington 197
1924 Dr. Roy Williams, Brainerd 195
1925 Jack Frink, Worthington 191
1926 Dave Fauskee, Worthington 197
1927 Dave Fauskee, Worthington 197
1928 F. Theirault, Pennington 193
1929 J. E. Dickey, Minneapolis 196
1930 Ed Zweiner, Blooming Prairie 194
1931 F. D. Saunders, Minneapolis 198
1932 Jack Cunningham, Sturgeon Lake 198
1933 Geo. Jewett, Anoka 198
1934 Jack Cunningham, Sturgeon Lake 197
1935 Horace Aldritt, Excelsior 198
1936 Harry Maginnis, Minneapolis 196
1937 J. E. Kelley, St. Paul 199
1938 Art Finney, Mankato 197
1939 Fred Menth, Robbinsdale 200
1940 L. H. King, Fergus Falls 198
1941 Otto Nelson, Albert Lea 198

Mississippi

1914 G. M. L. Key, Meridian 93
1915 G. M. L. Key, Meridian 95
1916 F. P. Fitzgerald, Clarksdale 99
1917 L. J. Matlock, Ocean Springs 92
1918 G. M. L. Key, Meridian 94
1919 Chas Williams, Greenville 288
1920 W. H. Griffin, Greenville 291
1921 Chas. P. Williams, Greenville 199
1922 R. W. Baird, Inverness 192
1923 C. P. Williams, Greenville 197
1924 S. D. Dodds, Clarksdale 197
1925 J. A. Hardy, Columbus 195
1926 R. E. Stratton, Jr., Clarksdale 191

Mississippi (Cont.)

Year	Name	Score
1927	S. C. Ryals, Hollandale	195
1928	Dr. C. T. Cully, Greenville	194
1929	S. C. Ryals, Hollandale	186
1930	S. C. Ryals, Hollandale	194
1931	S. C. Ryals, Hollandale	194
1932	Dr. W. L. Stroupe, Corinth	194
1933	C. T. Cully, Greenville	196
1934	W. D. Atterbury, Estill	191
1935	S. W. Lawson, Grenada	190
1936	Dr. R. J. Brown, Iuka	185
1937	W. D. Atterbury, Estill	173
1938	L. L. Paxton, Leland	193
1939	Jack Condrey, Tupelo	199
1940	L. L. Paxton, Wilmot	196
1941	Ray Underwood, Corinth	196

Missouri

Year	Name	Score
1914	W. L. Mulford, Kirksville	99
1915	D. J. Holland, Springfield	100
1916	C. B. Eaton, Fayette	98
1917	Harve Dixon, Oronogo	99
1918	George Nicolai, Kansas City	97
1919	J. W. Akard, Fair Play	286
1920	Harve Dixon, Oronogo	294
1921	Harve Dixon, Oronogo	198
1922	W. S. Dempsey, Marshall	192
1923	E. H. Thomas, Pleasant Hill	192
1924	Ira Carroll, Kansas City	195
1925	A. M. McCrae, Lamar	194
1926	Ira Carroll, Kansas City	199
1927	Count Smyth, Lamar	197
1928	Ira Carroll, Kansas City	186
1929	J. R. Elliott, Kansas City	189
1930	W. W. Bradbury, St. Louis	186
1931	F. F. Wilmas, St. Louis	195
1932	George Jewett, Kansas City	195
1933	Dan Zimmer, Creve Coeur	195
1934	Amos Joe, Independence	196
1935	O. B. Franz, St. Louis	193
1936	G. H. Allen, Belton	195
1937	Russ Elliott, Raytown	197
1938	Dave Henry, Kansas City	198
1939	Dave Henry, Kansas City	199
1940	Dave Henry, Kansas City	199
1941	J. T. Frakes, Dearborn	197

Montana

Year	Name	Score
1914	Lee Williams, Deer Lodge	95
1915	C. L. Parsons, Straw	99
1916	C. P. Tilzey, Moore	98
1917	H. Schnack, Forsyth	98
1918	E. W. Renfro, Warm Springs	99
1919	E. L. Robbins, Billings	286
1920	P. H. O'Brien, Butte	292
1921	E. W. Renfro, Warm Springs	197
1922	W. J. Berrer, Lima	197
1923	E. W. Renfro, Warm Springs	195
1924	Lee Kimmel, Kalispell	189
1925	P. O'Brien, Butte	197
1926	Frank Knight, Great Falls	195
1927	W. R. Wilcoxson, Great Falls	196
1928	J. J. Robinson, Anaconda	200
1929	Guy Robinson, Livingston	198
1930	Fred P. Young, Butte	194
1931	V. Rothrock, Billings	195
1932	Roy Forrester, Dillon	197
1933	E. B. Stennark, Glendive	198
1934	E. W. Renfro, Dell	200
1935	E. W. Renfro, Dell	197
1936	E. W. Renfro, Dell	199
1937	E. G. Simmons, Butte	196
1938	Joe Latimer, Butte	200
1939	Lloyd Humber, Butte	196
1940	Herman Peterson, Dillon	197
1941	Joe Latimer, Butte	198

Nebraska

Year	Name	Score
1914	D. B. Thorp, Eagle	95
1915	H. J. Rebhausen, North Platte	95
1916	F. H. Rudat, Columbus	98
1917	C. L. Waggoner, Diller	95
1918	J. A. Nelson, Boelus	98
1919	E. W. Varner, Adams	291
1920	Oscar Hanson, Fremont	286
1921	E. F. Stegman, Chappell	195
1922	S. C. Tappen, Hoagland	196
1923	Ray Kingsley, Omaha	197
1924	E. L. Rhodes, Kearney	193
1925	S. C. Tappen, Hoagland	192
1926	Wm. Kaufman, Columbus	197
1927	E. W. Rhodes, Kearney	194
1928	C. L. Waggoner, Diller	200
1929	John A. Nelson, Boelus	193
1930	E. L. Rhodes, Kearney	196
1931	H. F. Richter, Fremont	197
1932	Cal Waggoner, Diller	199
1933	Al Koyen, Fremont	197
1934	F. D. Dailey, Fremont	200
1935	Eddie Dygert, Omaha	191
1936	W. Harder, Lincoln	195
1937	F. D. Dailey, Fremont	196
1938	Eddie Dygert, Omaha	191
1939	Art Carmody, Trenton	196
1940	Cal Waggoner, Diller	197
1941	V. W. Van, Wakefield	197

New Hampshire

Year	Name	Score
1915	Elmer E. Reed, Manchester	96
1916	H. E. Thompson, Manchester	94
1917	Elmer E. Reed, Manchester	93
1918	Elmer E. Reed, Manchester	95
1919	Mayor E. E. Reed, Manchester	279
1920	Elmer E. Reed, Manchester	278
1921	Elmer E. Reed, Manchester	177
1922	Elmer E. Reed, Manchester	189
1923	Mayor E. E. Reed, Manchester	189
1924	W. C. Lombardie, Nashua	190
1925	W. C. Lombardie, Nashua	181
1926	Mayor E. E. Reed, Manchester	193
1927	C. S. Henry, Nashua	184
1928	C. S. Henry, Nashua	189
1929	Chas. L. Isola, Mt. Vernon	192
1930	J. W. Shuttlesworth, Portsmouth	194
1931	W. C. Goss, Henniker	190
1932	W. C. Goss, Henniker	191
1933	W. C. Lombardie, Nashua	189
1934	Herb J. Carpenter, Franconia	193
1935	Dr. H. T. Paul, Portsmouth	193
1936	W. C. Lombardie, Nashua	191
1937	Jack Shuttlesworth, Portsmouth	192
1938	Jack Shuttlesworth, Portsmouth	193
1939	Jack Shuttlesworth, Portsmouth	196
1940	Jack Shuttlesworth, Portsmouth	196
1941	W. B. Farmer, Hampton Falls	197

New Jersey

Year	Name	Score
1914	Dr. W. H. Mathews, Trenton	95
1915	Fred Tomlin, Penns Grove	97
1916	C. W. Speer, Passaic	99
1917	C. B. Platt, Bridgeton	100
1918	Fred Tomlin, Penns Grove	98
1919	C. B. Platt, Bridgeton	289
1920	Fred Plum, Atlantic City	289
1921	C. B. Platt, Bridgeton	196
1922	M. S. Haines, Mt. Holly	195
1923	C. B. Platt, Bridgeton	198
1924	J. L. Wright, Medford	192
1925	T. D. Hackett, Atlantic City	195
1926	Leon Marcus, Collingswood	195
1927	E. B. Springer, Wildwood	195
1928	E. B. Springer, Wildwood	196
1929	T. D. Hackett, Atlantic City	198
1930	Clarence Kinsley, Pemberton	193
1931	W. H. Emme, Richwood	195

New Jersey (Cont.)

1932 L. R. Slocum, Trenton.................... 196
1933 Harry Messlor, Trenton.................... 200
1934 Harry Messlor, Trenton.................... 196
1935 L. R. Slocum, Trenton.................... 198
1936 J. D. Rowland, New Brunswick............ 198
1937 Ezra Olt, Maple Shade.................... 197
1938 L. Pagliughi, Vineland.................... 198
1939 Paul Holloway, Clementon................ 198
1940 L. R. Slocum, Trenton.................... 195
1941 Paul Davis, Woodstown.................... 197

New York

1914 Frank Wright, Buffalo.................... 98
1915 Hank Pendergast, Phoenix................ 97
1916 Hank Pendergast, Phoenix................ 100
1917 Hank Pendergast, Phoenix................ 100
1918 Hank Pendergast, Phoenix................ 99
1919 Frank Wright, Buffalo.................... 286
1920 Frank Wright, Buffalo.................... 283
1921 A. C. Skutt, Morton....................... 200
1922 Frank Wright, Buffalo.................... 199
1923 Frank Huseman, Buffalo.................. 198
1924 Frank Wright, Buffalo.................... 196
1925 Frank Wright, Buffalo.................... 194
1926 Frank Wright, Buffalo.................... 197
1927 Frank Wright, Buffalo.................... 199
1928 Ed La Claire, Buffalo.................... 99
1929 George Dickhart, Albany.................. 193
1930 L. B. Smith, Milbrook.................... 200
1931 L. B. Smith, Milbrook.................... 193
1932 W. H. Patterson, Buffalo.................. 199
1933 M. T. Davidson, Jamestown................ 198
1934 M. T. Davidson, Jamestown................ 198
1935 Elmer Torge, Wales Center................ 197
1936 Elmer Torge, Wales Center................ 199
1937 G. C. Lindsley, Marcellus.................. 200
1938 Elmer Torge, Wales Center................ 195
1939 E. B. Chamberlin, Martville.............. 198
1940 Don McClelland, Williamsville............ 196
1941 G. C. Lindsley, Marcellus.................. 198

North Carolina

1914 J. B. Pennington, Tarboro................ 90
1915 W. L. Hefner, Hickory.................... 98
1916 J. B. Pennington, Tarboro................ 94
1917 J. B. Pennington, Tarboro................ 97
1918 C. C. Bates, Charlotte.................... 97
1919 H. A. Morson, Charlotte.................. 279
1920 H. A. Morson, Charlotte.................. 280
1921 H. A. Morson, Charlotte.................. 188
1922 L. P. Hazel, Durham...................... 181
1923 L. P. Hazel, Durham...................... 193
1924 H. A. Page, Aberdeen.................... 191
1925 W. B. Arey, Salisbury.................... 187
1926 W. B. Arey, Salisbury.................... 196
1927 W. B. Arey, Salisbury.................... 190
1928 L. P. Hazel, Durham...................... 188
1929 D. H. McCullough, Charlotte.............. 189
1930 D. H. McCullough, Charlotte.............. 187
1931 D. H. McCullough, Charlotte.............. 192
1932 D. H. McCullough, Charlotte.............. 193
1933 Albert Tufts, Pinehurst.................. 182
1934 H. B. Arey, Salisbury.................... 192
1935 D. H. McCullough, Charlotte.............. 191
1936 D. H. McCullough, Charlotte.............. 185
1937 W. E. Gladstone, Winston-Salem.......... 195
1938 J. C. Parker, Winston-Salem.............. 194
1939 W. E. Gladstone, Winston-Salem.......... 196
1940 T. G. Proctor, Greenwood.................. 194
1941 T. G. Proctor, Greenwood.................. 192

North Dakota

1914 A. R. Chezik, Portal...................... 89
1915 J. W. Sturgeon, Dickinson................ 96
1916 F. Holland, Devils Lake.................... 97
1917 A. R. Chezik, Portal...................... 92
1918 A. R. Chezik, Portal...................... 97
1919 A. R. Chezik, Portal...................... 291
1920 A. R. Chezik, Portal...................... 287
1921 A. R. Chezik, Portal...................... 197

North Dakota (Cont.)

1922 D. C. Rand, Jamestown.................. 191
1923 A. R. Chezik, Portal...................... 195
1924 A. R. Chezik, Portal...................... 196
1925 A. R. Chezik, Portal...................... 195
1926 J. W. Sturgeon, Dickinson................ 196
1927 J. B. Troeh, Grand Forks.................. 194
1928 J. R. Pence, Minot........................ 194
1929 Frank Ray, Dickinson...................... 193
1930 W. H. Lenneville, Dickinson.............. 195
1931 Dr. J. R. Pence, Minot.................... 195
1932 Dr. J. R. Pence, Minot.................... 191
1933 O. L. Spencer, Grand Forks.............. 196
1934 E. C. Lenneville, Dickinson.............. 193
1935 Frank Ray, Dickinson...................... 195
1936 L. A. Hughes, Fargo...................... 193
1937 Frank Ray, Dickinson...................... 197
1938 C. C. Hullinger, Devils Lake.............. 196
1939 John Tsoumpas, Grand Forks.............. 196
1940 C. C. Hullinger, Devils Lake.............. 189
1941 Otto Gullingsrud, Grand Forks............ 193

Ohio

1914 J. N. Knox, Convoy...................... 99
1915 J. Rummell, Niles......................... 98
1916 Mark Hootman, Hicksville................ 99
1917 F. E. Brint, Toledo...................... 99
1918 J. E. Cain, Dayton........................ 97
1919 L. M. Weeden, Cleveland.................. 288
1920 Fred Harlow, Newark...................... 292
1921 A. E. Kroehle, Cleveland Heights.......... 196
1922 Fred Harlow, Newark...................... 196
1923 Ward Sharp, Washington Court House...... 198
1924 Fred Harlow, Newark...................... 198
1925 Homer Hirth, Marion...................... 197
1926 Charlie Young, Springfield................ 196
1927 S. D. Geddes, Harrisburg.................. 198
1928 W. I. Spangler, Tarlton.................. 196
1929 Charlie Bogert, Sandusky.................. 198
1930 H. F. Roberts, East Fultonham............ 198
1931 Joe Hiestand, Hillsboro.................. 199
1932 Charlie Bogert, Sandusky.................. 198
1933 C. F. Morgan, Corning.................... 198
1934 Bill Eldred, Cincinnati.................... 199
1935 C. F. Morgan, Corning.................... 193
1936 Charlie Young, Springfield................ 197
1937 Joe Hiestand, Hillsboro.................. 200
1938 Mark Hootman, Hicksville................ 198
1939 Joe Hiestand, Hillsboro.................. 200
1940 P. O. Harbage, West Jefferson............ 199
1941 Karl Maust, Columbus.................... 198

Oklahoma

1914 C. B. Homer, Ardmore.................... 95
1915 J. A. Campbell, Tulsa.................... 99
1916 J. N. Walker, Spiro...................... 94
1917 George W. Lewis, Garber.................. 98
1918 W. H. Heer, Guthrie...................... 99
1919 V. H. Francis, Drumwright................ 292
1920 E. C. Wheeler, Pawhuska.................. 288
1921 Bill Lambert, Oklahoma City.............. 198
1922 W. H. Heer, Guthrie...................... 199
1923 Gus Payne, Tulsa.......................... 196
1924 W. H. Heer, Guthrie...................... 198
1925 Gus Payne, Tulsa.......................... 198
1926 H. West, Tulsa............................ 188
1927 Gus Payne, Tulsa.......................... 196
1928 H. West, Tulsa............................ 196
1929 Gus Payne, Oklahoma City................ 198
1930 Bill Lambert, Oklahoma City.............. 197
1931 Clarence Lambert, Oklahoma City.......... 198
1932 Gus Payne, Oklahoma City................ 200
1933 Gus Payne, Oklahoma City................ 197
1934 Homer Bryant, Henryetta.................. 195
1935 G. S. Hilly, Oklahoma City.............. 195
1936 C. F. Williams, Tonkawa.................. 194
1937 Clarence Lambert, Oklahoma City.......... 197
1938 Hod Brown, Oklahoma City................ 197
1939 J. L. Lewis, El Reno...................... 195
1940 Clarence Lambert, Stillwater.............. 197
1941 E. N. Alley, Oklahoma City.............. 199

Howard Kieffer — Casper Hoffman — John Martin, Ed Colosky

GRAND AMERICAN
SUB AND JUNIOR CHAMPIONS

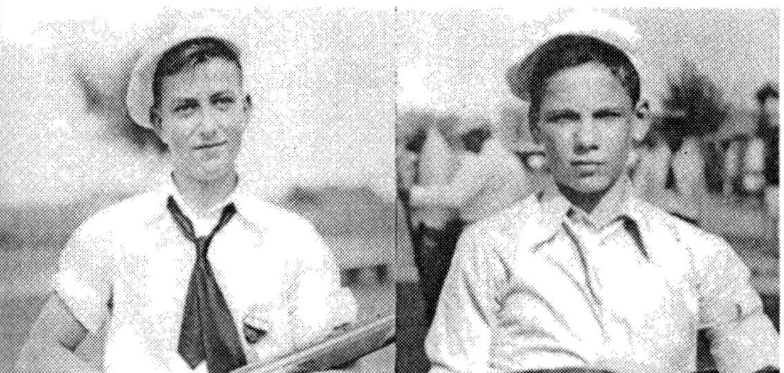

Bobby Stifal — O. B. Kiehl — Scotty Richards

S. Forsgard — Tobe Parks — Bobby Poore

Henry Rosenbrock (Champion), Bud McKinley (second) — Stanley Meadows, Ray Fienup, Rudy Etchen, Ned Lilly, Homer Clark, Jr.

Oregon

1914 Henry Wihlon, Portland.................... 98
1915 L. Rayburn, La Grande.................... 98
1916 P. H. O'Brien, Portland.................... 98
1917 J. W. Seavey, Portland.................... 98
1918 Frank Templeton, Portland................ 97
1919 J. W. Seavey, Portland.................... 293
1920 Jess Troeh, Portland...................... 289
1921 Abner Blair, Portland..................... 197
1922 J. W. Seavey, Portland.................... 195
1923 O. N. Ford, Portland...................... 194
1924 J. W. Seavey, Portland.................... 198
1925 Frank Troeh, Portland..................... 197
1926 R. F. Miller, Coquille.................... 197
1927 Frank Troeh, Portland..................... 198
1928 Frank Troeh, Portland..................... 199
1929 Frank Troeh, Portland..................... 193
1930 A. R. Parrott, Portland................... 197
1931-1940 (P.I.T.A. Shoots)
1941 R. D. Turner, Portland.................... 198

Pennsylvania

1914 W. S. Behm, Esterly...................... 98
1915 Charlie Newcomb, Philadelphia............. 98
1916 Allen Heil, Allentown..................... 100
1917 Roy McIntyre, Butler...................... 100
1918 Charlie Newcomb, Philadelphia............ 97
1919 Ed Hellyer, Jr., Alexandria............... 295
1920 Allen Heil, Allentown..................... 294
1921 Steve Crothers, Philadelphia.............. 196
1922 Steve Crothers, Philadelphia.............. 197
1923 W. C. Letterman, Lewiston................. 198
1924 Ed Hellyer, Alexandria.................... 197
1925 Steve Crothers, Philadelphia.............. 198
1926 Steve Crothers, Philadelphia.............. 197
1927 Allen Heil, Allentown..................... 197
1928 Steve Crothers, Philadelphia.............. 198
1929 W. B. Cochran, Kenneth Square............. 199
1930 Steve Crothers, Philadelphia.............. 200
1931 Steve Crothers, Philadelphia.............. 200
1932 Steve Crothers, Philadelphia.............. 199
1933 Steve Crothers, Philadelphia.............. 198
1934 Walter Beaver, Berwyn..................... 199
1935 Steve Crothers, Philadelphia.............. 199
1936 Steve Crothers, Philadelphia.............. 198
1937 Roy Hemming, Reading...................... 200
1938 Walter Beaver, Berwyn..................... 200
1939 Steve Crothers, Philadelphia.............. 199
1940 Steve Crothers, Philadelphia.............. 194
1941 Steve Crothers, Philadelphia.............. 199

Rhode Island

1916 W. J. Weaver, Providence.................. 95
1917 W. J. Weaver, Providence.................. 97
1918 W. J. Weaver, Providence.................. 93
1919 C. H. Dillon, Auburn...................... 282
1920 E. C. Griffith, Pascoag................... 278
1921 E. C. Griffith, Pascoag................... 189
1922 W. A. Barstow, N. Scituate................ 195
1923 A. T. Sisson, Providence.................. 192
1924 A. T. Sisson, Providence.................. 196
1925 E. C. Griffith, Pascoag................... 193
1926 A. T. Sisson, Providence.................. 191
1927 E. C. Griffith, Pascoag................... 190
1928 A. T. Sisson, Providence.................. 194
1933 A. J. Smith, Providence................... 190
1934 Dud Shallcross, Barrington................ 191
1935 K. A. Smith, Providence................... 178
1937 K. A. Smith, Providence................... 188
(Note: There was no state shoot in years that are missing.)

South Carolina

1915 J. H. Staples, Charleston................. 98
1916 J. H. Staples, Charleston................. 98
1917 J. H. Staples, Charleston................. 96
1918 R. G. McCants, Ninety-Six................. 94
1919 Paul Earle, Starr......................... 291
1920 Paul Earle, Starr......................... 288
1921 Paul Earle, Starr......................... 195

South Carolina (Cont.)

1922 J. H. Staples, Charleston................. 191
1923 Uley Brooks, Columbia..................... 196
1924 J. H. White, Spartanburg.................. 194
1925 Paul Earle, Starr......................... 193
1926 J. H. White, Spartanburg.................. 193
1927 Isaac Andrews, Spartanburg................ 194
1928 Paul Earle, Starr......................... 194
1929 Paul Earle, Starr......................... 194
1930 J. I. Chipley, Greenwood.................. 195
1931 J. I. Chipley, Greenwood.................. 194
1932 John G. Chafee, Aiken..................... 193
1933 M. T. La Fitte, Estill.................... 193
1934 John Chipley, Greenwood................... 198
1935 Paul Earle, Starr......................... 197
1936 Paul Earle, Starr......................... 188
1937 Paul Earle, Starr......................... 194
1938 Paul Earle, Starr......................... 195
1939 Paul Earle, Starr......................... 194
1940 Paul Earle, Starr......................... 192
1941 J. O. Rogers, Greenwood................... 196

South Dakota

1914 J. P. White, Watertown.................... 98
1915 A. J. French, Watertown................... 98
1916 J. C. Buzzell, Valley Springs............. 95
1917 E. T. Meyers, Mitchell.................... 98
1918 E. T. Meyers, Mitchell.................... 98
1919 Frank Hughes, Mobridge.................... 291
1920 George Kregor, Waubay..................... 295
1921 Frank Hughes, Mobridge.................... 190
1922 Ray Middaugh, Mitchell.................... 194
1923 H. G. Taylor, Meckling.................... 196
1924 Ray Middaugh, Mitchell.................... 196
1925 George Kregor, Waubay..................... 191
1926 Archie French, Watertown.................. 185
1927 Ed Smith, Aberdeen........................ 195
1928 Archie French, Watertown.................. 182
1929 A. Wallace, Canton........................ 193
1930 Wm. Bliss, Vermillion..................... 196
1931 Charlie Kaltschnee, Vayland............... 197
1932 Ben J. Mescher, Emery..................... 197
1933 Charlie Kaltschnee, Vayland............... 194
1934 Albert Seiner, Ethan...................... 194
1935 Archie French, Watertown.................. 194
1936 Archie French, Watertown.................. 197
1937 Ben J. Mescher, Emery..................... 198
1938 Jerry Wilson, Sisseton.................... 197
1939 H. Thoman, Huron.......................... 196
1940 Archie French, Watertown.................. 197
1941 H. Bloomenrader, Highmore................. 194

Tennessee

1914 Tom Hale, Mt. Pleasant.................... 97
1915 Tom Hale, Mt. Pleasant.................... 99
1916 Tom Hale, Mt. Pleasant.................... 97
1917 J. H. Fite, Mt. Pleasant.................. 99
1918 Boyd Duncan, Lucy......................... 95
1919 Ollie Williams, Nashville................. 288
1920 John Noel, Nashville...................... 295
1921 John Noel, Nashville...................... 197
1922 McGarock Hayes, Brentwood................. 192
1923 E. E. Buxton, Memphis..................... 184
1924 M. H. Cowan, Bristol...................... 187
1925 J. A. Kries, Knoxville.................... 191
1926 E. E. Buxton, Memphis..................... 193
1927 W. E. Rape, Chattanooga................... 195
1928 W. E. Rape, Chattanooga................... 193
1929 W. E. Rape, Chattanooga................... 194
1930 Tom Snowden, Memphis...................... 194
1931 Tom Snowden, Memphis...................... 198
1932 Tom Snowden, Memphis...................... 196
1933 W. E. Rape, Chattanooga................... 195
1934 J. A. Kries, Knoxville.................... 196
1935 J. A. Kries, Knoxville.................... 196
1936 John Noel, Nashville...................... 191
1937 Ed Luyben, Nashville...................... 191
1938 Ed Luyben, Nashville...................... 194
1939 John Noel, Nashville...................... 195
1940 Ed Luyben, Kingston Springs............... 194
1941 Boyd Duncan, Lucy......................... 198

Texas

1915 Tom Bryant, Houston...................... 99
1916 E. F. Forsgard, Waco...................... 95
1917 Forest McNeir, Houston................... 98
1918 Harley Woodward, Houston (15 years old).. 98
1919 Nic Arie, Menard......................... 289
1920 E. F. Woodward, Houston................. 295
1921 J. S. Day, San Antonio................... 197
1922 W. H. France, Houston.................... 199
1923 R. A. King, Wichita Falls................. 195
1924 A. V. Cocke, Wellington.................. 195
1925 E. F. Forsgard, Waco...................... 200
1926 E. F. Woodward, Houston................. 198
1927 E. F. Woodward, Houston................. 199
1928 E. F. Forsgard, Waco...................... 197
1929 E. F. Woodward, Houston................. 197
1930 E. F. Woodward, Houston................. 200
1931 E. F. Woodward, Houston................. 200
1932 John D. Clay, Houston.................... 197
1933 Harley Woodward, Houston................ 198
1934 H. A. Hausman, La Grange................ 200
1935 Forest McNeir, Houston................... 196
1936 Forest McNeir, Houston................... 198
1937 H. A. Hausman, Schuleberg............... 197
1938 Tommy Lovett, Houston................... 198
1939 H. A. Hausman, La Grange................ 200
1940 H. A. Hausman, La Grange................ 199
1941 Tom Lofland, Ft. Worth................... 198

Utah

1914 H. S. Mills, Salt Lake City................ 99
1915 C. H. Reilley, Jr., Salt Lake City......... 99
1916 A. P. Bigelow, Ogden..................... 100
1917 C. H. Reilley, Jr., Salt Lake City.......... 97
1918 Gus Becker, Ogden........................ 98
1919 C. H. Reilley, Jr., Salt Lake City......... 285
1920 C. H. Reilley, Jr., Salt Lake City......... 291
1921 E. F. Ford, Ogden......................... 196
1922 Sam Sharman, Salt Lake City............. 195
1923 Sam Sharman, Salt Lake City............. 194
1924 E. L. Ford, Ogden......................... 195
1925 E. L. Ford, Ogden......................... 194
1926 Sam Sharman, Salt Lake City............. 197
1927 E. L. Ford, Ogden......................... 198
1928 L. Hendershot, Ogden..................... 199
1929 Sam Sharman, Salt Lake City............. 200
1930 E. L. Ford, Ogden......................... 194
1931 Sam Sharman, Salt Lake City............. 198
1932 Sam Sharman, Salt Lake City............. 197
1933 C. B. Higgins, Ogden...................... 198
1934 Sam Sharman, Salt Lake City............. 195
1935 Alf Christenson, Ogden................... 194
1936 Dean Hurd, Salt Lake City................ 197
1937 Alf Christenson, Ogden................... 196
1938 C. B. Higgins, Ogden...................... 199
1939 Dean Hurd, Salt Lake City................ 198
1940 Dean Hurd, Salt Lake City................ 196
1941 Alf Christenson, Ogden................... 198

Vermont

1914 W. P. Twigg, St. Albans................... 89
1915 Dr. C. H. Burr, Montpelier................ 93
1916 D. M. Barclay, Barre...................... 94
1917 D. M. Barclay, Barre...................... 99
1918 D. M. Barclay, Barre...................... 95
1919 Dr. C. H. Burr, Montpelier................ 285
1920 Dr. C. H. Burr, Montpelier................ 277
1921 H. B. Moulton, Montpelier................ 193
1922 D. M. Barclay, Barre...................... 184
1923 Dr. C. H. Burr, Montpelier................ 190
1924 H. P. Sheldon, Montpelier................ 186
1925 H. F. Brugman, Rutland.................. 183
1926 L. L. Lane, Chester...................... 187
1927 H. B. Moulton, Montpelier................ 191
1928 L. L. Lane, Chester...................... 195
1929 L. L. Lane, Chester...................... 195
1930 Dr. M. P. Alexander, Rutland.............. 190
1931 L. L. Lane, Chester...................... 196

Vermont (Cont.)

1932 L. L. Lane, Chester....................... 198
1933 L. L. Lane, Chester....................... 196
1934 S. C. Wooden, Springfield................. 194
1935 M. K. Judd, White River Junction.......... 181
1936 W. E. Tresler, So. Hero.................. 176
1937 H. B. Moulton, Montpelier................ 176
1938 A. N. Practico, Rutland.................. 194
1939 A. N. Practico, Rutland.................. 190
1940 A. N. Practico, Rutland.................. 191
1941 H. B. Moulton, Montpelier................ 187

Virginia

1914 Dr. L. G. Richards, Roanoke............... 100
1915 W. D. Runnells, Staunton................. 98
1916 Dr. L. G. Richards, Roanoke............... 99
1917 R. A. Hall, Fisherville.................... 97
1918 E. C. Watson, Roanoke.................... 97
1919 W. D. Runnells, Staunton................. 291
1920 W. D. Runnells, Staunton................. 292
1921 E. M. Daniel, Lynchburg.................. 198
1922 H. C. Laird, Norfolk...................... 190
1923 A. F. Mercer, Norfolk..................... 197
1924 Dr. L. G. Richard, Roanoke................ 196
1925 W. D. Runnells, Staunton................. 193
1926 Miss Bessie Gleaves, Wytheville............ 192
1927 Dr. L. G. Richards, Roanoke............... 194
1928 Dr. H. M. Hayter, Abington............... 198
1929 C. B. Stickley, Vaucluse.................. 195
1930 H. C. Dodge, Tazewell.................... 196
1931 R. L. Bell, Norfolk....................... 196
1932 Dr. L. G. Richards, Roanoke............... 193
1933 Dr. L. G. Richards, Roanoke............... 197
1934 C. B. Stickley, Vaucluse.................. 196
1935 T. J. O'Connor, Ocean View............... 196
1936 C. J. Renner, Winchester.................. 198
1937 C. J. Renner, Winchester.................. 195
1938 C. J. Renner, Winchester.................. 197
1939 A. J. Wright, Roanoke..................... 193
1940 Col. J. R. Hall, Alexandria................ 198
1941 H. F. Mecum, Front Royal................. 196

Washington

1914 Frank Troeh, Vancouver................... 96
1915 E. J. Chingren, Spokane.................. 99
1916 Frank Troeh, Vancouver................... 97
1917 J. P. Hopkins, Seattle.................... 97
1918 Frank Troeh, Vancouver................... 98
1919 Frank Troeh, Vancouver................... 298
1920 Frank Troeh, Vancouver................... 295
1921 Frank Troeh, Vancouver................... 196
1922 Frank Troeh, Vancouver................... 198
1923 Jack McDonald, Yakima.................... 195
1924 H. B. Shuk, Yakima....................... 195
1925 Guy Egbers, Spokane...................... 197
1926 George Young, Sumner.................... 193
1927 George Young, Sumner.................... 194
1928 R. S. Searle, Seattle...................... 196
1929 Ed Schott, Yakima......................... 198
1930 J. D. Ankeny, Walla Walla................. 195
1932 Guy Egbers, Spokane...................... 194
1933 George Young, Sumner.................... 196
1934 Guy Chiesman, Spokane................... 198
1935 Guy Egbers, Spokane...................... 196
1936 Guy Egbers, Spokane...................... 198
1937 John D. Ankeny, Walla Walla.............. 197
1939 Guy Chiesman, Spokane................... 195
1940 Guy Chiesman, Spokane................... 198
1941 Earl Colson, Jr., Tacoma.................. 198

West Virginia

1914 W. A. Wiedebusch, Fairmont.............. 96
1915 H. L. Smith, Charleston.................. 100
1916 W. A. Wiedebusch, Fairmont.............. 99
1917 W. E. Meyers, Richwood.................. 98
1918 G. H. Meade, Huntington................. 96
1919 Richard Gerstell, Jr., Grafton............. 277
1920 J. B. Lallance, Huntington................ 289
1922 Ira Williams, St. Marys................... 186
1923 Dr. P. C. Showalter, Clarksburg........... 193

West Virginia (Cont.)

1924	L. E. Burrough, Parkersburg	190
1925	Ira Williams, St. Marys	189
1926	E. H. McDonald, Headsville	188
1927	Dr. Roscoe Stotts, Kenova	193
1928	C. H. Bivens, Elkhorn	194
1929	Wm. Beury, Algoma	196
1930	A. N. Davis, Charleston	195
1931	E. C. Sesler, Devilsfork	194
1932	E. H. McDonald, Headsville	197
1933	W. W. Pollack, Mullens	196
1934	C. H. Bivens, Elkhorn	194
1935	Ernie Wolfe, Charleston	192
1936	E. P. Smith, Jr., Fairmont	195
1937	C. H. Bivens, Elkhorn	191
1938	E. H. McDonald, Headsville	193
1939	L. M. La Follette, Charleston	198
1940	L. M. La Follette, Charleston	199
1941	E. H. McDonald, Headsville	199

Wisconsin

1914	F. J. Dreyfus, Muskego	95
1915	Guy Dering, Columbus	98
1916	A. Bushman, Burlington	99
1917	Charlie Larson, Waupaca	99
1918	Charlie Larson, Waupaca	97
1919	F. G. Fuller, Mukwonago	294
1920	Guy Dering, Columbus	293
1921	G. L. Landis, Milwaukee	196
1922	Oscar Larson, Waupaca	198
1923	Claude Olney, West Allis	200
1924	Claude Olney, West Allis	195
1925	Claude Olney, West Allis	189
1926	Dr. F. S. Cook, Eau Claire	196
1927	Harry Billett, Oconomowoc	198
1928	E. H. Alff, Columbus	199
1929	Fred Ludington, Wauwatosa	200
1930	Fred Ludington, Wauwatosa	197
1931	Guy Dering, Columbus	200
1932	Les Frint, Milwaukee	197
1933	Harry Billett, Oconomowoc	198
1934	Willis Spence, La Crosse	196
1935	Harry Billett, Oconomowoc	195
1936	Carl Koeffler, Milwaukee	197
1937	Roland Schroeder, Woodland	198
1938	Vic Reinders, Waukesha	196
1939	Vic Reinders, Waukesha	197
1940	Vic Reinders, Waukesha	198
1941	Vic Reinders, Waukesha	198

Wyoming

1914	See California	
1915	See California	
1916	Max Weick, Laramie	95
1917	J. H. Bradfield, Sheridan	91
1918	W. R. Tarrant, Buffalo	97
1919	A. C. Rice, Douglas	292
1920	E. C. Ward, Thermopolis	286
1921	E. C. Ward, Thermopolis	195
1922	John Evers, Green River	197
1923	L. E. Smith, Glen Rock	197
1924	Adam Helzer, Sheridan	195
1925	Carl Nelson, Green River	189
1926	Carl Nelson, Green River	191
1927	Carl Nelson, Green River	197
1928	A. H. Remington, Cheyenne	198
1929	Matt Katmo, Laramie	198
1930	A. H. Remington, Cheyenne	197
1931	Carl Nelson, Green River	192
1932	Max Weick, Laramie	194
1933	Carl Nelson, Green River	186
1934	A. H. Remington, Cheyenne	194
1935	E. C. Romine, Casper	192
1936	E. A. Schupbach, Torrington	192
1937	E. A. Schupbach, Torrington	197
1938	L. A. Reeves, Evanston	197
1939	O. E. Spangler, Casper	193
1940	C. W. Brock, Casper	195
1941	E. A. Schupbach, Torrington	187

Canal Zone

1921	A. C. Garlington, Balboa	184
1922	Albert Connor, Balboa	184
1923	A. C. Garlington, Balboa	196
1924	A. C. Garlington, Balboa	188
1925	A. C. Garlington, Balboa	193
1926	A. C. Garlington, Balboa	189
1927	J. R. Strauss, Balboa	190
1928	J. W. Ludlum, Balboa	192
1929	J. W. Ludlum, Balboa	179
1930	A. C. Garlington, Balboa	193
1931	A. C. Garlington, Balboa	194
1932	P. M. Disharoon, Balboa	189
1933	A. C. Garlington, Balboa	198
1934	P. M. Disharoon, Balboa	190
1935	A. C. Garlington, Balboa	193
1936	A. C. Garlington, Balboa	197
1937	P. M. Disharoon, Balboa	195
1938	P. J. Jones, Cristobal	194
1939	P. M. Disharoon, Balboa	194
1940	P. J. Jones, Cristobal	195
1941	P. J. Jones, Cristobal	193

Nevada

1925	H. M. Gallagher	194
1931	Al Brundige, Reno	189
1932	Walter Warren, Sparks	197
1933	Henry Rosenbrock, Gardnersville	194

British Columbia

1920	Dr. A. R. Baker, Vancouver	280x300
1921	E. J. Cameron, Vancouver	185
1922	C. W. MacLean, Vancouver	191
1925	True H. Oliver, Ladner	197
1926	C. D. Boardman, Vancouver	193
1927	True H. Oliver, Ladner	193
1928	C. W. MacLean, Vancouver	195
1929	C. W. MacLean, Vancouver	191

Alberta

1920	Walter Holmes, Edmonton	286x300
1921	W. B. McLaren, Calgary	189
1922	Chris Irgen, Edmonton	193
1924	H. A. Simpson, Calgary	167x175
1925	Rene Beese, Calgary	191
1926	C. A. Voight, Calgary	176
1927	H. A. Simpson, Calgary	195
1928	H. A. Simpson, Calgary	196
1929	Dr. J. D. Stewart, Calgary	188
1930	H. A. Simpson, Calgary	195
1931	W. J. Muirhead, Calgary	196
1932	Frank Pilling, Cardston	184
1933	H. A. Simpson, Calgary	193
1934	W. J. Muirhead, Calgary	194
1935	E. M. Rousch, Hardisty	194
1936	W. J. Muirhead, Calgary	195
1937	W. J. Muirhead, Calgary	196
1938	W. J. Muirhead, Calgary	197
1939	D. M. Blow, Calgary	193
1940	D. M. Blow, Calgary	194
1941	C. W. Davis, Clover Bar	196

Manitoba—Saskatchewan

1919	W. M. Hamilton, Winnipeg	288
1920	R. Dill, Saskatoon	253
1921	Johnny Black, Winnipeg	196
1922	Chummey Plummer, Swan River	188
1923	Wm. Geatros, Weyburn	188
1924	Chummey Plummer, Swan River	185
1925	Wm. Geatros, Weyburn	192
1926	P. G. Schwager, Dundurn	183
1927	P. G. Schwager, Dundurn	192
1929	P. G. Schwager, Dundurn	197
1930	Tom Harland, Winnipeg	195
1932	Jimmy Girgulis, Saskatoon	195
1933	Jimmy Girgulis, Saskatoon	199

Manitoba-Saskatchewan (Cont.)

1934	Jimmy Girgulis, Saskatoon	194
1935	Bert Brodie, Winnipeg	178
1936	Bert Brodie, Winnipeg	193
1937	Jimmy Girgulis, Saskatoon	195
1938	Jimmy Girgulis, Saskatoon	192
1939	Chummey Plummer, Flin Flon	190
1940	Chummey Plummer, Flin Flon	197
1941	No shoot held	

Ontario

1919	Sam Vance, Tilsonburg	290
1920	Sam Vance, Tilsonburg	294
1921	J. E. Jennings, Todmorden	199
1922	Sam Vance, Tilsonburg	198
1924	J. L. McQuaig, Toronto	195
1925	G. S. Abbott, Ottawa	189
1926	Sam Vance, Tilsonburg	194
1927	Sam Vance, Tilsonburg	194
1928	G. A. Marr, Woodstock	199
1929	G. A. Marr, Woodstock	197
1930	G. A. Reynolds, Montreal (Queb. & Ont.)	194
1931	R. J. Coleman, Hamilton	193
1932	Dr. P. C. Banghart, London	193
1933	J. E. Milne, Hamilton	190
1934	Dr. P. C. Banghart, London	192
1935	J. H. Kretschman, Hamilton	192
1936	W. Peters, Chatham	196
1937	J. E. Milne, Hamilton	200
1938	J. E. Milne, Hamilton	196
1939	J. H. Kretschman, Hamilton	193
1940	W. Peters, Chatham	191
1941	W. Peters, Chatham	192

Cuba

1941	Carlos Quintero, Havana	193

P.I.T.A. (Pacific Coast State Champions) 200 Targets

1931	Dr. H. W. Armstrong, Los Angeles	199
1932	O. N. Ford, Del Monte	195
1933	Dr. J. H. Bradfield, Monterey	196
1934	A. J. Stauber, Los Angeles	196
1935	A. J. Stauber, Los Angeles	198
1936	Don Traynham, Los Angeles	199
1937	Grant Ilseng, Los Angeles	195
1938	E. Carstens, Camino	198
1939	Al Elasho, Monterey	198
1940	Don Traynham, Woodland	197
1941	Gene Robertson, Los Angeles	196

British Columbia

1940	Dr. W. R. Leonard, Trail	98x100

Idaho

1931	W. A. Stevens, Boise	198
1932	Guy Chiesman, Lewiston	200
1933	W. A. Stevens, Boise	199
1934	W. A. Stevens, Boise	197
1935	J. C. Gray, Nampa	197
1936	J. C. Gray, Nampa	195
1937	Joe Cotant, Pocatello	194
1938	Joe Cotant, Pocatello	196
1939	Joe Cotant, Pocatello	195
1940	J. C. Gray, Nampa	198
1941	Floyd Deeder, Kellogg	196

Montana

1938	Joe Latimer, Butte	200
1939	Lloyd Humber, Butte	196

Oregon

1931	Frank Troeh, Portland	200
1932	Frank Troeh, Portland	196
1933	Frank Troeh, Portland	200
1934	Frank Troeh, Portland	198
1935	Frank Troeh, Portland	199
1936	Frank Troeh, Portland	197
1937	Frank Troeh, Portland	197
1938	Frank Troeh, Portland	198
1939	Frank Troeh, Portland	198

GRAND AMERICAN PRELIMINARY HANDICAP WINNERS

Billy Hoon (1912)

Johnny Fontaine (1929)

L. R. Slagle (1938)

M. L. Fox (1921) Harry Taylor (1922) Mike Weisman (1924)

C. E. Leek (1927) F. B. Hoggatt (1928) Jean Pope (1930)

Bobby Olds (1932) H. S. Shellito (1933) Henry Holbrook (1934)

/alter Winteringham (1939) Roy Miller (1940) Elmer Lucas (1941)

Oregon (Cont.)

1940	Frank Troeh, Portland	197
1941	O. S. Shiffer, Forest Grove	199

Utah

1931	C. B. Higgins, Ogden	196
1932	Cliff Anderson, Spring City	192
1933	Dean Hurd, Salt Lake City	200
1934	Gus Becker, Ogden	193
1935	Sam Sharman, Salt Lake City	197
1936	Sam Sharman, Salt Lake City	196
1937	Sam Sharman, Salt Lake City	196
1938	C. B. Higgins, Ogden	195
1940	Dean Hurd, Salt Lake City	198
1941	R. E. Fergason, Salt Lake City	196

Wyoming

1940	George Robinson, Evanston	183

Washington

1931	R. D. McFarland, Ritzville	198
1932	George Young, Sumner	196
1933	George Young, Sumner	197
1934	George Young, Sumner	197
1937	Dr. Richard Flaherty, Spokane	197
1938	L. A. Marks, Castle Rock	194
1939	Guy Chiesman, Spokane	195
1940	W. V. Henderson, Seattle	188
1941	E. E. Colson, Jr., Tacoma	198

When it comes to all-around sportsmen and all-around shooters, don't overlook this fellow E. L. Hawkins from Ft. Wayne, Indiana. Listen to this: He won the Indiana State Skeet Championship in 1940 with 197 out of 200, won the Grand American Preliminary Handicap in 1936 and the world's doubles championship in 1940

HISTORY OF SKEET

PART II

HISTORY OF SKEET

The seed of this great outdoor sport, skeet, was planted on the grounds of the Glen Rock Kennels in the town of Andover, Massachusetts. Here a small group of upland shooters, composed principally of the late Bill Foster and C. E. Davis, proprietor of the Glen Rock Kennels, his son, Henry W., used to shoot at clay targets as a means of obtaining wing-shoot practice with their favorite upland guns. There was nothing remarkable about this since similar groups of sportsmen, realizing the possibilities of the clay target as a substitute for live game, have done the same thing before and since.

This form of practice was followed at the Glen Rock field between the years 1910 and 1915. Between 1915 and 1920 a friendly rivalry had sprung up between the trio that led to the establishment of a program that gave each shooter the same series of shots in order that the competition might be even.

This arrangement was a complete circle of twenty-five yards radius with the circumference marked off like the face of a clock. The trap was set at "12 o'clock" and set to throw the targets over "6 o'clock." The competitive program consisted of shooting two shots from each of twelve stations. The shell that was left over from the box was used, first just as a stunt, to shoot an incomer from the center of the circle. This later proved to be a shot offering real snap-shooting practice and has since developed into the plan of Station 8 shots of the regulation program.

The "shooting around the clock," as it was informally called in 1920, had most of the elements of modern Skeet shooting and several local sportsmen besides the original trio tried their hand at this sport; their enthusiastic efforts soon indicated that this form of shooting had the earmarks of a new and separate sport.

A commonplace incident then occurred that had a distinct bearing on the shooting program. In "shooting around the clock" shots were fired to all points of the compass. In the clock shooting what there was of a gallery followed the shooter around as did the trap attendant who pulled the trap with a long cord. Over in an adjoining lot a neighbor started a hen farm that put a stop to shooting in that direction. W. H. Foster solved the difficulty by producing a second trap and placing it at "6 o'clock" so that it would throw its target over "twelve." This gave the same problems as were found in the original clockface, but restricted the danger zone to an area only about half the size of the original one.

Mr. Foster entered the employ of National Sportsmen, Inc., publishers of National Sportsman and Hunting and Fishing magazines, as assistant editor in 1920. He published articles on "clock" shooting in the November, 1920, and November, 1922, issues of National Sportsmen.

Between the years 1920 and 1926, the same small group, now and then augmented by a few enthusiastic visitors, continued to shoot clay targets for practice during the closed season on game, using the half clockface arrangement with the two traps. Occasionally some improvement was made to give a closer parallel to game shooting situations. Chief among these was the elevation of one of the traps in order to obtain a target of flatter flight in contrast to the rising target from the other trap.

Noting the appeal that this form of shooting held for all who had a chance to try it, Mr. Foster became convinced that development of the idea could be made nationally accepted. He therefore set about to complete a shooting program that would contain all the necessary elements of a practical form of wing-shooting practice and a competitive sport. Among the additions was the introduction of four sets of doubles and the optional shot.

When the details of the sport had been worked out and tested and a set of shooting rules drawn up, the idea was introduced to the public in 1926. At the same time the National Sportsmen's magazine offered a prize of $100.00 for the most appropriate name for the new sport. Mrs. Gertrude Hurlbutt, of Dayton, Montana, suggested "Skeet," an old Scandinavian form of the word "shoot," and her suggestion received the award.

Henry Ahlin, Boston, is manager and president of the National Skeet Association. Mr. Foster died in 1941.

NATIONAL SKEET CHAMPIONS

1935—L. S. PRATT

L. S. Pratt, Indianapolis, Indiana, won the first National Skeet tourney staged at Cleveland, Ohio, August 25 to 31, 1935. Pratt, comparatively a youngster, broke 244 out of 250 to score a clean-cut victory.

On Thursday, the first day of the National championship, Pratt broke 99 out of 100, which found him in a tie with the famous Ollie Mitchell of Natick, Massachusetts, who was an All-American at that time.

On Friday, Pratt continued his march to victory with a 97, while Ollie dropped to 95. In the meantime, Phil Conway of New York, 17 years of age, and W. A. Jackson, the Keystone "ace," had forged up in the runner-up spot—these three gunners had 194's, two targets behind the fast-stepping Indianapolis star. Two targets might seem a big lead in the final 50 targets which were to be shot on the following day to determine the champion, but clay birds are slippery and the strain was terrific on the Hoosier lad.

Pratt, in an early squad, missed two targets, finished with 244 out of 250. Conway, too, felt the strain, and dropped two birds, while Mitchell and Jackson each muffed three. In the meantime, E. L. Marshall, the Birmingham policeman, had been plugging along and he finished with the good score of 242

Billy Clayton

Esther Abbie Ingalls and Max Marcum

as well, which placed him in a tie with Conway for second honors. The New York gunner won the shoot-off.

Other leaders were Ollie Mitchell, 241; Jack Tway, Atlanta, Georgia, 241; W. A. Jackson, 241; Fred Nordin, Minneapolis, 240; Dave Sklar, Brooklyn, New York, 240; L. C. Delmonico, New Jersey ace, 240, and G. E. Crosby, Missouri, same score. Nordin won the shoot-off for seventh place.

Curly haired Max Marcum, Louisville, Kentucky, captured the Junior championship with 98 out of 100, followed by Bobby Stack, Los Angeles, and Billy Clayton of Calvin, Oklahoma, both of whom scored 96's. Stack won the shoot-off. Right here might be a good place to mention the 13-year-old Dick Shaughnessy of Boston, who broke a 95 for fourth place. This was the first time that I had watched him shoot. In future years he was to become one of the greatest skeet shots of all times.

Harold Russell, for years one of the leading trapshooters in Minnesota, scored a clean-cut victory in the Professional or Industry race, when he scored 97 out of 100. Clyde Mitchell, Minneapolis, was second with 95 out of 100; Buddy Jones of Atlanta, Georgia, was third, while Charlie Van Studdiford, Detroit, Michigan, placed fourth with 94.

It was a walkaway for Miss Abbie Ingalls in the Women's race, when she scored a 95. Abbie lives in Hot Springs, Virginia. Mrs. Sid Small, a great shot at that time, from Detroit, Michigan, was second, with 92.

Henry Joy, Detroit, was the star of the tournament. This popular gunner won the 20-Gauge championship with 98 out of 100, edging out Bobby Stack of California by one target. Then came C. H. Seymour with 96, and L. S. Pratt and J. G. Dimond with 94's.

The Smallbore championship was a thriller, with Billy Clayton, the junior gunner, and Henry Joy breaking 94's for first position. The 17-year old Clayton copped the title with 25 straight in the shoot-off. Clarence Mitchell, brother of Ollie, from Waltham, Massachusetts, was third with 93, while Max Marcum came up with 92 for fourth place.

It was Clarence Mitchell's turn in the Sub-smallbore championships, but only after a heated shoot-off with Henry Joy, who had shot well during the entire meet. They had broken 89's. Four gunners, J. T. McMillan, Detroit; Phil Conway,

Ed Garland, Belleville, New Jersey, and D. R. Nichols, West Orange, New Jersey, followed with 88's. J. T. McMillan won the shoot-off for third place.

Clay "Boid" John Couzens was in charge of the referees. Several years ago John's eyes went bad on him, so Henry Ahlin made him a big league skeet umpire . . . I took great pleasure in taking a buck out of "Dead Eye" John Hession of New Haven on the outcome of the shoot . . . Jake Taylor, the guy with the broad smile, is a big attorney from "way down yonder in Alabam' " . . . John Olin, the Western executive, and Cap Crossman were late for the banquet. . . . Lt. Jim Culley is a New York police officer and a swell fellow.

Jack Guenveur and John Du Puis made a couple of fine toastmasters at the banquet and were louder than a couple of Lake of the Woods loons on a stormy night. . . . The kids, Marcum, Stack, Clayton, Joy and Conway stole the show, and, as Frank Traeger, the All-American, said, "I spent a hundred bucks to come down here and let a bunch of school kids show me the ins and outs of skeet."

The Nationals attracted 168 different gunners from 27 states for the first shoot, reminding us that the first Grand American trapshoot at New York in 1900 had 74 shooters. . . . It was my suggestion that we start class shooting at the Nationals, just as they do at the Grand American. . . . After the main race Pratt and Jack Tway were challenging everybody, beating nobody. . . . I'd like to see a special race between five-foot, 100-pound Abbie Ingalls and Atlanta's Buddy Jones. They tied with 95 out of 100 Thursday. . . . Harry Fleischmann brought along young Bobby Stack to trim him. (Both, by the way, are now in the movies, and Bobby is still trimming him.)

Morris Ackermann, an outdoor editor, enjoyed every minute of the shoot. . . . Ralph Shattuck did the announcing and didn't mind it a bit. His side-kick, Jim Scholl, worked day and night. What a bunch, these Cleveland boys; Shattuck, Scholl, Turnock, Conkey and Carson. . . . Buddy Jones brought along a squad of youngsters from Atlanta and Tom Yawkey, multimillionaire owner of the Boston Red Sox, entertained them and yours truly at the Boston-Cleveland game Wednesday.

Every winner was presented with his trophy and given a

nice sendoff from Manager Henry Ahlin and President Bill Foster. . . . Ed Cave spent the week taking photos for his yearly booklet, and we must all agree that Ed knows his onions. . . . Big "Bill" Jackson from Conneaut Lake, Pennsylvania, who tied with Ollie Mitchell and Jack Tway for fourth place, is quite a guy. . . . Fred Nordin, the Minneapolis photographer, was as steady as Gibraltar when he edged out Sklar, Delmonico and Crosby for seventh place in the Championship race.

Nothing missed the eagle eye of Charlie Hopkins, the Western "dynamo," who watched the champs churn up the clays. . . . Mrs. Sid Small, Detroit, whom we hailed as the world's greatest woman skeet shot a few years ago, shot below her average. . . . Art Farian, Al Ormsbee, Henry Winchester and Jack Guenveur took care of the office and did a bang-up job. . . . Red Boardman, freckles and all, aged nine, was the center of attraction with his big, double gun. Red lives in Georgia. . . . Fritz Howell, A. P. sports writer from Columbus, Ohio, who handles the A. P. at the Grand American each year, did a good job on getting the results of the first Nationals to all parts of the country.

1936—DICK SHAUGHNESSY

Richard Shaughnessy, 14-year old Boston schoolboy, won the second annual Skeet championship, staged at St. Louis, Missouri, in 1936.

Shaughnessy, who had broken 92 out of 100 earlier in the week to win the Junior title, blasted his way to the highest pinnacle of skeetdom, winning the Individual championship with 248 out of a possible 250.

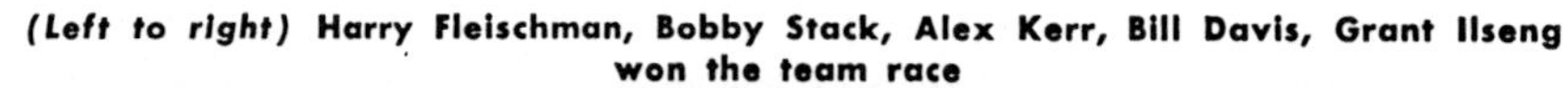

***(Left to right)* Harry Fleischman, Bobby Stack, Alex Kerr, Bill Davis, Grant Ilseng won the team race**

Kenneth Miller won the Smallbore title with 100 straight. Miller *(at the left)* is pictured with Charlie King of Texas and big Dutch Heath of Oklahoma

Dick's victory was decisive only by the narrow margin of one clay target. A young polo playing millionaire from Santa Monica, curly headed 17-year-old Bobby Stack, was right behind the eastern "flash" with 247. Stack still shoots, is now better known as a movie star.

Billy Clayton, Oklahoma star, and big Grant Ilseng of Los Angeles, followed in the big race. Walter Forest, another California "ace," turned in the lone 245 for fifth rung. There were two 244's, Harry Fleischmann's, California, and Henry Joy's, of Detroit.

Bobby Stack won the 20-Gauge championship with 99 out of 100. Again Billy Clayton showed his prowess with his shotgun when he broke a 98 in this competition. He tied for second place but was defeated by Phil Conway of New York in the shoot-off. Walter Forest and Harry Fleischmann finished with 97's.

Kenneth Miller, from Texas, created somewhat of a furore when he crashed 100 straight to win the Smallbore championship. He led this fast field by three targets, and Alex Kerr, the Beverly Hills, California, sporting goods proprietor, turned in the lone 97 for second honors. Grant Ilseng and Phil Conway followed with 96's.

The Sub-smallbore title went to Billy Clayton, who scored 95 out of 100. W. P. Conway, New York City, was next with 94 while Dick Shaughnessy hung up a 93 for third.

Miss Betty Small, Detroit, captured the Women's cham-

(Left to right) Betty Small, Mrs. Sidney Small, Mrs. H. B. Joy and Mrs. W. H. Simons. Mrs. Small won the Lordship Women's title in 1932 and 1934

pionship with 89 out of 100, but only after a shoot-off with Mrs. Dan Rice of Wheaton, Illinois.

The Team race, a new feature at the Nationals, was won by the Los Angeles Santa Monica club by a city block when they scored 1,217 out of 1,250. Their lineup included Bob Stack, Bill Davis, Alex Kerr, Grant Ilseng and Harry Fleischmann.

Bobby Parker, Tulsa, won the Sub-junior with 48 out of 50, with Junior Baldridge of Terre Haute in second position. Billy Clayton proved that he was the best all-around pointer of the tourney when he led the entire field by four targets, breaking 530 out of a possible 550. Harry Fleischmann and Phil Conway followed with 526. The professional All-around title went to Ed Lindsay of Paris, Texas, who scored 513 out of 550. He also won the professional Individual title with 241 out of 250, three targets in front of another great Texan, Herman Ehler.

Phil Conway won the class A championship with 242 out of 250 and the other class victors were J. P. Harvey, B, with 241; R. M. Wilson, C, with 233; Miss Viola Siedhoff, D, with 221, and Bobby Parker, E, with 216.

There were 210 entries in the Individual championship race. The shoot was held at the Bridlespur Hunt Club and much of the success of this great shoot was due to the efforts of the popular and well known St. Louis sportsman, Joe Werner. Henry Ahlin, secretary of the National Skeet Association, was in charge of the shoot.

George Sisler, the noted St. Louis baseball star, and I announced results of the shoot each night over KWK in St. Louis, where George conducts a daily sports broadcast. . . . Emmett Marshall, Birmingham star, crashed through with a 99 Friday. . . . "It just wasn't my week," moaned T. K. Lee of Alabama, one of the world's greatest all-around shots. . . . O. L. Harrison, Dayton, Ohio, sportsman, was one of the men responsible for trapshooting's permanent home at Dayton. . . . Bottles Ketchum, the St. Louis beer king, was one of the outstanding entertainers. . . . Grand bunch of boys from Tyler, Texas, all oil men, are Kenneth Miller, Staley, Strickland, Wiley and Peavey. And don't overlook John Lawhon, the attorney, Wooley from Longview and McCarter from Corsicana.

If the National championship had been decided on 100 targets, Harry Fleischmann, with his 100 straight, would have been the winner. It was the only 100 straight on opening day. . . . Vic Bracher, now of San Antonio, Texas, was busier than a hen mallard at nesting time taking photos of the various shooters. . . . Doug Hadden wore the classiest shooting jacket on the grounds. . . . "Doc" Wallace and his pretty wife were on hand from St. Joe, Missouri. . . . California's second team, with Mel Morgan, H. F. Byrd, Dick Bloomfield, Walter Forest and Odis Walding in their lineup, staged a whirlwind finish and broke 125 straight. "That's one record that they can't take away from us," smiled Mel Morgan, who is interested in the Sunkist orange plant at Pasadena.

"We wuzz robbed," yelled Paul Osterbeck of Michigan when Shaughnessy busted 248 to win. . . . Ted Lyons, Sugar Cain and Joe Morrissy of the Chicago White Sox were visitors Friday. . . . Genial Roy Swan, who puts on the Lordship show each year, can't sit still a minute. . . . Viola Siedhoff, Wichita, Kansas, gunner, took class D over all men and women. . . . Bobby Parker, 12-year old, won the Sub-junior and E class Individual championships. . . . It was just about all Missouri in the C class contest, with R. M. Wilson, Monroe City, in first place; P. E. Conrades, second, and Dr. W. P. Birney, fifth. . . . Johnny Manlove, Minneapolis, took third place over the big Indian boy, Harry Bolton, from Oklahoma, who placed fourth.

Everett Herrick was the only Missouri gunner to place in the Championship race. Herrick busted 242 out of 250, tying with W. P. Conway for tenth place. . . . Six out of 10 high gunners in the 250 target championship race were from California. . . . We can't overlook the popular Louis Grammes from York, Pennsylvania, who tied Viola Siedhoff for D class honors. . . . Three top places in the B class 20-Gauge competition went to Wolverines Osterbeck, Sperry and Dick Hecker. . . . Thursday was an off day for the St. Louis Browns, so Russ Van Atta, who winters in Florida, and never misses a trapshooting tourney down there, and Beau Bell, the slugger, and Augi Guiliani, the catcher, took in the shoot.

1937—ODIS WALDING

Odis Walding, 38-year old dry cleaning plant operator from Hollywood, who had been shooting skeet only 20 months, was the victor of the third National championships staged at Detroit, Michigan, in 1937. Walding won that year with a score of 248 out of 250. Again it was Bobby Stack of California who placed second with 247, but only after breaking 75 straight in the shoot-off to defeat Paul Osterbeck of Michigan, Dave Sklar of Brooklyn and the famed Frank Kelly of New Jersey, one of the skeet leaders of this era. They finished in that order after the shoot-off.

Walding shot a fine race from start to finish. After the first day's shooting, which he finished with 100 straight, he was tied up with Frank Kelly and Don Searls of South Lynn, Michigan. The leaders were Walding and Dr. C. W. Scranton with 198's at the close of the second day, with eight 197's barking at their heels. That left 50 targets on Saturday morning to decide the championship. Scranton shot targets in his sleep at a Detroit hotel, with the result that he missed four in his final 50, while Walding, as confident as a Joe Louis, broke the 50.

L. S. Pratt, who had won the Championship in 1935, broke 243 out of 250 to lead the Professionals, while Jackie Horton, 13-year old Edgewood, Rhode Island shooter, copped the Junior title with 99 out of 100. The Sub-junior was won by Clayton Boardman, the freckled faced Georgian, who came up with 44 out of 50.

Miss Viola Siedhoff, hotel proprietor from Wichita, Kansas, garnered the Women's championship with 95 out of 100, but only after a heated shoot-off with Mrs. E. C. Crossman of Los Angeles. Jack Lindsay, Oklahoma, won the A class honors with 244 out of 250, while Ray Marshall of Detroit took the

Dr. C. W. Scranton, Carl Schweinler, Frank Traeger, Frank Kelly, Ed Garland. They won the team championship

Don Sperry *(left)*, winner of the Sub-Small and All-Around Championships, lines up with three other noted Michigan gunners, Paul Osterbeck, I. Jacobs and S. Dockson

B class laurels with 242. It was Dr. R. C. Brown of Snyder, N. Y., in the C class division, with his 239, and Mrs. James McMillan of Detroit in class D, with 238. G. D. Hubbard, Elwood, Indiana, won E class, with 227.

The National Team championship was won by the Roseland quintet. They registered 1,213 out of 1,250. In this team was Ed Garland, Frank Kelly, Frank Traeger, Dr. C. W. Scranton and Carl Schweinler.

Don Sperry, Flint, Michigan, and Frank Kelly were the stars of the shoot. Sperry won the Sub-smallgauge championship with 96 out of 100, after shooting out Frank Kelly in a hectic shoot-off. Sperry won the All-around championship with 537 out of 550 and the Smallgauge title with 98 out of 100 and 25 straight in the shoot-off. Sperry again demonstrated that he was one of the world's greatest shoot-off competitors by defeating the famed Grant Ilseng and Henry Joy in a spirited shoot-off for the Smallgauge crown.

The 20-Gauge crown went to Frank Kelly, who clicked off 99 out of 100 in the main event and 25 straight in a heated shoot-off to erase Carl Schweinler, the New Jersey state and Lordship champion, and young Jackie Horton, the Junior king, who had tied him.

Tom Davis, who started working around trapshoots in 1898, handled the bulletin board in the publicity tent. . . . Henry Ahlin always wears a smile, no matter how tough the going. . . . Bob Wilfong, winner of the California state championship with 100 straight, is a banker. . . . Earl "Bull Pickerel" Feitz, who for years handled the Grand American bulletin board, was in charge of the big board again. . . . Harold Siebens'

Missouri Mules came up with 125 straight on Thursday. In their lineup we noted Harold, Dando, Herrick, Weber and Montgomery.

Henry Ford and his wife dropped around to the shoot. "You fellows have a great time with your clay ducks, while I am bothered with directors' meetings and strikes," smiled the automobile magnate when we asked him how he liked the clay target sport. Mr. Ford is a personal friend of Henry Joy.

The capable Bill Harris and Elmer Christian were in charge of the Western traps and did a swell job. . . . John McManus of the Detroit News worked like a Trojan. So did Don Gillis, who helped with the publicity. . . . Don Searls, who busted 100 straight to tie Kelly and Walding on Thursday, teams up with Ray Marshall of the Hi Gun Club of Detroit, and this pair of birds hasn't been out of money this year. . . . Eddie Kost, the Los Angeles Mesa maestro, and Major Slater showed their best form in the dining hall. . . . Likable Bob Nichols was on hand for Field and Stream.

Ross Miller and Russ Baldwin handled the traps for the green-shirted Remington clan and there wasn't a slip up. . . . Sterling Dockson, Captain of the Hi Gun Club, broke 376 straight a few weeks before the shoot, a new record. . . . Most consistent gunner, A. Beam of Buffalo, who registered a 96, 96 and 48, which is 96 per cent flat. . . . On the final day in the Championship race, Harkins, Ring, Clayton, Heath, Stack, Doc Nichols, Sperry, Doc Sydow, Osterbeck, Harvey, Perry, Henderson, Traeger, Kelly, Walding and Dave Sklar broke the 50 straight. . . . The skeet shooters in Atlanta wired Buddy Jones, their championship threat, "If 78 is the best you can do, pack up and come home." Which reminds us of John Hesston of Winchester the time he wired his wife that he had won the world's rifle championship, years ago, and wife wired back, "It's time you won the championship. You have shot long enough."

I still treasure that picture of Clyde Mitchell, Bernie Strader, R. H. Coleman and Dave Flannigan, taken at the shoot, even if they didn't break any records. Grand bunch of boys. . . . Jimmy Wallace of South Lynn, Michigan, was second in the Sub-junior race. R. H. King, Jr., of Danville, Indiana, was third.

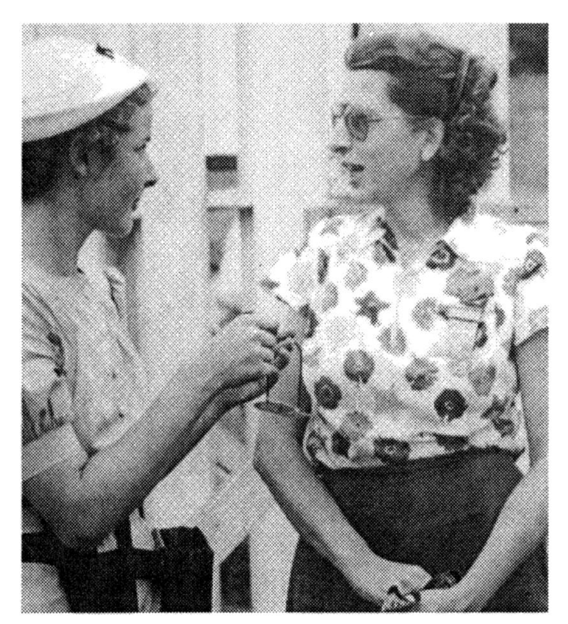

Pat Laursen and Viola Siedhoff

1938—HENRY JOY

Tulsa, Oklahoma, staged the fourth annual Skeet championships and none other than popular Henry Joy, Jr., 28-year-old Detroit sportsman, was the winner with the first perfect score ever recorded in this event—250 straight hits. Joy, however, had a battle on his hands from start to finish, but was equal to the task when he crashed 50 straight on the last day in the finals to rub out Grant Ilseng's chances. Ilseng had been tied with Henry on the previous day with 200 straight. Grant dropped one target, which gave him 249 out of 250. He still had a job on his hands, because Alex Kerr and Ed Williams from Redwood City, California, had moved up with 249's and it took Grant another 125 straight to defeat them in the shoot-off for second rung. Score in shoot-offs: Ilseng, 125 out of 125; Kerr, 124 out of 125, for third place; Williams dropping a target in his first round, fourth.

Interesting are the 248's for fifth position, with big Dutch Heath from Morris, Oklahoma, busting 75 straight to defeat Dud Shallcross of Rhode Island, who broke 74 out of 75, and others with 248's following in order were: Lowrey Booth, a fine shot out of Chicago; Odis Walding; Kenneth Miller, Tyler, Texas, and C. J. Colby, the famed Corpus Christi, Texas, gunner.

Tom Mettler broke 247 out of 250 and another 125 straight in the shoot-off to win A class; R. W. Canfield, Locust Valley,

(Left to right) Odis Walding, Ed Williams, Grant Ilseng, Capt. Ralph Scott, Tom Mettler won the team championship

NATIONAL ALL-BORE SKEET CHAMPIONS

A GREAT JOB SAID COLONEL W. F. SIEGMUND *(right)* to Odis Walding (1937)

"Coley" Coleman *(right)* congratulates Junior Joy (1938)

Dick Shaughnessy

New York, took B with 243 out of 250; C. J. Dando, Springfield, Missouri, won C with 244 out of 250; Bob Naegele, a new shooter from Minneapolis, captured D class honors with 232 out of 250; while Al Epplerly, Indianapolis, paced the E class gunners with 226.

Pretty Pat Laursen, Akron, Ohio, who came highly recommended by Roy Swan from the Lordship shoot where she won the Women's title, captured her first National championship when she banged out 96 out of 100. Viola Siedhoff won A class with 90 and Mrs. R. C. Porter won B with 92. Viola lives in Kansas, Mrs. Porter in Texas.

Bob Chandler, Muskogee, Oklahoma, won the Professional crown with 244 out of 250, but only after a heated shoot-off with Herman Ehler, noted Texas pro. Jackie Horton, Providence, Rhode Island, roared down the line with a 100 straight to cop the Junior laurels. Freckled faced Red Boardman, one of my favorites, captured the Sub-junior with 95 out of 100. Red lives in Georgia. The Kerr-Ilseng "duo" were much too rough in the Two-Man team championship—their scores, 498

L. S. Pratt, 1935 All-Bore Champ *(left)*, is being congratulated by his friend Junior Baldridge

"That was a great piece of work," said big Jim Smith *(right)* to Walt Dinger, who had just won the 1939 National Skeet Championship. Jim lives in Los Angeles

Jack Lindsay, Okmulgee *(extreme right)* cleaned up the Small Gauge, Sub-Small Gauge and All-Around titles at the 1938 Nationals. This is the team he shot with—Bobby Parker, *(left)* Walt Dinger, G. C. Parker, Sr., and G. C. Parker, Jr., all from Oklahoma

out of 500. The Parkers, Bobby and G. C., were the Father and Son victors.

The Gilmore Red Lions, with Walding, Ilseng, Mettler, Williams and Captain Ralph Scott, won the Team race with a record score of 1,238 out of 1,250.

Jack Lindsay, Okmulgee, had no trouble in winning the Sub-smallbore title when he shattered 98 out of 100. S. L. Hutcheson, New York, won the A class honors with 93 out of 100; M. L. Smythe, Aurora, Ohio, the B class with 87; S. J. Dando, Louisville, Kentucky, C class with 87, and Bill Adkins of Louisville, Kentucky, led the pros.

Lindsay came right back the next day with his second major victory of the week in the Small-gauge contest, when he crashed 99 out of 100 in the main event and 25 straight in the shoot-off to defeat Odis Walding, California, and Johnny Wray of New York, who had tied him in the regular race. Wray took second place. The class winners were: Tom Mettler, A, with 97 out of 100; Mrs. M. L. Smythe, Aurora, Ohio, B, with 92 out of 100, and L. Kennedy, Tulsa, C, with 94 out of 100. L. S. Pratt, Indianapolis, won the professional honors with 97.

It was Dick Shaughnessy of Boston all the way in the 20-Gauge championship race which he won with 100 straight. Barking at Dick's heels were Bottles Ketchum, St. Louis, Missouri; Henry Adler, Dallas, Texas; Art Davidson, Chicago;

ob Chandler (1938) Harold Russell (1935) Ed Lindsay (1936)

PROFESSIONAL ALL-BORE CHAMPIONS

Fred Missildine (1941)

Graydon Hubbard, Elwood, *(center)* won the Professional Crown in 1940. He is pictured with Dave Arnette *(left)*, Junior Baldridge, H. K. Spaulding and H. M. Beanblossom, all from the Hoosier state

Felix Hawkins, Dallas, Texas, and Bobby Parker of Tulsa with 99's.

Bill Sweet, Minneapolis, belongs to the Sioux Indians and it was his first National shoot. Ditto Doc Bouma of St. Paul, another prominent Indian. Both won trophies. . . . Jack Guenveur, Wilmington, was in charge of the office, enough said. . . . Viola Siedhoff busted just 98 out of 100 Friday. . . . Eddie Kost was on hand from Los Angeles with a banner on his car —"World's Greatest Shot." Must have meant Johnny, his youngster, surely not himself.

This boy Van Schaack from Denver is a pretty gun pointer. . . . Pratte and Geiger came all the way from Florida. . . . Young Harry Harkins led the Florida gunners with 246 out of 250. . . . Mose Browning and Dutch Heath were looking for side matches for dollars. . . . Bill Ragsdale from Boston visited his old home town friends in Claremore, Will Rogers' home town. . . . Sports editor B. A. Bridgewater of the Tulsa World didn't do a thing but work. . . . Hats off to G. C. Parker, Grant, Piggott, Klein, Bothwell, Richards, Clarke, Canterbury, Sherman and Catlett, sponsors of this great shoot.

With 110 above weather, I moved from the hotel out to a tourist camp with Grant Ilseng and Ed Williams. . . . Doc Cullpepper came all the way from Honolulu. . . . Gus Alexander was there with his famous wardrobe of shooting jackets. . . . When it comes to digging up facts, don't overlook Al Ormsbee. . . . Hughes Richardson was in there pulling for San Francisco next year, which was okay with me. . . . Among the 100 straights the first day in the big race we noted Harold Siebens, noted St. Louis sportsman; Charlie King and Landon Cullum, both of Wichita Falls, Texas; Howard Sherman, one of the sponsors of the shoot from Tulsa and Joe Witt, of Beverly Hills, that "feller" who owns several dry ice plants that we could have used at Tulsa. . . . L. S. Pratt, Indianapolis, won the Pro title with 97 out of 100. . . . At the end of the shoot, my score card gave Jack Lindsay the All-around championship, with 540 out of 550, his third major victory of the week.

1939—WALT DINGER

Walt Dinger, Tulsa, Oklahoma, won the fifth National Skeet championship at the Pacific Rod and Gun Club, San Francisco, California. Dinger's victory was the most dramatic in skeet history. When the smoke had cleared away in the National championship event, five nationally known gunners, Dinger, Joe Puckett and George Scott of Fresno, California, little Bobby Parker of Tulsa, and Dudley Shallcross of Providence, Rhode Island, were locked in a tie with 247's.

After the first shoot-off of 25 targets, the score sheet showed Bobby, Walt and Puckett straight and still in the running. Scott and Shallcross had each dropped two targets.

The second event told the tale. Puckett was the first to miss —then Bobby blew a target. Dinger apparently was not to be denied. He ground his targets to ink spots and when he crashed his 25th target the large crowd gave him a great ovation. It was a popular win with everybody.

The shoot-off between Bobby Parker and Puckett was a thriller, just as spectacular as the championship contest, in fact. They shot at 200 targets and Bobby broke 199, which gave him second honors. Puckett automatically took third place, while Scott eventually captured fourth honors and Dud Shallcross took fifth.

Don Sperry, Flint, Michigan, won the A class honors with 244 out of 250 while C. F. Stoner of Culver City, California, took B class with the same score. John Urabe, Salinas, California, captured the C class honors with 236 out of 250, while Bob Hare of Indianapolis went out in front of the D class claybusters with 222. Mrs. R. W. Canfield, Long Island, New York, was the E class winner with her score of 205 out of 250.

Pretty Pat Laursen, Akron, Ohio, retained her Women's

Fresno won the Team Championship: *(Left to right)* J. L. Puckett, Lloyd Sciaroni, George Scott, F. Mosier and Joe Yrulegui

A group of movie stars who shot skeet at the Fred Stone Birthday shoot at Alex Kerr's Santa Monica Club, Los Angeles: *(Left to right)* Jack Holt, Fred Stone, Wendie Barrie, Clark Gable and Jimmy Gleason. Buster Collier standing

championship with 236 out of 250 in the main event and 24 out of 25 in the shoot-off to defeat Mrs. M. L. Smythe of Aurora, Ohio.

The Fresno, California, team scored somewhat of an upset when it captured the Team championship with 1,219 out of 1,250. Their lineup included Joe Puckett, George Scott, Joe Yrulegui, Lloyd Sciaroni and Earl Howard.

Bobby Parker and Walt Dinger won the Two-Man championship with 494 out of 500. G. C. Parker and Bobby captured the Father and Son laurels and Bobby won the All-around honors for the entire shoot with a score of 534 out of 550.

Resting between shots at the Indianapolis skeet tourney: *(Left to right)* Bill Ragsdale, Boston, who helped win the team championship; Don Speery, Michigan; Mrs. Potter Palmer, III, and Gerald Batten, both of Chicago, and Mrs. D. Mead Johnson

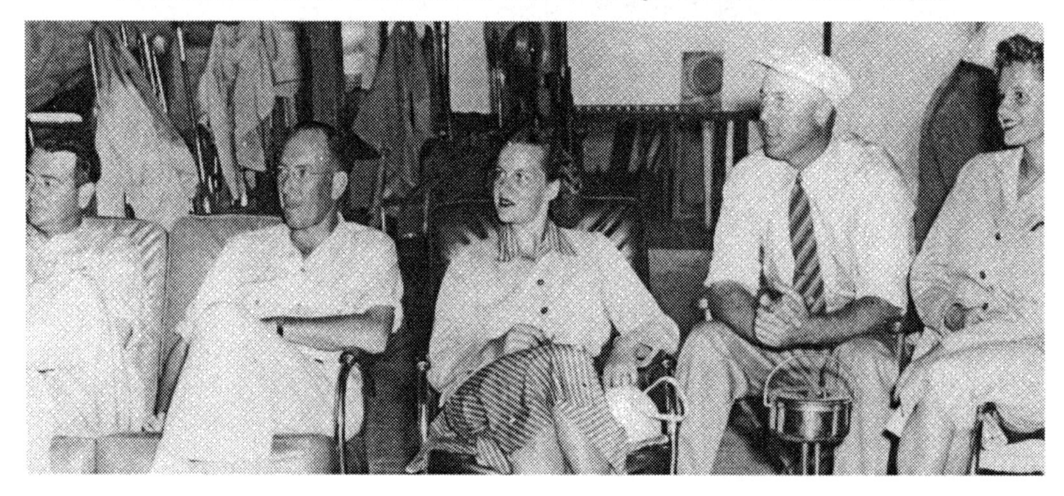

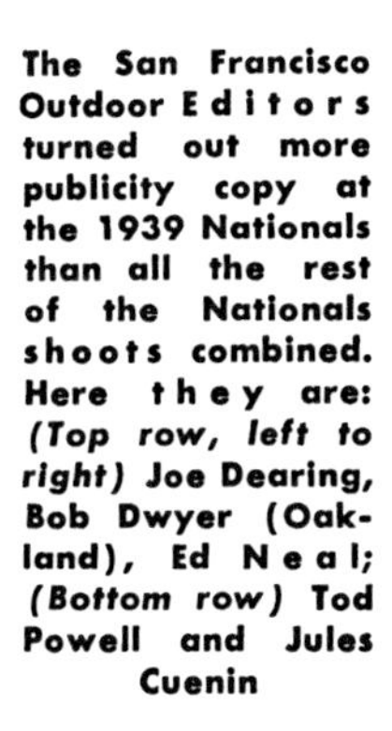

The San Francisco Outdoor Editors turned out more publicity copy at the 1939 Nationals than all the rest of the Nationals shoots combined. Here they are: *(Top row, left to right)* Joe Dearing, Bob Dwyer (Oakland), Ed Neal; *(Bottom row)* Tod Powell and Jules Cuenin

The Professional championship went to E. L. "Skinny" Ilgner, the Los Angeles trapshooter, who broke 244 out of 250. We might add that Colonel W. F. Siegmund of East Alton, Illinois, had quite a week for himself when he won the professional 20-Gauge, the Smallgauge and All-around. Harold Russell took the Sub-smallgauge back to Minneapolis.

It was Bobby Parker again in the Junior competition when he banged out 100 straight and little Johnny Kost of Los Angeles carried off the Sub-junior championship.

Dick Shaughnessy, the hot shot from Boston, started off with a rush in the opening Sub-smallbore championship race, when he crashed 94 out of 100 to easily lead this field. Henry Adler, Dallas, Texas, was next, with 92.

The Smallgauge title went to the great Don Sperry, who busted 99 out of 100 in the regular event and 25 straight in the shoot-off to defeat Alex Kerr, Beverly Hills, California (second), and Dick Shaughnessy.

Don Sperry hung up his second victory in two days when he again broke a 99 in the 20-Gauge race and again defeated two other noted gunners, Dick Shaughnessy and George Scott. Mrs. E. B. Hockwalt, Edmonds, Washington, won the Women's event with the fine score of 94 out of 100.

The shoot was a tremendous success from every standpoint. The newspaper publicity was the best of any National skeet shoot before or since.

Charlie Rapp from California had tough luck—led the entire field on Thursday and Friday with 198 out of 200. . . . Harold Lang and C. C. Rogers handled the shoot-offs in grand style. . . . Jim Smith, Los Angeles, manager of the Arabian team, was our official photographer. . . . John Urabe was the first National Japanese champion, and he is a real fellow. The Jap squad, composed of Urabe, Okamoto, Shirachi, Doc Kita and Tsukamoto, was captained by "Wild Bill" Bergschicker and coached by C. C. Rogers.

The outdoor editors, Uncle Joe Dearing, Tod Powell, Ed Neal, Bob Dwyer and Jules Cuenin, did a grand job on about two hours' sleep each night. Tod Powell didn't have any, chasing around with Minneapolis' Bob McDonald. . . . Bumped into Ed Hammond, the famous trapshot, who was a visitor. . . . Joe Tobin, one of the owners of the San Francisco Chronicle, put on a cocktail party that was a hummer.

Al Reihl, famed Portland gunner, cashiered the shoot, then took off for the Grand American at Dayton. . . . Dutch Heath, the Oklahoma star, is equally as good at trapshooting and that's saying something. . . . Tom Menzies, popular Los Angeles gunner, is a member of the insurance firm of Thornton, Menzies and Taylor, outstanding on the Pacific coast. . . . Joe Springer is the main spoke in the Pacific Rod and Gun Club. . . . Doc Alkalay, popular president of the club, took sick before the shoot. Doc is a great booster for Ducks Unlimited.

A shoot wouldn't be a shoot without Gilbert Orr, from Brownsville, Pennsylvania. . . . Mrs. L. S. Webb from Richmond was as attractive as ever. . . . Joe Darcey, the San Mateo gunner, owns one of the finest sporting headquarters on the coast. . . . Don't think Mrs. E. B. Hockwalt, the 20-Gauge Women's champ, can't shoot. . . . Charlie Lindemann and O. N. Ford, both world known trapshooters, were visitors. . . . Salt Lake McGanney, the former Grand American professional Doubles champ, was buried with bulletin sheets.

Gus Peret, big game hunter, was Sally Rand's instructor—which reminds us that Sally, who had a show at the Fair, shot a few skeets and broke her first two straight, by golly. . . . Al Ormsbee, the New Haven "Count," broke a snappy 98 the

JUNIOR SKEET CHAMPIONS

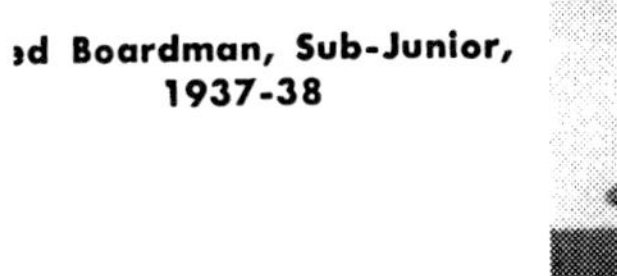

ed Boardman, Sub-Junior, 1937-38

Jackie Horton, Junior, 1937-38

F. Lutcher Brown *(left)*, Junior, 1941, and Bill Handy, Sub-Junior, 1940

ohnny Kost, Sub-Junior, 1939

Newton Newman, Sub-Junior, 1941

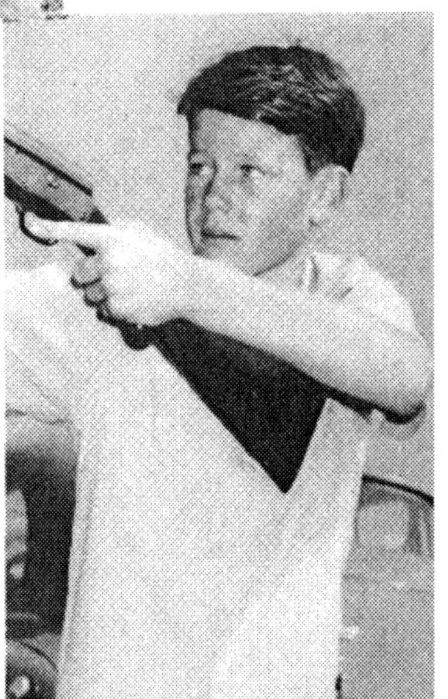

first day to lead the pros, which gave Al and this writer a great thrill. . . . Verne Marlow and L. S. Hawxhurst, a couple of popular coast pros, were there with bells on. . . . Yes, and Captain A. H. Hardy, the famous all-around exhibition shooter, was there with his showy gun cases.

Uncle "Louie" Lewis brought his Choate Prep school team from Wallingsford, Connecticut, with Charlie Lyman as a sub. In their lineup were four Lymans—Charlie, Charles III, Bob, the captain, and Dick. Leonard Graham completed the squad. The natty blue and gold jackets added color to the shoot.

Weather was fine, the San Francisco hospitality marvelous. . . . Jack Conway, MGM director, busted 93 out of 100 to pace C class gunners in the Smallgauge contest. . . . Mrs. Morrie Orr from New York was present with her usual charming manner. . . . Lloyd Kahn, chairman, lost five pounds and was glad when it was over. . . . Don Westwater is a real guy and so is Dynamo Crowley. . . . Bob Draper, who came all the way from Hopedale, Massachusetts, really enjoyed the shoot. Bob winters in Florida and has a real reputation as a deep sea angler. . . . Mrs. Jules Cuenin, wife of the outdoor writer, Jules Cuenin, is quite a writer herself.

We're not forgetting some of our dinners at Clark Gable's country estate on our way to the shoot. . . . Director Jack Conway's luncheon at the MGM studios. . . . Jim Smith's feed at Lyman's in Los Angeles, and Major Ralph and Earl Gilmore's luncheon at the University Club.

Here is 1940 Star-Journal All-State Skeet team from Minnesota: ***(Left to right)*** **Johnny Manlove, John Dick, Jr., Jay Laidlaw, Dr. L. R. Bouma and Fred Nordin**

1940—DICK SHAUGHNESSY

Richard "Dick" Shaughnessy, Boston, proved beyond all doubt that he was the greatest skeet gunner in the game by winning the sixth annual Skeet championship at Syracuse, New York, when he led this fast field with 249 out of 250 in the main event and 50 straight in the shoot-off to defeat F. S. Hawkins of Dallas, Texas, and Alex Kerr of Beverly Hills, California, who had tied him. Dick's victory marked the first time in skeet history that a shooter had won this championship twice. He won it in 1936 at St. Louis, when he was 14 years of age. After the shoot-off, the Dallas gunner took second position, Kerr, third.

Eight gunners carried 100 straights to bed with them Thursday night. The field dwindled down to six on Friday night with Shaughnessy and Charlie Poulton of San Antonio, leading the field with 200 straights, trailed by Miss Pat Laursen of Akron,

The famous Hill Top Team Champions at Lordship in 1939-40: ***(Left to right)*** **J. Guenveur (mascot), Elliott Moore, Jack Horton, Dick Shaughnessy, Dud Shallcross and Bob Canfield**

Ohio; Alex Kerr; Dr. E. L. Lewis of Jackson, Michigan, and F. S. Hawkins, who had 199's.

Pat Laursen again won the Women's championship with 246 out of 250, while O. L. Baldridge, better known as "Junior," paced the Juniors with a 97. Graydon Hubbard, Elwood, Indiana, was the big gun among the professionals, winning the Individual Sub-smallgauge, Smallgauge and All-around, while Leslie Webb of Richmond, Virginia, captured the professional 20-Gauge title. Webb broke 98 out of 100.

Dick Hecker, Detroit, the Skeet Statistician

A good looking youngster, W. E. Handy of Bridgeport, Connecticut, stalked off with the Sub-junior championship, and Felix Hawkins, the Dallas druggist, copped the All-around amateur title with the great score of 544 out of 550.

Hawkins, a soft spoken Texan, captured the Sub-small championship with 98 out of 100, which equalled Jack Lindsay's record score in 1938 at Tulsa. Brooklyn's noisy Dave Sklar placed second with 97. Pat Laursen won the Women's championship with 87 out of 100, and Diana Bolling, the great Greenwich, Connecticut, gunner, was next.

Shaughnessy showed his metal in the Smallbore championship, which he won with 99 out of 100 in the regular race and 125 straight in the shoot-off, a new record, to defeat the great George Deyoe of Washington, D. C., Felix Hawkins, Bobby

***(Left to right)* Mrs. Dick Hecker, Mrs. J. T. McMillan, Jr., Elizabeth Small (1936 Women's Champ)**

Parker and H. Lutcher Brown. Deyoe, Brown and Hawkins fell by the wayside early, but Bobby Parker hung on like a tiger. The two youngsters broke their first 100 straight with no decision. Then Bobby faltered on his tenth bird in the next event, while Dick went straight for the title. Mrs. M. L. Smythe, small but mighty Ohio gunner, copped the Women's laurels with 92, but she had to defeat Pat Laursen in a shoot-off.

Bobby Parker, Culver student at the time, and fresh from victory at Asheville, North Carolina (where he won $1,000 in cash, busting 200 straight), won the 20-Gauge championship with 100 straight in the main program and 75 straight in the shoot-off to beat George Deyoe and Morrie Orr of New York City. Deyoe dropped out in the first 25 targets of the shoot-off, but Morrie held on until he missed in his third event. Dr. R. F. Westermier, and Dave MacEllven, both of Buffalo, followed with 99's. Pat Laursen won the Women's event, but had to outshoot Mrs. M. L. Smythe and Mrs. Morrie Orr of New York City.

Fred and Henry L. Brown of San Antonio, Texas, captured the Father and Son All-gauge championship when they scored 492 out of 500. Shaughnessy and Dud Shallcross won the Two-Man team championship with 495 out of 500 and Bobby Parker and his dad were victors in the Family 20-Gauge competition. Edward Dooley, Binghamton, New York, scored an easy victory in the Veterans' contest.

The great Texas team, with Charlie Poulton, Henry Adler, Felix Hawkins and the two Browns won the Team championship with 1,228 out of 1,250.

Mrs. M. L. Smythe was one of the eight 100 straights the first day in the All-gauge and it marked the first time that a woman had broken 100 straight in this event.... Ray L. Vande-Vate, the Bausch and Lomb expert from Rochester, spent most of his time talking goose hunting and fishing....Felix Hawkins, Herman Adler and A. Fifley drove to the shoot from Dallas and all figured in some kind of a win. Fifley won the C class crown in the Smallbore event, with 94.

Dick Porter and Danny Taylor, former big league baseball stars, bosses of the Syracuse Chiefs, took time out to watch the gunners. Dick is a well known duck hunter. . . . Statistician Dick Hecker of Detroit wore out two pencils chalking up the

Michigan leaders. . . . Ed Garland, as usual, was the best dressed man on the grounds. Ed had 40 victory badges on his jacket, all won before 1882.

Corwin Spencer called our attention to their great Ohio shooters, with Miss Pat Laursen and Mrs. M. L. Smythe topping all Buckeye gunners in the All-gauge race. . . . Won a buck from Moe Collett when I bet he couldn't break 75. Moe got the jitters, wound up with 74 out of 100. . . . Ray Trullinger, popular New York World-Telegram scribe, shot the entire 250 target program and turned in a neat score. . . . Howard Kemp covered the event for his Rochester Democrat-Chronicle in his usual highclass manner. . . . Leo Bolley, noted WFBL and WGY sports announcer, got a great kick out of the shoot and announced it nightly over his chain.

Bill Higgins of the Savage Arms Company recalled one of his Minnesota moose hunts years ago when he lived in Grand Rapids, Minnesota. . . . Jack Durkin of the Syracuse Herald-Journal and Jerry Ash of the Post-Standard were right on the job and gave the shooters a big play. . . . The fast stepping Foresters Gun Club of Williamsville, New York, broke 249 out of 250 in their last half of Thursday's program. In their lineup we noted Lloyd Bissell, C. A. Brown, Dr. R. F. Westermier, B. Brown and A. B. Beam—four B's.

A hand to John Couzens, the faithful referee and to Howard Kaslin, main spoke of the club, who worked day and night. . . . And when Alex Kerr busted his 250th target, it gave him the highest average of the season, .9924 on 1,450 registered targets.

S. L. Hutcheson won the National 20-Gauge Championship in 1941 with 100 straight. *(Left to right)* Dave Sklar, E. A. MacMillan, Morrie Orr, (Hutcheson) and Grad Sears

A group of famous Women gunners at Lordship: *(Left to right)* Mrs. H. E. Rogers, 1937 Lordship Champ, Mrs. M. L. Smythe, National Women's Champion, Mrs. R. A. Fletcher, Mrs. Morrie Orr and Mrs. A. W. Walker. Mrs. Orr and Alex Kerr won the Mixed Team race at the 1941 Nationals

1941—CHARLIE POULTON

A Texan, Charlie H. Poulton of San Antonio, won the seventh annual Skeet championship at Indianapolis in the screwiest shotgun event the world has known. The entire shoot was a heartbreaker from start to finish and you will agree after you read our story that everything happened except an earthquake, and had it not been for the fact that S. L. Hutcheson of New York broke 100 straight in the main event and 25 straight in the shoot-off to defeat the big, husky, 95-pound Mrs. M. L. Smythe of Ohio, I am sure that many of the old-timers would have chucked away their guns. That would have been something that the skeet gunners would have a hard time explaining to their hero worshippers at home—and to the wives as well. The climax was the heated shoot-off for the automobile in the Calcutta Auto Sweepstakes, which was won by Alex Kerr, but only after a terrific last stand by Junior Baldridge (second), Dick Shaughnessy, Poulton and Bill Clark.

Ted Doremus of the Du Pont Powder Company *(left)* and Henry Ahlin, Manager of the National Skeet Association

H. Lutcher Brown *(left)* was the star at the 1941 Lordship tourney, winning the All-Around and .410 Short Shell Here he is pictured with Mrs. R. C. Porter, Texas Women's Champion and Landon Cullum, who won the '41 Texas State Championship with 299 x 300. All are from the Lone Star State

The National Individual championship race was a thriller. Poulton and the great Alex Kerr tied for first place with 250 straights. Then came the record-breaking shoot-off. A more even match could not be found. They each broke 25 straight, then again and again. Finally Kerr muffed one, his 155th, and the race was over, Poulton winning with 175 straight. The 249's followed in this order: Junior Baldridge, third; George Deyoe, fourth; Henry B. Joy, Jr., fifth; Bill Ragsdale, sixth, and Dick Hecker, seventh. Fred Missildine, manager of the Sea Island, Georgia, gun club, won the Professional championship with 249 out of 250.

Anthony Zugates, Indiana, Pennsylvania, won the A class title with 249 out of 250, while M. O. Devers, Dayton, Ohio, captured the B class laurels with 247. L. R. Ford, Indianapolis, paved the way for the C class shooters with 245, and a Chicago gunner, S. Hawxhurst, topped D class marksmen with 239. Chicago was again high in E class with C. L. Barnett the big gun, with 237.

Mrs. M. L. Smythe, Aurora, Ohio, won the Women's championship with 245 out of 250, five targets in front of

Phil Conway of New York, teamed up with his Dad, (Conway) to win the first Father and Son Championship at St. Louis in 1936

Billy Perdue, Mobile, Alabama, won the 1941 Smallgauge title

Mrs. Barr Patterson of Chicago and Jane Hoffman of Lakeview, Ohio. The Father and Son championship was again won by the popular H. Lutcher and F. Lutcher Brown of San Antonio, Texas.

The Team championship went to the West Brook Cardinals with Dick Shaughnessy, S. L. Hutcheson, Bill Ragsdale, Dave Sklar and Ed Garland in their lineup. Total score—1,237 out of 1,250.

Poulton and Billy Perdue won the Two-man Team championship with 498 out of 500 in the regular event and 50 straight in the shoot-off to defeat Henry Joy and Dick Hecker of Detroit. John M. Kerr, Detroit, a distinctive new shooter, won the Veterans' title with 229 out of 250.

Alex Kerr captured the Amateur High-over-all with the remarkable score of 543 out of 550. Mrs. Smythe outclassed the women's field with 527 out of 550, while big Grant Ilseng took the professionals into camp with 534.

W. C. "Billy" Perdue, 19-year-old real estate agent from Mobile, Alabama, making his start in the Nationals, was the winner of the Small-gauge championship with 100 straight hits. Perdue, who claims he would rather hunt birds than eat, had to break the 100 straight to win. Close on his heels were three dangerous gunners, Bobby Parker, H. Lutcher Brown and E. R. Pratte, the restaurant man from Miami, who came up with 99's. Brown won the shoot-off for second place with 25 straight.

The Women's Small-gauge title went to Diana Bolling of Greenwich, Connecticut, who scored 93 out of 100, but only after she had defeated Mrs. Smythe in a shoot-off with 25 straight. A. R. "Bing" Crosby, likable Detroit professional, turned in 97 out of 100 to lead the pros.

The National Junior championship went to F. Lutcher Brown, 15-year old San Antonio gunner, when he busted 99 out of 100. Billy Coombs, Rochester, New York, placed second with 98 and Lester Varn of Jacksonville, Florida, was third with 97.

The Sub-junior title winner was Newton Newman of Evansville, Indiana, who scored 83 out of 100. Joe Devers, Dayton, Ohio, was next with 76.

The 20-Gauge championship race was a scorcher with S. L. Hutcheson of New York City the victor. Hutch broke 100 straight in the regular event and 25 straight in the shoot-off to defeat Mrs. M. L. Smythe, of Ohio. George Deyoe, Washington, won third place honors with 99 out of 100 and 75 straight in the shoot-off from Charlie Poulton and D. W. "Boots" Allen, the Michigan state champion from Detroit.

Bobby Parker captured the A class honors with 99 out of 100 and W. W. Rapley, Washington, took B class with the same score. The C class honors went to J. A. Kleinhausen of Chicago, who rang up 95, while Mr. and Mrs. M. L. Smythe, Ohio, won the Family championship with 196 out of 200.

Alex Kerr, who operates a sporting goods store in Beverly Hills, California, scored a cleancut victory in the Sub-small-gauge championship race when he shattered 99 out of 100. It was his first National victory. Dick Shaughnessy was second with 98 and dapper Dave Arnette of Indianapolis was third with 96. Bobby Parker won the A class honors with 93 out of 100 while Wm. Rapley, Washington, D. C., paved the way for B class shooters with the same score. Ralph Meli, Chicago, who is quite an expert at trapshooting, led the C class gunners with 94.

Mrs. M. L. Smythe edged out Mrs. Potter Palmer, III, of Chicago, when she scored 89 out of 100 to win the women's championship. Mrs. Palmer broke 88. Pat Laursen won the class A honors with 82 out of 100 while Mrs. J. L. Younghusband, quite a noted field shot from Chicago, copped the B class laurels with Mrs. L. Childs of Lake Kerr, Florida, second. Grant Ilseng, Chicago, won the professional championship.

After breaking 250 straight in the Championship race, Alex Kerr had to bust another 400 straight to win the Calcutta and De Soto car. Two cars were put up, and Jane Hoffman had the lucky number, which was Kerr. . . . Bing Crosby and Grant Ilseng tied for second place with 248's in the Industry race, Bing winning the shoot-off. . . . E. R. Davis came all the way from Honolulu and busted a sweet 248. . . . L. S. Pratt and his charming wife worked like Trojans. Pratt is manager of the Indianapolis gun club.

Don Gillis handled the INS and Detroit Times. . . . Dick Steinhoff broke 72 straight in his first 100, then a mourning dove flew into his pattern. Same thing happened to Diana Bolling a few weeks before and it was the first wild bird she

Five Women(?) Champs from Maryland: ***(Top row, left to right)*** **Tom Offutt, Colin Thomas, Harry Wright;** ***(Bottom)*** **Joe George and Jack Groves**

had ever killed. . . . Tom Metzger is known as the Michigan potato king. Also owns a 350-acre onion farm. . . . Charlie Van Studdiford finally landed in the news column when he broke 96 out of 100, dropped his four optional birds. Charlie likes dogs and quail hunting. . . . Boots Allen from Detroit had hard luck in the 20-Gauge race; missed his first target, then ran 99 straight. . . . Ollie Rodman, popular National Sportsman prexy, talked ducks.

One-armed Andy Anderson from St. Paul broke his first 50 straight Friday. . . . Charlie Hopkins and Gail Evans staged a little side wager, with the latter collecting. Mr. Hopkins had fully recovered from his last auto accident. . . . Tom Sullivan, president of the Lincoln Park gun club, and a real fellow, favors optional shooting at the Nationals. . . . Al Reihl and Henry Winchester, two old faithfuls, cashiered the shoot. A

Texas won the 1940 team championship. ***(Left to right)*** **Henry Adler, Fred Brown, Felix Hawkins, H. Lutcher Brown and Charlie Poulton**

couple of heavyweights, Uncle John Couzens and Jay Bouknegt, handled the bulletin board. Both jobs are thankless ones.

Shaughnessy busted 100 straight to win the Champion of Champions race, but had to bust another 175 straight to beat state champions Anthony Zugates of Pennsylvania; John Ginter, Florida; Bill Clark, Illinois, and Dr. J. H. Nichols of Ohio. . . . Bill Clark, who works for Marshall Fields in Chicago, was hotter than a firecracker all week. Bill sells sporting goods. . . . Frank Kracht's mask had the girls at the hotel guessing. . . . Missildine, the new pro champ, is 25 years old, has been shooting just three years.

Coley Coleman is getting serious about his shooting. Did a fine job, breaking 245 out of 250, best score of his career. . . . E. H. Boone, Lexington, who auctioneered the Calcutta, is a brother of F. E. Boone, the Lucky Strike tobacco auctioneer. . . . Pete Quick, Romeo, Michigan, shot 242 out of 250, best score he ever made. . . . Bob Nichols, well known gun editor of Field and Stream, talked ballistics when he wasn't tearing up and down the line with his camera, shooting the boys in action.

SKEET RECORDS

STATE SKEET CHAMPIONS

Alabama

1931 Emmett Marshall, Birmingham.......... 95x100
1932 C. D. Norris, Birmingham............... 95x100
1933 J. H. Cumby, Birmingham.............. 96x100
1934 Joe Biddle, Birmingham................ 92x100
1935 Emmett Marshall, Birmingham.......... 95x100
1936 T. K. Lee, Birmingham................. 98x100
1937 A. M. Feltus, Mobile.................... 99x100
1938 F. C. Owens, Woodward................. 99x100
1939 W. C. Perdue, Spring Hill.............. 99x100
1940 T. K. Lee, Birmingham.................148x150
1941 W. C. Perdue, Mobile...................145x150

Arizona

1941 George Williams, Glendale.............. 49x 50

Arkansas

1933 E. S. Van Sickel, Little Rock.......... 91x100
1934 W. K. Lemley, Hope.................... 94x100
1935 Julius Petty, England.................. 97x100
1936 W. P. Smead, Camden.................. 97x100
1937 Sibley Ward, Little Rock...............144x150
1938 Beck Morgan, Texarkana...............147x150
1939 C. H. LaDue, Little Rock..............147x150
1940 Julius Petty, England..................198x200
1941 W. P. Smead, Camden..................197x200

California

1931 Burr Perkins, Los Angeles............. 92x100
1932 Bob Wilfong, Pasadena................. 97x100
1933 Fred Carr, Pasadena.................... 97x100
1934 R. Stockberger, Los Angeles............100x100
1935 Jules P. Cuenin, San Francisco.........100x100
1936 Harry Fleischmann, Los Angeles....... 99x100
1937 Bob Wilfong, Pasadena..................100x100
1938 Grant Ilseng, Los Angeles..............100x100
1939 Charlie Warren, Los Angeles............ 99x100
1940 Don Westwater, San Francisco..........193x200
1941 Tom Mettler, Bakersfield...............100x100

Colorado

1936 H. C. Van Schaak, Jr., Denver.......... 86x100
1937 H. C. Van Schaak, Jr., Denver.......... 98x100
1938 H. C. Van Schaak, Jr., Denver.......... 98x100
1939 Chas. E. Gast, Denver................. 97x100
1940 C. L. Lathrop, Golden.................. 98x100
1941 F. DeBell, Denver...................... 97x100

Connecticut

1932 C. A. Pickering, Middletown............ 99x100
1933 E. Field White, W. Hartford............ 97x100
1934 Fred Needham, New Haven............. 98x100
1935 Frank Rockwood, N. Franklin........... 99x100
1936 Frank Rockwood, N. Franklin.......... 98x100
1937 Frank Rockwood, N. Franklin........... 96x100
1938 Jas. Ott, Chester....................... 98x100
1939 Frank Rockwood, N. Franklin........... 97x100
1940 A. W. Warner, Fairfield................. 98x100
1941 R. Dukat, Handen...................... 99x100

Delaware

1933 John Bancroft, Jr., Wilmington......... 47x 50
1934 D. A. Parks, Wilmington................ 88x100
1935 H. P. Scott, Jr., Wilmington........... 95x100
1936 F. G. Tallman, Wilmington............. 96x100
1937 W. B. Denham, Wilmington.............. 89x100
1938 F. G. Tallman, Wilmington............. 94x100
1939 H. B. Slater, Clayton.................. 96x100
1940 W. H. Slater, Claymont................. 95x100
1941 I. Keil, Wilmington..................... 97x100

Florida

1934 Tubby Price, Miami..................... 92x100
1935 George Handley, St. Petersburg........282x300
1936 George Long, West Palm Beach.........185x200
1937 Frank Fisher, Miami....................144x150

Florida (Cont.)

1938 Don L. Smith, Miami..................142x150
1939 W. H. Sand, Orlando.................... 99x100
1940 John Ginter, Jacksonville............... 99x100
1941 Dr. L. W. Childs, Lake Kerr............ 99x100

Georgia

1932 H. J. Fields, Decatur.................. 96x100
1933 Wm. Jones, Atlanta...................... 96x100
1934 Jack Gray, Atlanta...................... 97x100
1935 Jack Tway, Atlanta...................... 96x100
1936 Tom Cassels, Atlanta...................190x200
1937 Addison Smith, Atlanta................194x200
1938 Dr. LeRoy W. Childs, Atlanta..........148x150
1939 Jack Boardman, Augusta...............147x150
1940 W. F. Golden, Columbus...............148x150
1941 W. F. Golden, Columbus...............147x150

Illinois

1933 H. Behm, Maywood...................... 95x100
1934 Forest H. Norris, Riverside............. 96x100
1935 Lowrey Booth, Chicago.................. 99x100
1936 Chas. Beeder, E. St. Louis.............143x150
1937 Art Davidson, Chicago..................146x150
1938 M. Shoup, Kankakee.................... 99x100
1939 Wm. Clark, Chicago.....................197x200
1940 Jimmy Anderson, Chicago..............100x100
1941 Art Hultberg, Kankakee...............100x100

Indiana

1933 Connie Stumph, Indianapolis........... 99x100
1934 C. O. Free, Indianapolis................ 97x100
1935 C. C. Lumpkin, Indianapolis........... 98x100
1936 Sam Griffith, Indianapolis............. 96x100
1937 Sam Griffith, Indianapolis.............. 96x100
1938 Graydon Hubbard, Elwood.............149x150
1939 Graydon Hubbard, Elwood.............150x150
1940 E. L. Hawkins, Ft. Wayne, Ind..........197x200
1941 Lyman Stahl, Indianapolis..............199x200

Iowa

1932 K. E. Kelley, Altoona................... 95x100
1933 K. E. Kelley, Altoona................... 95x100
1934 Ralph Mead, Des Moines................ 94x100
1935 Birney Baker, Des Moines.............. 93x100
1936 Birney Baker, Des Moines...............186x200
1937 Claude Smith, Davenport...............144x150
1938 H. D. Anderson, Davenport.............148x150
1939 John Lensch, Eldridge.................142x150
1940 Birney Baker, Des Moines..............148x150
1941 D. A. Decker, Mason City............... 97x100

Kansas

1933 R. O. Bills, Wichita...................... 93x100
1934 R. C. Wise, Wichita..................... 90x100
1935 Fred Etchen, Wichita.................... 93x100
1936 Galen Spencer, Pittsburg............... 98x100
1937 John Crane, Wichita.................... 91x100
1938 Viola Siedhoff, Wichita.................. 99x100
1939 Ralph Wise, Wichita..................... 99x100
1940 Ralph Wise, Wichita..................... 96x100
1941 Ralph Wise, Wichita..................... 98x100

Kentucky

1935 Max Marcum, Louisville................. 99x100
1936 Bruce Sloan, Albany.................... 95x100
1937 Bruce Sloan, Albany.................... 96x100
1938 Max Marcum, Louisville................ 98x100
1939 Max Marcum, Louisville................ 98x100
1940 Max Marcum, Louisville................150x150
1941 Max Marcum, Louisville................149x150

Louisiana

1936 Jim Dockery, Shreveport...............190x200
1937 Paul Cook, Monroe......................193x200
1938 Mose Browning, Vivian.................196x200
1939 C. H. Devlin, Chalmette................149x150

THEY BROKE PERFECT SCORES TO WIN THEIR STATE SKEET CHAMPIONSHIPS

Ollie Mitchell, Mass. (1933-34)

Bob Wilfong, Calif. (1937)

Jack Kerr, New York (1941)

Frank Kracht, Mich. (1940)

Art Hultberg, Ill. (1941)

Maine

1933 Carl Hayden, Portland.................. 94x100
1934 Carl Hayden, Portland.................. 95x100
1935 Jim Whitney, Portland.................. 91x100
1936 Richard J. McWilliams, Lewiston........ 93x100
1937 A. D. Wing, Richmond................... 95x100
1938 Ransom P. Kelley, Fairfield............ 98x100
1939 Ransom P. Kelley, Fairfield............ 98x100
1940 Dr. A. O. Yates, Bangor................ 96x100
1941 James H. Whitney, Portland............. 92x100

Maryland & D.C. (100 Targets)

1932 E. M. Cheston, Ruxton.................... 95
1933 E. M. Chester, Ruxton.................... 93
1934 C. B. Gillet, Baltimore.................. 95
1935 C. B. Gillet, Baltimore.................. 100
1936 Geo. Radebaugh, Towsen................... 98
1937 Mrs. A. W. Walker, Westmoreland.......... 98
1938 George Deyoe, Washington................. 99
1939 Wm. Snyder, Baltimore.................... 99
1940 George Deyoe, Washington................. 99
1941 R. M. Watson, Laurel..................... 99

Massachusetts (100 Targets)

1932 Oliver Mitchell, Natick.................. 99
1933 Oliver Mitchell, Natick.................. 100
1934 Oliver Mitchell, Natick.................. 100
1935 Clarence Mitchell, Waltham............... 97
1936 Bob Canfield, Cambridge.................. 97
1937 Dr. Robert Vance, Wabon.................. 98
1938 Dick Shaughnessy, Boston................. 99
1939 Dick Shaughnessy, Boston................. 100
1940 Dick Shaughnessy, Boston................. 100
1941 Dick Shaughnessy, Boston................. 100

Michigan (100 Targets)

1931 L. D. Bolton, Detroit.................... 95
1932 L. D. Bolton, Detroit.................... 96
1933 L. D. Bolton, Detroit.................... 94
1934 Mrs. Sid Small, Detroit.................. 96
1935 Henry B. Joy, Detroit.................... 98
1936 Henry B. Joy, Detroit.................... 99
1937 Don Sperry, Flint........................ 99
1938 George Patterson, Grand Rapids........... 99
1939 Henry B. Joy, Detroit.................... 100
1940 Frank Kracht, Detroit.................... 100
1941 Dwight Allen, Detroit.................... 99

Minnesota

1933 Forest D. Saunders, Minneapolis.......... 94
1934 Forest D. Saunders, Minneapolis.......... 98
1935 John Dick, Jr., Minneapolis.............. 98
1936 Jack Mitchell, Worthington............... 95
1937 Dr. John Dick, Minneapolis............... 98
1938 Fred Nordin, Minneapolis................. 98
1939 Jay Laidlaw, Minneapolis................. 98
1940 John Dick, Jr., Minneapolis.............. 100
1941 Fred Nordin, Minneapolis................. 99

Mississippi

1935 Morrell Feltus, Vicksburg..............233x250
1936 George Hunt, Jackson...................196x200
1937 S. J. Lindamood, Columbus..............190x200
1938 George Guyton, Tuplelo................. 96x100
1939 E. L. Mahaffey, Jackson................196x200
1940 E. L. Mehaffey, Jackson................191x200
1941 George Hunt, Jackson...................194x200

Missouri

1933 G. E. Crosby, Lakeside.................... 92
1934 Everett Herrick, Springfield...........187x200
1935 Everett Herrick, Springfield...........191x200
1936 G. E. Crosby, Eldon....................196x200
1937 Ted Dahlke, Baldwin....................192x200
1938 Everett Herrick, Springfield...........194x200
1939 Dr. V. Blakemore, Columbia.............197x200
1940 Walter L. Harrison, Hannibal...........198x200
1941 Walter L. Harrison, Hannibal...........198x200

Montana (100 Targets)

1940 Lyle Pressy, Ronan....................... 91

Nebraska (100 Targets)

1933 Eddie Dygert, Omaha...................... 95
1934 James Stuart, Lincoln.................... 95
1935 Eddie Dygert, Omaha...................... 91
1936 Eddie Dygert, Omaha...................... 97
1937 W. F. Harder, Omaha...................... 93
1938 E. J. Morehead, Falls City............... 96
1939 R. L. Schainost, Fairbury................ 94
1940 James Stuart, Lincoln.................... 96
1941 James Stuart, Lincoln.................... 97

New Hampshire (100 Targets)

1934 Herb J. Carpenter, Franconia............. 91
1935 Chas. Adams, Nashua...................... 93
1936 Mark Chamberlin, Jaffrey................. 95
1937 P. Lampros, Dover........................ 90
1938 Chas. Adams, Nashua...................... 94
1939 Addison G. Smith, Laconia................ 99
1940 Emerson Chamberlin, Jaffrey.............. 97
1941 Chas. Adams, Nashua...................... 94

New Jersey

1932 Frank Traeger, Montclair............... 96x100
1933 Frank Traeger, Montclair...............100x100
1934 Ed Garland, Belleville................. 96x100
1935 Dr. Chas. Scranton, E. Orange.......... 99x100
1936 Frank R. Kelly, W. Orange..............199x200
1937 Carl Schweinler, W. Orange.............147x150
1938 L. C. Delmonico, Morristown............146x150
1939 Carl Schweinler, W. Orange............. 99x100
1940 Frank R. Kelly, W. Orange..............100x100
1941 Frank Traeger, Montclair............... 99x100

New York (100 Targets)

1933 Orson D. Munn, S. Hampden................ 98
1934 Dave Sklar, Brooklyn..................... 96
1935 Harry Eschenbach, Elmhurst............... 97
1936 Wallace Ketchum, Port Washington......... 99
1937 S. L. Hutcheson, Larchmont............... 99
1938 Dave Sklar, Brooklyn..................... 100
1939 S. L. Hutcheson, Larchmont............... 100
1940 Dr. Richard Westermeier, Buffalo......... 100
1941 Jack Kerr, Buffalo....................... 100

North Carolina

1934 W. R. Jones, Statesville................ 94x100
1935 J. L. Morehead, Charlotte..............192x200
1936 W. E. Gladstone, Winston-Salem.........187x200
1937 W. E. Gladstone, Winston-Salem.........193x200
1938 J. L. Putnam, Lincolnton...............193x200
1939 W. E. Gladstone, Winston-Salem.........199x200
1940 A. R. Idol, High Point.................192x200
1941 W. E. Gladstone, Winston-Salem.........149x150

North Dakota

1933 C. C. Hullinger, Devils Lake............ 92x100
1934 Ed Bovette, Grand Forks................186x200
1935 Ed Bovette, Grand Forks................188x200
1936 Ed Bovette, Grand Forks................188x200
1937 Ed Bovette, Grand Forks................183x200
1938 Ed Bovette, Grand Forks................189x200
1939 C. C. Hullinger, Devils Lake............193x200
1940 M. M. Knutson, Rugby...................189x200
1941 Gale Frosaker, Minot...................195x200

Ohio (100 Targets)

1932 Chalmers Hoyt, Cleveland................. 97
1933 H. W. Helwig, Youngstown................. 99
1934 H. F. Carson, Shaker Heights............. 94
1935 Art E. Hart, Cleveland................... 92
1936 M. C. Taylor, Youngstown................. 95
1937 Dr. J. H. Nichols, Cleveland............. 96
1938 E. B. Kennedy, Findlay................... 97
1939 O. L. Harrison, Dayton................... 99
1940 M. L. Smythe, Aurora..................... 99
1941 John Oros, Bay Village................... 98

Captain A. H. Hardy, Earl Gilmore who sponsors the Gilmore Red Lions Skeet team and Irvin S. Cobb, take in one of Eddie Kost's shoots at Los Angeles

John Couzens—The Referee

The Missouri Mules broke 249 out of their last 250 at the Tulsa tourney. *(Left to right)* Bottles Ketchum, Harold Siebens, Ed Montgomery, Dr. Virgil Blakemore and Everett Herrick

No, this isn't a gun factory Just Dudley Decker, the low champ, trying out one of hi many guns

DR. R. G. VANCE, Lordship .410 Champ in 1933, '34, '35

At Syracuse—The popular Forester Gun Club—C. A. Brown, Dr. R. C. Brown, A. A. Beam, Dr. R. F. Westermeier and Lloyd Bissell

Oklahoma

1934 Billy Clayton, Calvin.................. 47x 50
1935 Billy Clayton, Calvin.................. 97x100
1936 Billy Clayton, Calvin.................. 97x100
1937 Bobby Parker, Tulsa..................148x150
1938 Bobby Parker, Tulsa..................200x200
1939 Walt Dinger, Tulsa....................150x150
1940 Jack Lindsay, Okmulgee...............100x100
1941 Bobby Parker, Tulsa..................150x150

Oregon

1935 M. G. Henkel, Portland................ 47x 50
1936 Chet Rehfield, Portland............... 47x 50
1937 H. W. Dickson, Pendleton.............. 47x 50
1938 Dr. C. Mathews, Pendleton............. 94x100

Pennsylvania (100 Targets)

1933 W. A. Vincent, Morristown.............. 97
1934 W. A. Vincent, Morristown.............. 93
1935 W. A. Vincent, Morristown.............. 96
1936 C. R. Binkley, Ephrata................. 97
1937 R. C. Purnell, Fracksville............. 96
1938 C. R. Binkley, Neffsville.............. 97
1939 D. W. Lied, Ephrata.................... 99
1940 A. Zugates, Indiana.................... 99
1941 W. F. Thompson, Boothwin............... 99

Rhode Island (100 Targets)

1932 A. J. Smith, Providence................ 95
1933 Robert Sherman, Exeter................. 95
1934 Dudley Shallcross, Providence.......... 99
1935 Dudley Shallcross, Providence.......... 93
1936 Fred Hirsch, Pawtucket................. 97
1937 Dudley Shallcross, Barrington.......... 94
1940 Elliott Moore, Allenton................ 98
1941 Elliott Moore, Allenton................ 97

South Carolina

1935 J. W. Peterson, Charleston............. 93x100
1936 Claude A. Taylor, Spartanburg..........140x150
1937 F. P. Barry, Summerville...............184x200
1938 W. O. Boatle, Charleston...............285x300
1939 W. O. Boatle, Charleston...............295x300
1940 W. O. Boatle, Charleston...............148x150
1941 Fresh Nash, Spartanburg................192x200

South Dakota (100 Targets)

1935 G. M. Richardson, Lemmon.............. 93
1936 John Buzzell, Valley Springs.......... 86

Tennessee

1934 A. B. Case, Memphis.................... 87x100
1935 Mack Phipps, Knoxville................196x200
1936 L. L. Harrell, Trenton................. 96x100
1937 J. G. Roe, Paris......................194x200
1938 J. G. Roe, Paris......................100x100
1939 M. G. Radcliffe, Kingsport............. 99x100
1940 Tom May, Dyersburg.................... 97x100
1941 F. D. Hancock, Chattanooga............ 99x100

Texas

1933 Chas. Pickle, Austin..................194x200
1934 George Debes, Houston.................196x200
1935 Sam Barcelona, Houston................197x200
1936 D. W. Conway, El Paso.................292x300
1937 Roy Cherry, Dallas....................287x300
1938 C. J. Colby, Corpus Christi...........295x300
1939 K. C. Miller, Tyler...................297x300
1940 Landon Cullum, Wichita Falls..........298x300
1941 Landon Cullum, Wichita Falls..........299x300

Vermont (100 Targets)

1933 Russell G. Merriman, Montpelier........... 93
1934 Dr. P. C. Davis, Burlington............... 95
1935 Fred H. Kelly, Richford................... 97
1936 Fred H. Kelly, Richford................... 91
1937 Dr. W. G. Townsend, Burlington........... 99
1938 Dr. W. G. Townsend, Burlington..... 96
1939 Dr. W. G. Townsend, Burlington........... 94

Virginia

1934 N. Clyde Britt, Roanoke............... 96x100
1935 Dr. F. E. Markley, Staunton........... 96x100
1936 B. Wayne Erskine, Staunton............ 99x100
1937 J. P. Coyner, Staunton................ 96x100
1938 R. E. Stuart, Alexandria..............194x200
1939 Dr. F. E. Markley, Staunton........... 99x100
1940 W. B. Strickler, Roanoke.............. 98x100
1941 M. C. Britt, Roanoke.................. 99x100

Washington

1935 Joe Warren, Tacoma.................... 49x 50
1936 O. S. Ballew, Wenatchee............... 94x100
1937 O. S. Ballew, Wenatchee............... 98x100
1938 Les Peck, Mt. Vernon.................. 94x100
1939 H. H. White, Spokane.................. 97x100
1940 Chas. A. Libby, Jr., Spokane..........144x150
1941 Chas. Morton, Yakima..................146x150

West Virginia (100 Targets)

1934 Gale Davis, Charleston..................... 94
1935 Gale Davis, Charleston..................... 94
1936 Sam Roberts, Milton........................ 93
1937 Clyde Roberts, Milton...................... 96
1938 G. W. Easley, Williamson................... 98
1939 O. C. Fulks, Weston........................ 99
1940 O C. Fulks, Weston......................... 99
1941 John Kafer, Weston......................... 99

Wisconsin (100 Targets)

1933 Harry Billett, Oconomowoc.................. 95
1934 Harry Billett, Oconomowoc.................. 94
1935 Frank Mazanet, Madison..................... 99
1936 Walter Allen, Sparta....................... 96
1937 Jim Nagel, Eau Claire...................... 91
1938 Frank Mazanet, Madison..................... 95
1939 Ed Zemlica, Milwaukee...................... 95
1940 Ed Zemlica, Milwaukee (registered shoot).. 92
1940 Vic Reinders, Waukesha (not registered)... 95
1941 Alex Nabor, Shawano........................ 93

Hawaii

1938 R. M. Turrill.......................... 98x100

British Columbia

1938 J. A. Garrett, Vancouver.............. 88x100

Manitoba

1936 Bert Brodie, Winnipeg................. 43x 50
1937 Ross Screaton, Winnipeg............... 94x100
1938 Bert Brodie, Winnipeg................. 92x100
1940 Ross Screaton, Winnipeg............... 98x100
1941 Johnny Baldner, Winnipeg.............. 93x100

Ontario

1940 D. Nasmith, Toronto................... 97x100

LORDSHIP CHAMPIONS

1929 Ed Sransky, Palisades Park, N. J.........48x50
1930 Art Strahlendorf, West Englewood, N. J..... 100
1931 Augie Macone, Concord, Mass.............. 96
1932 Harry Hathaway, Dighton, Mass........... 99
1933 Glenn Watts, Lynbrook, L. I., N. Y........ 98
1934 K. K. Nielson, Essex, N. Y............... 98
1935 Augie Macone, Concord, Mass.............. 100
1936 Frank R. Kelly, W. Orange, N. J.......... 99
1937 C. L. Schweinler, W. Orange, N. J......... 99
1938 Frank Wirth, Flushing, N. Y............... 99
1939 Dick Shaughnessy, Boston, Mass........... 100
1940 Bob Canfield, Locust Valley, N. Y......... 100
1941 George Deyoe, Washington, D. C........... 100

All-Around Champions (300 Targets)

1936 Frank R. Kelly, W. Orange, N. J........... 285
1937 Frank R. Kelly, W. Orange, N. J........... 287
1938 Dick Shaughnessy, Boston, Mass........... 287
1939 Alex Kerr, Beverly Hills, Calif............ 296
1940 Dick Shaughnessy, Boston, Mass........... 296
1941 H. Lutcher Brown, San Antonio, Texas.... 295

The Northwest Gun Club of Chicago won the National Telegraphic shoot in 1937. *(Left to right)* Bill Clark, Gerald Batten, Lowrey Booth, Jimmy Anderson and Art Davidson who is shooting

(Left to right) **E. D. Holcomb, Paul Weeks, Paul Weeks, Sr., and Mose Browning, all are Louisiana quail hunters**

At the Tulsa Nationals were *(left to right)* Harry Moore, Powell Briscoe, Sr., Clarence Strong, Powell Briscoe and Dutch Heath, all from Oklahoma

The 1941 Lordship Team Champions: *(Left to right)* George Deyoe, who won the Individual Championship, Rufe Watson, John Hawkins, L. A. Singer and V. A. Frank, Jr. They shoot for the National Capitol Club of Washington, D. C.

20-Gauge (100 Targets)

1937	Frank R. Kelly, W. Orange, N. J.	97
1938	Frank R. Kelly, W. Orange, N. J.	97
1939	Grant Ilseng, Los Angeles, Calif.	99
1940	Dick Shaughnessy, Boston, Mass.	100
1941	Dick Shaughnessy, Boston, Mass.	100

National Telegraphic (500 Targets)

1931	Waltham, Mass.	470
1932	Houston, Texas	481
1933	Izaak Walton, Los Angeles	473
1934	Gilmore Red Lions, California	483
1935	Los Angeles, Santa Monica	487
1936	Los Angeles, Santa Monica	487
1937	Northwest Gun Club, Chicago	488
1938	Gilmore Red Lions, California	491
1939	Capitol City Gun Club, Washington, D. C.	493
1940	Gilmore Red Lions, California	497
1941	Los Angeles, Santa Monica	497

Great Eastern Team Race (500 Targets)

1929	Concord, Mass.	222x250
1930	Hudson County, New York	482
1931	Waltham, Mass.	470
1932	East Hampton, Mass.	469
1933	Waltham, Mass.	466
1934	Gilmore Red Lions, California	483
1935	Roseland, New Jersey	482
1936	Loantaka, New Jersey	471
1937	Roseland, New Jersey	481
1938	Roseland, New Jersey	485
1939	Hilltop Gun Club, Holliston, Mass.	489
1940	Hilltop Gun Club, Holliston, Mass.	494
1941	National Capital, Washington, D. C.	492

(.410 Gauge—Short Shell)

1932	Harry Hathaway, Dighton, Mass.	44x
1933	Dr. R. G. Vance, Waubon, Mass.	42x
1934	Dr. R. G. Vance, Waubon, Mass.	44x
1935	Dr. R. G. Vance, Waubon, Mass.	91
1936	Frank R. Kelly, W. Orange, N. J.	95
1937	Dick Shaughnessy, Boston, Mass.	95
1938	Dick Shaughnessy, Boston, Mass.	96
1939	Alex Kerr, Beverly Hills, Calif.	98
1940	Dick Shaughnessy, Boston, Mass.	97
1941	H. Lutcher Brown, San Antonio, Texas	99

(x denotes 50 target program. Others 100 targets.)

Women's Championship (100 Targets)

1932	Mrs. S. R. Small, Detroit, Mich.	88
1933	Mrs. R. G. Vance, Waubon, Mass.	90
1934	Mrs. S. R. Small, Detroit, Mich.	95
1935	Mrs. R. G. Merriman, Montpelier, Vt.	92
1936	Mrs. R. G. Vance, Waubon, Mass.	91
1937	Mrs. M. E. Rogers, Waltham, Mass.	96
1938	Miss Pat Laursen, Akron, Ohio	95
1939	Diana Bolling, Greenwich, Conn.	98
1940	Mrs. M. L. Smythe, Aurora, Ohio	99
1941	Mrs. M. L. Smythe, Aurora, Ohio	99

Junior Championship (50 Targets)

1933	J. Chisnall, Jr., Bridgeport	40
1934	M. L. Pitman, Bridgewater, N. Y.	43
1935	R. E. Rosien, New Haven, Conn.	45
1936	Dick Shaughnessy, Boston, Mass.	49
1937	Jack Horton, Providence, R. I.	48
1938	Johnny Wray, Rochester, N. Y.	50
1939	Clayton Boardman, Augusta, Ga.	49
1940	John Reed, Rochester, N. Y.	49
1941	F. L. Brown, San Antonio, Texas	50

Charlie Phellis, New York City, famous trapshooter and horseman

SHOTGUN HINTS

There are two types of shotgun shooting—field shooting and target shooting (trap and skeet shooting). A suggestion to the skeet or trapshooter is to procure from the Arms and Ammunition Manufacturers Institute, 103 Park Avenue, New York City, the Handbook on Shotgun Shooting, which is a complete treatise of the subject and is well written and begins with the fundamentals of the game.

The next step in trapshooting or skeet is to visit the gun club and to practice. You will be received with open arms and will receive instruction and practical tips.

What type of gun? Double, overunder, pump or autoloader. Choose the type that you prefer for all-around shooting. There are very few men or women taking up trapshooting or skeet who do not expect to improve their field shooting by practice gained at the gun club.

How will I get a gun to fit me? All American manufacturers supply standard dimension stocks for trap, skeet and field shooting. The dimensions of these stocks are suitable for 95% of the shooters. A rather straight stock is the best for trapshooting, with the usual dimensions being 14⅜, 1⅞, 1½; for skeet 14, 2¼, 1½, and for field shooting about the same as for skeet. If you are short-armed, short-necked, shorten the stock from ¼ inch to ½ inch; and by the same token, if you are unusually tall and long-armed, lengthen the stock to the same amount.

How shall I choose the bore? Trapshooters prefer full choke. Skeet shooters choose skeet boring which is 50, 55% choke or designated on and overunder type or double as skeet in and skeet out. For upland shooting specify improved cylinder or modified, depending upon the type of upland game you wish to shoot. For all-around work in the field, the average shot will do better with a modified choke bored gun.

What load will I use? For trap and skeet, use the loads designated as Trap and Skeet. For field shooting, you will have the choice of many combinations of powder loads and shot sizes. You will find that your game hunting friends are divided in their opinion as to proper size of shot. You will be safe in choosing size 6 shot for all upland game and duck hunting

Indian Trapshoots are popular. Here is a squad of the famous Illini Tribe. ***(Left to right)*** **Jim Heckard, Dr. C. D. Hermon, H. F. Wilson, P. Ludendorf and Joe Donahue**

when used in a full choke or modified choke, and 8 shot when using the open bored guns for quail, doves, snipe, etc.

For aquatic fowl, the heavy loads with larger sizes of shot are obtainable in all sizes of shots from BBs to 7.

There are just as many opinions as to proper loads as there are opinions on the best all-around dog.

Any gun or load combination will do the job if you point it properly.

No standard gun or load is a poor shooting combination.

It's up to you to learn to put the load in the right place at the proper time.

To sum up the entire situation, learn to handle a gun properly and safely. Practice when possible your "swing of follow through" and make your gun shoot where you look.

In the field, learn to shoot at game "in range" and avoid crippling game. This can only be gained by observation and experience.

HOW AND WHAT TO SHOOT

(By Fred Etchen, famous shooting instructor and Captain of the 1924 Olympic Trapshooting Team)

I believe more shotguns have been purchased with less knowledge on the part of the individual as to what he really needs for the purpose he intends using it for, than any other sport equipment.

Many hunters buy a small bore gun, such as a .410 or 20 gauge to shoot ducks, pheasants and grouse. This is all right for the expert shot, but certainly too small for the beginner, as these guns require too much accuracy. Many hunters buy a 12 gauge cylinder bore or improved cylinder and expect to kill ducks and pheasants at 50 to 60 yards. This is impossible. On the other hand, many hunters purchase a 20 gauge full choke and wonder why they can't kill quail at a short range, or doves coming into a water hole.

They do not understand that the full choke 20 gauge requires an expert marksman to hit his game. We advise the beginner, if he wants to shoot ducks, to forget the full choke until he can hit his birds. He should use a wide spreading gun for small game, such as quail.

Many parents start their youngsters off with a heavy 12 gauge gun. They are unable to handle this gun which has a tremendous recoil, and will no doubt make them gun-shy.

They should start off with a .410 gauge, using a 2½-inch shell, or a gun not larger than a 20 gauge with a very light load. It should have a recoil pad. I have instructed youngsters in all parts of the country and have found that the ones using heavy guns invariably closed their eyes and missed their targets. After we convince the youngsters that they should use a smaller gun and light load, they immediately respond and start breaking their targets.

The fit of a gun is very important. If it fits, it will handle easier and have less recoil. If the average hunter would only go out to the gun club, or make the acquaintance of a professional shooter who works for an ammunition company, he would soon learn his troubles. Here he will learn if his gun fits, what kind of shot he should use at different kinds of game, safety and other things.

SYSTEM OF MONEY DIVISION FOR CLUB OR TOURNAMENT SHOOTING

CLASS SHOOTING OR THE PERCENTAGE SYSTEM. In the old days, when there were but few trapshooters and a small number of entries, the purses were usually divided 60 and 40 per cent. As the number of entries increased the number of moneys increased to four or five. This system gives rise to injustice and encourages "dropping for place" and has, therefore, been almost wholly discontinued, except for live birds. It is still in use in live bird shooting to quite an extent, therefore the principal divisions are given below.

Two moneys, 60 and 40 per cent; Three moneys, 50, 30 and 20 per cent; Four moneys, 40, 30, 20 and 10 per cent; Five moneys, 30, 25, 20, 15 and 10 per cent; Six moneys, 27, 23, 17, 13, 11 and 9 per cent.

HIGH GUNS

The most recent addition to the system of purse divisions is the high guns. This system, used almost entirely in live bird shooting, is rapidly becoming very popular—the more so as it becomes better understood. The opposition that this system met with at the start arose from the belief that but a very small percentage of the entries would get into the money, but when considered as made use of in the Grand American Handicap, with two moneys for every ten entries, or as made use of in many of the gun clubs, two moneys for every five entries—in the latter case making ten moneys in every twenty-five entries—the opposition died away, and the system has become quite popular. The money is divided by percentage but the system is entirely distinct from class shooting.

1 to 10 entries, two moneys—60 and 40 per cent.

11 to 20 entries, four moneys—40, 30, 20 and 10 per cent.

21 to 30 entries, six moneys—30, 20, 15, 13, 12 and 10 per cent.

31 to 40 entries, eight moneys—25, 20, 15, 12, 10, 8, 5 and 5 per cent.

41 to 50 entries, ten moneys—22, 18, 11, 10, 9, 8, 6, 5, 4, 4 and 3 per cent.

The above is based upon two moneys for each ten entries. However, one money for each three entries is a more popular division.

ROSE SYSTEM

The Rose system is used in money division at tournaments. A nominal entry of from fifty cents to $1.50 per event, is the entrance fee. The division is made on the point system. Rose 4, 3, 2, 1. Rose 5, 3, 2, 1, 1. The purse per event is divided by number of points accumulated, paying as follows: For 25, 4. For 24, 3. For 23, 2. For 22, 1. Establish the value per point and multiply it by number of points obtained. Under this system there is no dividing of purses in case of ties, as equal points are credited for each score made. In other words, you get paid for what you break.

JACK RABBIT SYSTEM

The Jack Rabbit system is used in many parts of the country. It is based on paying back to the shooter the full amount of his entry fee for each target he breaks. It also divides what is left, among those who take first, second and third places, in the proportions of 50 per cent, 30 per cent, and 20 per cent.

Example: In a 25-target event the management charges 2 cents each for targets and has a fixed valuation of 10 cents a target. This makes a value of 12 cents a target thrown or $3.00 for the entry. The management pays $2.50 to the shooter who runs straight and also gives him his share of the other moneys in proportions of 50 per cent for first place, 30 per cent for second, and 20 per cent to the third out of the sum accumulating by retaining 10 cents for each target fired at and lost. This enables a man to cash in nicely even though he may have but one or two 25 straights in a 150 or 200 target event.

There are other good systems of money division, such as the Siefken High Gun System, Lewis Class System (see explanation in the Hunters' Special story), the (Luther) Squier Money Back, the KWB System, etc. Other systems of money division are possible but they are modifications of, or combinations of systems listed. Your local ammunition trade representative is always willing to assist you in writing programs and assisting you in conducting a tournament.

SLIDING HANDICAPS

The sliding handicap rehandicaps shooters after each five shots. All start at 16 yards. Those breaking five straight go back a yard, and keep on moving back a yard for each additional five straight. When a man misses one target in five, he stays where he is for the next five; when he misses two targets, he moves forward one yard. In this system of handicapping, no one shoots from closer than 16 yards, nor from farther than 25 yards.

When large numbers of contestants of comparatively equal yardage handicaps are competing, they are squadded so that those in each squad will shoot from about the same distance. When men shoot from 16 and from 25 yards in the same squad, the 16-yard men are annoyed by muzzle blast, and the back-distance men by seeing those in front.

THE GRAND AMERICAN GROUNDS AT VANDALIA, OHIO—Art Stifal, Earl Thompson, both of Illinois

GAME SHOOTING—UPLAND

Any one who is fond of nature will appreciate upland hunting. As the name implies, it is the hunt of upland game birds, and it differs in almost every respect from water shooting. The principal difference is that in waterfowl shooting, the gunner sits still and lets the bird come to him; while in upland shooting he goes after the birds. One of the pleasantest features of upland shooting is watching the dogs work.

Skeet was designed both as a substitute for upland shooting, and as a tuning-up process for such shooting as remains in most sections of North America. Even the variable delay in the trapping of Skeet targets is intended to school the shooter in alert watchfulness without "freezing" his controls. But if practice at Skeet is not enough, a little hand-trap shooting with a few boon companions, or several sessions at a "quail shoot" or "walk up," should finish the education of any gunner. There remains only the time-honored ailment of buck fever to be reckoned with, and since this corresponds to the fault of flinching in target shooting, the cure is strictly up to the shooter and to nobody else.

Buck fever ordinarily is diagnosed as over-anxiety in the presence of game. Over-anxiety, that is, to bag the flying game before it gets away. The shooter either freezes his eyes and body muscles and fires too slowly, or else hurries his eyes and bangs a hole in the air. The whir of a rising covey of quail or explosion of a grouse in the dry leaves will tend to unnerve any gunner.

The gunner must hurry—but not to the point where he bangs an unaimed shot in the general direction of the speeding game. He must take time to do these three things: Advance the pivot foot in the direction and SELECT ONE BIRD. Mount his gun quickly and press his cheek to the stock, covering with the sighting plane the theoretical zero point of his imaginary vertical clock—which will be that point on or near the path of the target which the target occupied when so identified. Estimate the angle with the sighting plane of the gun formed by the continuation of the flight of the target, and swing along the arc between the gun muzzle and the actual target, firing the shot as the target is passed by the muzzle.

Remember—if any shooter merely learns to follow the

target with the sighting plane of his gun, he will take a lot of game, whether he does anything else correct or not. It will help if he keeps his head down, if he keeps his eyes open, if he pulls or slaps the trigger firmly but not roughly. Most upland hunting is accomplished without a dog—and the shooting is just so much harder because the game must be located in air after it has flushed, rather than located as to general whereabouts before it takes wing. Birds in the open should always be flushed toward the nearest cover, rather than attempt to drive the game farther out into the open.

Modern firearms, even the most inexpensive kind, are so efficient that any gun, with smokeless shot shells, will kill plenty of game. There is a tendency on the part of the American hunter to take pride in the tools of his hobby, and his own technique with these tools. This tendency is responsible for the increasing popularity of small-gauge guns, 16's and 20's for upland shooting. Even the hardy old grouse and pheasant will succumb readily to a full ounce of chilled 6's from a light 20-gauge gun—and these slim, beautiful little weapons are a joy to carry in comparison to the greater weight of the old American standard, the 12-gauge.

Most famous character at dog trials in the northwest is Joe MacGaheran, noted writer and radio commentator. Here we have Joe pictured with a couple of his fine pointers. Rap's Hillcrest Joe *(front dog)* was an entry in the prairie chicken championships at Pierson, Manitoba, last fall. The other dog is Kettle River Mary

DUCK DECOYS

Decoys are almost as important a part of the duck and goose hunter's equipment today as his shotgun. Because of the vast increase in the numbers of hunters, waterfowl are warier and more alert than ever before. Decoys must be used to lure wildfowl within shooting range.

The use of decoys will prove to be an effective conservation measure. Usually, when shooting over decoys, waterfowl are shot at closer range, reducing cripples to a minimum. Furthermore, decoys will prove to be an aid to the shooter's pocketbook, as shooting at closer ranges eliminates many misses, thereby saving shells.

First to use decoys in North America were the Indians. White shooters followed in their footsteps. In general, decoys may be divided into two classes—field decoys for field shooting and floating decoys for shooting over water.

Ten million decoys are used annually in North America. Most of them are mallard decoys. The ratio in favor of mallard decoys is 10 to 1. Bluebills or scaup are next. Goose decoys – either field or water—virtually are in a class by themselves.

You may spend as much as you like for decoys. They range in price from about $5 a dozen to $75 a dozen. Well made, properly shaped decoys are more effective than crude chunks of wood. It pays to use good decoys. There are times, of course, when ducks will decoy to almost anything—but those occasions are few and far between.

Modern decoys are infinitely better than those which were in use as recently as 10 years ago. Decoy making is big business and decoy makers are using all the knowledge which science has placed at their disposal to produce better decoys.

There are a great many different kinds of decoys. Some are made from wood, others from rubber, paper, cork, plastics and other materials. Among the woods used are white pine, cedar, basswood, redwood, cork, whitewood, etc.

Selection of decoys is largely a matter of personal preference. How and where he will use his decoys influences the hunter in making his choice. Some wildfowlers prefer small decoys, others large ones. I lean to the large ones. Some prefer a plain black decoy, others insist upon highly decorated ones.

The section of the country in which one hunts generally is

the determining factor in decoy selections. Wise hunters are quick to adopt the decoys in vogue in the region where they intend to hunt. If the local gunners use large decoys, then the stranger will be assured of success if he uses large decoys, too. If the home crowd shoots over small decoys, it's a 100 to 1 shot that small decoys are the type to adopt.

Where blinds may be reached with comparative ease by motor car or boat, any number of decoys of every kind—heavy wooden blocks or lighter models—may be transported. If, however, it is necessary to travel by canoe or boat and to make extensive portages, then lightweight decoys are virtually a necessity.

The wooden decoy has been found to be the most durable. Old-timers swear by it. The factor of weight, however, has influenced many hunters to prefer lighter decoys made from cork, rubber and other lightweight substances.

Many hunters make their own decoys. Great care should be taken when carving a duck head. Don't have your head too pointed or sharp, or your duck gives the appearance of being scared. Your heads should imitate perfectly feeding or resting ducks.

Eyes are important. Select the correct type of eye for the decoy and position them in a lifelike manner. A keel is a worthwhile addition; it helps to prevent rolling and tipping.

How many decoys to use in a stool is a question many new hunters ask. Some gunners use two or three decoys—others set up several dozen. I like a large stool of decoys.

Here's a tip—if you want decoy shooting like you've never had before, set out three or four goose decoys about 20 yards to one side of your duck decoys.

Here is Russell Hofmeister who makes goose calls for Herters Decoy Company at Waseca, Minn. Russell is one of the world's greatest goose callers. George Herter says Russ is the best

WATERFOWL SHOOTING

The most vital factor in a successful shoot is a good knowledge of the habits of wild fowl; as here conditions change so that even the veteran hunter is sometimes at fault. Every move in a day's duck hunting is based on what the hunter thinks the game will do on that particular day; and if his reasoning is sound, a heavy game bag will be his reward.

First, in shooting ducks, your equipment is indeed important. You should dress warmly, or if you have light clothes, you should always be prepared for a storm. Nobody knows what the weather will do on the following day. The hunters of the northwest were taught a costly lesson during the Armistice storm in 1940, a storm which cost many lives and that came with the rush of a tornado. You should carry along an extra pair of sox. You should have a pair of rubber boots, your hunting coat should be tan or brown. Do not wear conspicuous colors.

Your boat should be tested before you open the duck season. The boat must be wide enough, should preferably have a rounded bottom so that it will push easily over the mud and weeds, and it should have sufficient length so that it can ride the waves if you pass over a large body of water. Take along some clothes line or heavy string—plenty of it, to tie your boat. Most duck boats are painted an olive drab green. A dead grass green is the best. Always take along an extra paddle. Several years ago while hunting with Walter Bush on Lake Manitoba, we nearly lost our lives when we lost our paddles.

I have always found No. 6 shot in my 12 gauge the best pattern for ducks. Some prefer 5's or 4's. I also use 5's and 6's for geese. In the south, where they shoot over decoys, a 16 or 20 gauge gun is sometimes the choice of the hunter with a

Here are a couple of happy hunters with a bag of geese. *(Left to right)* Ki Steiner, President of the American Linen and Sam Nickerson, Director of Johnson-Gokey Sporting Goods Store, Minneapolis

lighter load. However, a hunter soon learns to shoot the load that he prefers. During the past few years, the Magnum guns have proved very popular, especially for pass shooting or geese. A three-inch shell is shot in a Magnum. Don't shoot out of range. Let your ducks come in. A kill at more than 50 yards is only luck, and you will cripple more ducks than you will kill at this range. Calling ducks is an art. If you are an expert, take your call, if not, leave it at home. A poor caller will turn ducks away.

TRAINING THE DOG

There has been much written about choosing a young dog. Very little can be told of a young dog. The one safe way is to select your dog after he is six months old, and then you can gain some inkling of what the future ability of dog will be. If we wait until the dogs can be taken afield we have better grounds for selection. The dog that displays a natural ability to hunt, and seems to want to do this above everything else, is the one to bank on.

One of the first demands in starting the training of a hunting dog is to cure it of "gun" fright or "gun" shyness. A dog that fears a gun will never be a good hunting dog. Gun shyness must be cured at an early age. Start with a cap pistol or .22 rifle and fire when the dog eats. At the start, fire but once, then increase it to several times within a few days. Then you can use a .410 shotgun and if this doesn't bother him, use a 12 gauge.

The lessons with a dog should not be long. At the very beginning, speak with a mild voice. A dog can hear you just as well when you speak in a mild voice as when you shout. Never hasten matters and never lose your temper. Fifteen minutes a day is sufficient to train a puppy.

The commands to "Charge," "Stop," "Steady," "Come in," etc., can be regulated to suit the individual and the dog. They are easily taught in the yards and easily forgotten the first day afield by the pupil. Another thing, while on this important subject, is that yard work instills in the mind of the dog who is master, besides cultivating a love in the dog for his handler which only association can develop. Instant obedience with the whistle is desirable.

Labradors are popular duck hunting dogs. Here we have pictured Nick Kahler, who promotes the Northwest Sportsmen's Shows *(third from left)* with his famous Labrador, Banter. *(Left to right)* Stan White, Webb Coffee, (Kahler), Warden Ed Porthe, Joe Paranteau and Red Johnson, outdoor editor of the Chicago Daily News and Vic Johnson, tourist director for Minnesota. They had been hunting at the Lake of the Woods, Minnesota

It is a good thing immediately to teach a dog to lead. When you have a dog that wants to pull against you all the time, use the choke collar, one without spikes in it, or else a lead with a similar noose, and jerk rapidly each time he tries to strain at it.

The command, "Down," "Drop," or "Charge" is one that should be instructed early. With most dogs there is no need of the force collar to teach this. Grasp the dog firmly with your hand at its coupling in the back and force it to the ground while uttering the command "Down" or "Charge." It will drop easily in this manner. Do not let it get up until you say the word "Up." This can be done with a light switch also. After the command is absorbed, keep the dog under observation of your eyes and then walk around him, not permitting him to arise until you wish. Do this fifteen minutes each day for fifteen days.

Later have him drop and walk off farther, as far as you desire, but never permitting him to get up until you do by command. He will then learn to obey quickly.

Now take a short lead and walk around with the dog, the lead being attached to his collar, and after walking a few paces say in a low voice, "Steady" or any other word that you want to represent stopping instantly. Stop a few minutes without moving or paying the slightest attention to the dog, and the very fraction of the second that you start on again say "On." Do this fifteen minutes each day for fifteen days.

A dog can be made to heel at command by using a switch or the end of the lead forcing him back of you with it and uttering the word "Heel." He can be permitted to advance only at the word "On." Again this becomes mechanical if persisted in regularly each day for a period of fifteen days.

Have patience with your dog. Some dogs that turn out to be fine hunting dogs, react very slowly when trained. Never continue training when you see that the dog is tiring. Many good dogs have never been trained until they were four years old. Dogs should be in good shape for the hunting season and should be exercised before the season opens.

Great attention should be given to his food. Changes in food will affect him in the same manner as his owner. Poor food and bad quarters are the chief causes of dogs losing flesh so rapidly when on a hunt in a strange country. Proper food should be shipped with the dog. Feed the dog two hours before the hunt. A dry food is the best. It won't hurt to give the dog a warm meal in the evening. It doesn't do any harm to give your dog a good rub-down after the hunt. If his feet are sore, bathe them with hot water and witch hazel.

Our good friend Bob Becker, outdoor editor of the Chicago Tribune, a real friend of dogs, claims that most puppies have worms, but that doesn't mean that every owner of a new puppy should buy worm medicine. It is best to talk to a veterinarian. Among the common symptoms of worms in puppies are: enormous or finicky appetite; a harsh, unthrifty coat which lacks sheen; loss of weight; a soft, hacking cough or watery eyes.

All dogs are susceptible, although distemper occurs most frequently in young dogs, especially those under a year old. Keep your dog in good physical condition, then if distemper strikes he may be able to defeat the disease with the help of a reliable veterinarian.

If your puppy loses his pep, doesn't want to play, becomes very sluggish, and won't eat, and generally doesn't look or act right, better take him to a "vet" because distemper often starts with these symptoms. The easiest way to prevent distemper is to have a "vet" inoculate your puppy.

Printed in the United States
142392LV00001B/5/A

9 781432 572563